5 conversations you must have with your Son

Vicki
Courtney

REVISED AND EXPANDED

5

conversations you must have

with your *Son*

B&H
PUBLISHING GROUP

NASHVILLE, TENNESSEE

978-1-4627-9630-4

Published by B&H Publishing Group
Nashville, Tennessee

Dewey Decimal Classification: 306.874
Subject Heading: BOYS \ PARENT AND CHILD \
PARENTING

Cover design by Jennifer Allison of Studio Nth.
Cover photo © Westend61 / getty.

1 2 3 4 5 6 7 • 23 22 21 20 19

To my sons, Ryan and Hayden—
Thank you for patiently enduring the conversations
contained in this book (or at least pretending to!). One of
my greatest joys in life has been watching you grow in your
faith and become the godly young men you are today.

And to my grandsons, Walker, Micah, Fletcher,
Nicky, and baby boy McMichen who is due
shortly after this book releases—
May you follow the God of your parents and grandparents
and make Him your absolute everything.

Acknowledgments

● ● ● ● ● ●

Keith, I continue to acknowledge and thank you in every book, but it bears repeating: I could not do what I do were it not for you picking up the slack. As I read through the final manuscript, I was struck with how intentional you have been in discipling our sons over the years. Truly you should be the one writing this book . . . or at least, one to follow for dads, perhaps? Our sons (and daughter) have been so very blessed to have you for a dad. What a reward to be on the other side of this parenting journey and see the reward for your faithfulness—the biggest of which is our fast growing brood of grandchildren!

To my sons, Ryan and Hayden: when you were little, I would often tell you, while tucking you in at night during our bedtime prayers: *"I'm so glad God picked me to be your mama."* I mean it more today than ever before. I'm so glad God picked me to be your mom! I couldn't be more proud of the godly young men you've become. It is such a joy to watch you embark on your own parenting journey and raise your sons with a firm foundation of faith.

To my son-in-law, Matt: You far exceeded anything I could have imagined when I prayed for my daughter's future spouse all those years. Even though I didn't get the privilege of raising you, I count you as my own. You are an amazing father to Molly and I am beyond excited that you are about to experience the joys of having a son.

To my publisher, B&H: thank you so much for partnering with me to get this message out to moms with sons.

To the many moms of sons who encouraged me to write this book and shared your own parenting journeys with me: Thank you so much for your support. Your sons are blessed to have such caring and concerned mothers.

And last of all, the acknowledgments would not be complete without giving thanks to the one who enables me to write, speak, live, breathe, and love. I pray this book will bring glory and honor to my Savior, Jesus Christ.

Contents

● ● ● ● ● ●

Introduction

● ● ● ● ● ●

When my publisher approached me about updating this book, I eagerly accepted the challenge. Many of the conversations I had presented in the original book had proven relevant to a generation of children growing up in a rapidly changing culture. In the nearly decade that has since passed, new challenges have emerged requiring a tune-up to the original conversations, or in some cases brand new conversations. When I wrote the original book, my older son was wrapping up his final semester of college and engaged to be married. My daughter was halfway through college and also engaged to be married. My youngest son was months shy of graduating from high school and preparing to move out for college. I was nearing the end of my parenting journey and about to enter a new season of life.

The reality of that new season hit me in full force when I returned home after moving my youngest son into his college dorm. The house was eerily quiet. My children's rooms stayed miraculously clean. My driveway no longer looked like a used car lot. There were blank spaces in my calendar. Weekends that had once been reserved for sporting events were free. For the most part, the hard work was behind me. I was done with staying on top of homework assignments, worrying about grades, and shuttling my children to their many extracurricular activities. I was done with curfews, managing screen time, and monitoring my children's peer groups. I was done with arguing with my sons about haircuts, hygiene, and messy rooms. I was done with training them in regard to finances, manners, and self-discipline. I was finally done. In the immediate aftermath of my last child leaving, it was hard to know whether or not to mourn or celebrate. (For the record, I did both.) In the months that followed, I adjusted to this new normal where my role as a mother took on a completely different identity. My children needed me every now and then, but overall, they were on their way to becoming independent, self-sufficient young adults. Or so I hoped!

In the years that followed my children's launch out of the nest, I held my breath to see if they would successfully make the transition into adulthood and most importantly, carry their faith with them. There were some bumps along the way, but that was to be expected. And yes, there were times when I wondered if they had paid any attention to the conversations we had had along the way, especially when some of their choices indicated otherwise. In those moments, God was faithful to remind me that my ultimate calling was to make "holy deposits" in their lives and trust Him for the results.

Today, all three of my children are grown adults who are now married and have embarked on their own parenting journeys. They all have a deep faith and are committed to raising their children to know and love God. My empty nest has transitioned into a full nest of a half dozen grandchildren and counting. My husband and I feel extremely blessed that our children live nearby and we see them often. In fact, my youngest son's bedroom has been converted into a nursery where my grandchildren nap on occasion in the same crib that my children once slept in. I love this season of life and wouldn't trade it for anything. I often joke with my friends that "if I'd known how awesome it was to be a grandmother, I would have started with grandkids first!"

All this to say, I have enjoyed being somewhat ignorant regarding the challenges facing children today. Updating this book required me to reenter the parenting fray and get back into the trenches, so to speak. In doing so, it didn't take me long to realize that a great deal has changed since the original book released. A whole new generation (iGen or Generation Z) has emerged in place of the millennials that had been the focus of the previous book. This new generation has some similarities to millennials, but overall, they are very different. Ironically many of the young parents who will pick up this book (including my own children), are now millennial parents raising iGen or Generation Z children. Essentially, I was faced with the challenge of writing to a brand-new audience of parents raising a brand-new audience of children who are facing a brand-new set of challenges. In an effort to better understand this new generation, I immersed myself into researching what makes this generation tick. I read countless books and articles focused on iGen or Generation Z children, as well as participated in an online training geared to those who work with this current generation.

Needless to say, I was caught off guard by much of what I discovered related to this emerging generation—record levels of mental illness, depression, loneliness, gender confusion, a lack of identity and purpose, a decreasing interest in marriage and parenthood as future goals, a detachment from the God of the Bible and a rebellion toward His standards and principles, and the list goes on. I would be lying if I told you it didn't take an emotional toll on me at times. My grandchildren are in this generation, so it was personal. I have skin in this game. There were days when I had to take a break from my research and immerse myself in God's Word to be reminded that there is hope. Fortunately, Jesus Christ is the same yesterday, today and forever and none of this has caught Him off guard. His Word never changes and His principles are true for all times. The generation of children today may be growing up in a culture that is resistant to that answer, but that doesn't mean we throw in the towel and give up. God has tasked us with the awesome responsibility to "train up [our] children in the way [they] should go" (Prov. 22:6 ESV), and He never intended that we go it alone.

Ralph Waldo Emerson once said, "It's not the destination, it's the journey." I'm not sure I fully understood that beautiful truth when I wrote the original book. Truth be told, at some level I bought into the naïve belief that if a parent invested enough time and heartache into the rearing of their children, they were guaranteed to arrive safely at the ultimate destination. The problem was, I had the destination all wrong. The destination wasn't an end goal of raising obedient children who have an unblemished track record of devotion to God coupled with a long list of good deeds. Rather, it's about a journey that, much like ours, includes poor choices, many missteps along the way, and hard life lessons that hopefully lead to a better understanding of God's love, patience, and forgiveness.

I couldn't be more proud of where my children are today, but I'm not naïve enough to believe it's because I devoted myself to the conversations contained in this book. I've always said there are no foolproof parenting formulas when it comes to raising children. The conversations in this book are simply a tool to better aid you in the journey. Nothing more and nothing less. My children knew that nothing was off limits to talk about—whether they wanted to discuss it or not! The conversations we had over the years encouraged a healthier pattern of communication that has contributed to the deep friendship I have with each of my children today. For that I am extremely thankful. My children are where they are today because somewhere along the way, they concluded for themselves that the ultimate destination in this journey is a relationship with Jesus Christ. Now, as they are faced with the task of raising their own children, my prayer is that they would set their coordinates on that same destination and point them to Jesus in these uncertain times. He alone is the answer.

And that, my friend, is my prayer for you as well. I won't promise you it will be an easy task. There will be days when you'll want to give up. Fortunately, God never gave up on us! Point your children to Jesus. Model to them that He is your absolute everything. And whatever you do, don't forget to enjoy the journey. It goes by quicker than you think.

Conversation 1

Don't let the culture define you.

Chapter 1

A Time for Everything

●　　●　　●　　●　　●　　●

"I prayed for this child, and the LORD has granted me what I asked of him. So now I give him to the LORD. For his whole life he will be given over to the LORD." (1 Sam. 1:27–28)

Most every mother remembers an incident beyond the "It's a boy!" announcement that marked their sudden induction into the Boy Mama Club. For me initiation day began with special instructions from a nurse in the hospital on how to clean the navel area and (ahem) . . . you know, "it." When I tried to follow her instructions, I was awarded with a golden waterworks display and a chuckle from the nurse who responded to the show with, "Welcome to the wonderful world of boys!" It was almost as if my new son was sending out an advance warning: "Get ready, lady! You ain't seen nothin' yet!" And bless my heart, I hadn't. I didn't have a clue about the world of boys until I found myself smack-dab in the middle of raising my own little bundle of testosterone. And I wouldn't trade the experience of raising my two boys for anything. In fact, they both captured my heart from day one.

Nothing compares to raising boys. Recently I was going through a box of keepsake items and stumbled upon a letter I received from my youngest son, Hayden, when he was away at camp for a week. He was nine years old at the time, and it was his first summer camp experience. He had begged to go to summer camp like his two older siblings, and finally I relented and signed the boy up. His older brother and sister had been two years older when they experienced their first summer camp, so I went back and forth after turning the paperwork in, wondering if I had made the right decision. When the time came to drop him off, I could hardly tear myself away. He looked so small next to some of the older campers! Of course, he was excited and could hardly wait for his father and me to leave. I had packed paper and self-addressed, stamped envelopes in his trunk and given him strict instructions to write home at least every other day (yes, to assuage my own worries!).

I worried myself sick during the week that followed and checked the mailbox daily hoping for a letter from him. I waited. And I waited. And I waited. Finally, toward the end of the week, I received the one and only camp letter I would ever receive from my son during all his camp years combined. Mind you, I discovered this rare camp letter from my son in the keepsake box that contained a sea of camp letters from my daughter. In her letters she provided detailed descriptions of her days and full-length bios on each new friend made. As a bonus she often added stickers or doodle drawings to jazz up her letters. Needless to say, Hayden's camp letter did not follow his sister's previously established protocol.

Following is a transcript of my much-anticipated camp letter from Hayden:

Dear parents,

We had bean burritos for lunch today and Andrew
and I couldn't stop tooting so we started a tooting
contest in our cabin during bunk time. I won. Camp
is fun.

Love,
Hayden

That's it. No details about canoeing, horseback riding, or roasting marshmallows by a campfire. Just tooting. Which for the record, he could have done at home, for free. On the upside, at least the letter brought an end to my worry. Clearly the little lad wasn't *crying* himself to sleep each night. *Tooting* himself to sleep maybe but not crying. For the record, on pickup day, I raced toward him and was greeted with, *"Mommy, I love camp! Can I go for two weeks next summer?"* When we returned home, I opened his trunk to begin the post-camp laundry washathon, and to my absolute horror found an unused bar of soap along with five of the seven prematched and neatly folded outfits still prematched and **neatly folded**! On the upside, I didn't have much wash to do.

Welcome to the world of boys where post-burrito flatulence is considered a competitive sport and hygiene, much to a mother's dismay, is optional. In this chapter we are going to discuss some factors that make our boys unique (beyond hygiene and flatulence issues). We will also discuss the unique role we, as mothers, play when it comes to communicating with our sons in order that we might set a proper foundation for the conversations to come. Somewhere at the top of our list should be an ongoing pep talk on proper hygiene, including instructions on raising the toilet seat and putting it back down. Because we all know that particular skill needs to be mastered *before* marriage.

Paving the Way for Open Communication

Author and clergyman Henry Ward Beecher once noted, "The mother's heart is the child's schoolroom." Boys view their mothers as a safe haven or a shelter from the storms of life. Whether they take a tumble off their bikes at age four or fail to make the basketball team at fourteen, Mom will be there to offer encouragement and support. Author Meg Meeker, in her book *Boys Should Be Boys*, says, "When a mother extends outstretched arms to a son who has failed in sports, or school, or socially, or been deemed not smart enough, 'manly enough,' or just plain not good enough, he begins to understand what love is all about. The moment a mother extends her grace, he begins to understand that goodness in being a man isn't all about his performance. It isn't about his successes or his failures. It is about being able to accept love from another and then return that love."[1]

The love a boy receives from his mother will set the tone for his future relationships. I remember shortly after I met Keith, the man who would become my husband, telling my two closest girlfriends, "I think I met *him—you know, the one*." One of their first questions was, "What kind of relationship does he have with his mother?" If a boy has loved and been loved by his mother, he is at an advantage when it comes to loving others. While fathers typically model acts of service to their sons and focus more on *doing*, mothers typically model acts of love and help their sons find value in *being*. If a boy is to develop into a well-rounded young man, he will need both a primary male and female influence in his life. If your son is lacking a primary male influence, set out to find positive and trusted male role models. (I will address this more in-depth in Conversation 5.)

In addition to modeling love to our sons, we also hold the primary position of influence when it comes to character and spiritual development. E. W. Caswell (eighteenth-century hymn writer) said, "The mother, more than any other, affects the moral and spiritual part of the children's character. She is their constant companion and teacher in formative years. The child is ever imitating and assimilating the mother's nature. It is only in after life that men gaze backward and behold how a mother's hand and heart of love molded their young lives and shaped their destiny." Your willingness to pick up this book and read it speaks volumes about your commitment to the spiritual and character development of your son(s).

A Listening Ear

It can be difficult for boys to open up and talk about their feelings, emotions, fears, and things that matter most to them. In the book *Boys Should Be Boys*, author Meg Meeker notes, "Boys usually form stronger emotional bonds with their mothers during the early boyhood years, and it is important not to sever those bonds unnaturally or too soon. Mothers can encourage sons in areas where fathers typically don't. Being more emotionally attuned than fathers, they can see their sons' feelings and motivations more readily, and try to understand and direct them. Because many boys feel emotionally safer with their mothers, they feel less inhibited in front of them."[2]

As your son begins to pull away in his adolescent years, he may be more resistant to talk about his feelings, but that doesn't mean he doesn't have them. Look for signs of stress or indications he may need to process something that may be weighing heavy on his heart.

You might offer a simple, "Hey, is everything okay? Remember, I'm here if you need to talk about anything." Resist the temptation to try to force him to open up or share more than he is comfortable sharing at the time. By simply making yourself available, it sends a message that you care and are on call to listen should he need you.

As your son gets older and begins to interact more with girls, you can be a great source of wisdom to your son when it comes to unraveling the mysterious female mind. Meeker says, "A mother can teach her son about girls, because a son respects his mother even when he finds it hard to tolerate the girls at school. She teaches him to tolerate girls at various ages, to excuse their feminine behaviors that he finds ridiculous, and to appreciate that the differences between boys and girls are not good and bad, but two beneficial aspects of human nature."[3]

Mothers are in a unique place to help their sons better understand girls. The irony is, I gave my sons pep talks and described the kind of girls they might want to steer clear of only to realize later, I've just described myself as a girl! It's funny how your perspective suddenly changes when you have a son who could fall prey to the kind of girl drama their own mama doled out! I recall one poor guy in the sixth grade whom I broke up with after three hours because one of my friends told me another guy (whom I had a big-time crush on) liked me. If some girl had attempted to pull that stunt on one of my boys, there's a chance I would have signed up for a martial arts class and paid her a friendly visit. For the record, justice was served because the object of my crush dumped me within twenty-four hours!

Finally, if your son confides in you or shares something that is sensitive in nature, do not share it with your friends. This is especially true when it comes to social media. While it may seem harmless to post a transcript of a cute conversation you had with your son or upload a picture of a sweet note they wrote to you or someone else, it can come back to haunt you years later if your son concludes that anything he shares with you is fair game to post on social media. It takes boys a great deal of courage and trust to share their innermost thoughts and feelings, and when they do so, it's an honor and a privilege to be on the receiving end.

Entertainment Industry: The Joke's on Men

The entertainment industry has tremendous power of persuasion when it comes to viewers and how they perceive the world around them. This is especially true when it comes to the portrayal of men in movies and television. The standard prototype seems to be a weak, emasculated male who is incapable of formulating an intelligent, rational thought on his own.

Consider one commercial that aired during a Super Bowl game. CBS's Jim Nantz delivered an injury report on a guy (Jason) whose girlfriend "removed his spine." Microphone in hand, Jim delivers his lines in newscaster fashion as Jason is forced to shop with his girlfriend during game time. The first scene shows poor Jason standing in a lingerie shop with a red bra draped over his shoulder staring in a static gaze as his girlfriend flips through the sales rack in the background. The ad is for FLO-TV, which would allow Jason to watch the game on his mobile phone.[4] Voilà, problem solved for the army of emasculated men who were fortunate enough to be tuning into the Super Bowl game with their buddies, and platters of buffalo wings. I imagine there was a chorus of high-fives among game watchers when Jim Nantz delivers the final line in the ad: "Change out of that skirt, Jason."

And then there was the Dockers "Men without Pants" thirty-second ad spot that addressed the emasculated state of manhood by showing a group of childish men marching onto the field (pantless) and singing, "I wear no pants." They were interrupted with the message: "Calling all men, it's time to wear the pants."[5]

Dodge capitalized on the all-too-common stereotype of the emasculated male by airing an ad during the Super Bowl that showed a series of men who stared into the camera lens with a hollow and expressionless look on their faces as the laundry list of male indignities were listed one by one by a narrator.

- I will get up and walk the dog at 6:20 a.m.
- I will eat some fruit as part of my breakfast.
- I will shave, and clean the sink after I shave.
- I will be at work at 8:00 a.m.
- I will sit through two-hour meetings.
- I will say yes when you want me to say yes.
- I will be quiet when you don't want me to say no.
- I will take your call and listen to your opinion of my friends.
- I will listen to your friends' opinions of my friends.
- I will be civil to your mother.
- I will put the seat down.
- I will separate the recycling.
- I will carry your lip balm.
- I will take my socks off before getting into bed.
- I will put my underwear in the basket.

The narrator's tone began with an edge of quiet confidence that by the end of the ad turned into a raw anger that culminated with the line, "And because I do this. I will drive the car I want to drive.

Charger, Man's Last Stand."[6] The ad was a rally cry for men to rise up and take back their masculinity.

Add to this the "idiot husband and dad" portrayal of men in the average TV sitcom family, which has been around for so long most of us have subconsciously come to expect it as the norm. We've all been guilty of laughing at the vaudevillian caricatures of TV husbands and dads who behave more like immature adolescents than grown adults. We'd be naïve to believe it hasn't influenced our view of men at large.

In movies, television shows, and commercials, men have become nothing more than a punch line to a joke; laughable, but certainly not respectable. Our sons are absorbing this message and it has, at least on a subconscious level, had an impact on their perception of manhood and masculinity. I am not suggesting we ban our sons from watching these shows, but rather, let's take advantage of the opportunities as they arise to teach our sons to recognize the negative portrayal of men, and in turn, point them to real-life examples of men who are noble representations of godly manhood.

The Feminization of Education

For decades, boys have been falling behind girls in school. Girls now outperform boys at every grade level from kindergarten through twelfth grade.[7] Boys have more trouble graduating high school and are less likely to attend college. Consider that in the 1970's 58 percent of college students were men and 42 percent were women. Today, that percentage has nearly reversed and women comprised approximately 56 percent of college students nationwide in the fall of 2017. To put it into perspective, there were nearly 2.2 million fewer men enrolled in college.[8] Sadly, the trend shows no signs of letting up.

Why are boys lagging behind in school? Albert Mohler Jr., theologian and author of the book *Culture Shift*, speculates, "Many young men consider the educational environment to be frustrating, constricting, and overly feminized."[9] Decades ago there was an outcry to funnel more attention into addressing the weak links in educating girls. Special interest groups sprang forth with blueprints in place to address and cater to the learning patterns in girls in the years leading up to college, with the higher goal of increasing female enrollment in colleges and universities. New female-friendly approaches in education (for example, The Women's Educational Equity Act) were implemented to cater to the educational needs of girls and help them succeed in subjects like math and science, which had previously proven to be weak links for many girls.

Rick Johnson, author of the book *That's My Son*, notes:

> The war cry of these groups in the past has been that boys were given preferential treatment in schools much to the detriment of girls. This was epitomized a dozen years ago when Wellesley College researcher Susan Bailey wrote a report that made national headlines. Titled, "How Schools Shortchange Girls," the study chronicled how teachers paid more attention to boys, steered girls away from math and science, and made schools more inviting to boys than to girls. However, a review of the facts today shows that boys are on the weak end of the educational gender gap.[10]

Take into consideration the fact that in the United States girls capture more academic honors, outscore boys in reading and writing, and score about as well on math at the fourth-, eighth-, and twelfth-grade levels on the National Assessment for Educational

Progress exam.[11] "Brain research has shown differences in male and female brains that can affect preferred learning styles and communication," says Mary Ann Clark, UF associate professor of counselor education and principal investigator of an international study exploring the gender gap in education. "It has been suggested that public school curriculum may not be teaching 'to the boys' and that teaching styles are more suitable for girls."[12]

Michael Gurian, family therapist and author of *The Minds of Boys*, has trained thousands of teachers to handle the differences between girls and boys, showing them brain scans to point out the specific gender differences, and making suggestions on how to help boys in the classroom. "They need to touch and move things around and they need to move their bodies around and they'll learn better," he says. "The male brain many times per day just shuts down. So (boys) get bored very easily."[13] Clark agrees, stating, "The use of physical space and need for movement should be taken into consideration."[14]

Yet in spite of the finding that boys need space to move around in order to engage their brains and learn more efficiently, recess time is being drastically reduced or done away with altogether in schools across the country. Peg Tyre, author of *The Trouble with Boys*, notes "In Atlanta, Georgia, and elsewhere, recess has become such a marginal part of the school day that elementary school buildings are being erected without playgrounds. Taking test scores seriously means giving up recess."[15] The American Academy of Pediatrics has deemed recess "a crucial and necessary component of a child's development." Studies show it offers important cognitive, social, emotional, and physical benefits, yet many schools are cutting down on breaks to squeeze in more lessons, which may be counterproductive, it warns.[16] Other schools have imposed restrictions on recess such as Zeeland Elementary School in Grand Rapids, Michigan, which in 2013 banned games like tag and all chasing games for fear of someone getting hurt. That same year, CBS News reported that Weber Middle School in Port Washington, New York, placed a ban on "footballs, baseballs, soccer balls, lacrosse balls, or any other equipment that might harm a child or school friends." Nerf balls were deemed an acceptable replacement.[17] No wonder men today feel emasculated. At every turn they are forced to temper their testosterone. In the book *Wild Things*, authors (and therapists) Steven James and David Thomas say, "Instead of fighting against boys and their basic character, we must learn to work with how they were created and redirect them toward a noble vision of masculinity. Helping boys grow and mature into men means providing an environment that acknowledges and supports them in their maleness, not one that demands they be different.[18]

As mothers, we have been given a tremendous privilege to raise and nurture our sons in a way that honors God. While the culture that surrounds them seeks to demean and emasculate them at every turn, we must be their defenders, and more importantly, their cheerleaders. In the past, boys received preferential treatment simply because they were born male, and I am in no way advocating for a return to those days. I am thankful for the progress we have seen when it comes to equal rights for men and women. However, in an effort to offset the damage done in the past when women were treated as inferior, we have overcorrected to the detriment of our boys.

In spite of the culture's confusion over what constitutes masculinity and manhood, we are called to a higher standard—to raise our sons to be the men God called them to be, and to see themselves through His eyes. God values our sons, just as He values our daughters. They are not to be given an advantage, but rather a fair chance to cultivate their distinct qualities. As mothers, we will set the tone when it comes to how our sons view themselves. The culture may tell them they are burdens, but we know better. They are wonderful blessings to be celebrated in every season of life.

Chapter 2

Wired for Adventure

● ● ● ● ● ●

Now John wore a garment of camel's hair and a leather belt
around his waist, and his food was locusts and wild honey.
(Matt. 3:4 ESV)

Recently my kids were all home for a visit, and we decided to watch old home videos. In one particular video my oldest son, Ryan (age five at the time) had set a trap for his younger brother, Hayden (age eleven months). In the clip, he was explaining to the video camera his "secret plan" to trick his brother into getting caught in the "trap." The "trap" was an empty cardboard appliance box sitting on its side in the corner of our living room. Leading to the entrance of the trap was about a ten-foot long trail of Cheerios (coincidentally, Hayden's snack of choice).

Sure enough Hayden fell for the trap, crawling (and eating) his way into the cardboard prison one Cheerio at a time. Once Hayden made his way into the box, Ryan proceeded to close the flaps and quickly drag a chair in front of the box to impede his brother's escape. The tape ended with Ryan doing a victory dance of some sort while Hayden's muffled cries could be heard in the background.

Chances are you could fill a book with similar accounts documenting your own son's innate sense of adventure. I doubt any mother of a son needs to be convinced that her son is wired from birth for adventure. In the book *That's My Son*, author Rick Johnson notes, "Mothers, because of their nurturing tendencies, are often overprotective of their children. After all, it's a mother's job to civilize a boy."[1] He further explains that if a boy is missing a male influence, he can end up failing to learn the valuable link between taking risks and attaining success in life. This would likely explain the head-butting that commonly occurs between husbands and wives related to their sons' questionably "dangerous" adventures.

In my book *Your Boy*, I described a time when both my sons begged to pitch a tent in the backyard during the summer months. They were ages thirteen and eight at the time, and I relented at the prompting of my husband. One night turned into two nights, two nights into three, and before long my boys had practically moved their bedrooms into the tent. After one particular night of their campout adventure, they came in the following morning and excitedly shared that they had forgotten to zip up the entrance to the tent and had awakened to find a raccoon rifling through their food stash. I just about lost it; and with visions running through my mind of a raccoon showdown that resulted in trips to the ER to get a necessary series of rabies shots, I declared the campout officially over. My husband vetoed my camping ban, insisting these sorts of adventures are what separate the men from the boys. *(Exactly my point, I thought. Wouldn't age eight and thirteen fall into the "boy" category?)*

Today I am grateful for my husband's intervention in green-lighting many of the boyhood adventures I would have otherwise squelched.

What a Mother Doesn't Know Won't Hurt Her

As mothers, one of our greatest challenges in raising our sons is finding a healthy balance when it comes to monitoring the adventures our boys may pursue. Our goal should be to protect them without stifling their innate need for adventure. In the book *Wild Things*, authors Stephen James and David Thomas note, "The male brain has more spinal fluid in the brain stem, which makes boys more physical than girls. Add to that the high level of testosterone in a boy's brain, and it's easy to see that he is programmed to be more aggressive than girls and more of a risk taker."[2]

John Eldridge adds, "The recipe for fun is pretty simple raising boys: Add to any activity an element of danger, stir in a little exploration, add a dash of destruction, and you've got yourself a winner."[3] This brings to mind one of my oldest son's adventures that contained every element in Eldridge's suggested recipe for fun. During his college years, I had asked him to describe a memorable and "potentially dangerous" adventure he had experienced to see if there was any truth to Eldridge's theory. In return I promised him immunity for any story he shared. No scolding, no lectures. Basically, a free pass. Ryan took me up on the offer and began to share about an adventure he and one of his friends had experienced. Boy, I wish I'd never asked!

To give you a bit of background, both boys were good students who have since graduated, married, and are now raising children of their own (boys, as a matter of fact!). Ryan and his friend's adventure involved rappelling from a second-story apartment window to the ground below. I followed with the obvious question on most any mother's mind, "What in the world would possess you to do something so stupid?" His answer? Get ready because it may offer you some insight into the mysterious male mind: "Somehow it just came up, and we both admitted we'd always wanted to try it." Gulp.

With a ring of pride in his voice, Ryan went on to describe how they had stripped the bed sheets off of two twin beds in the apartment (as a side note, I doubt they had ever been washed). They then knotted the sheets together to form a makeshift rappelling rope and tied it securely to a heavy dresser. They leaned the dresser against the window, gave their rope a few test tugs, and then one at a time made their descent out the window and to the ground below. Did I mention that "the ground below" was a concrete sidewalk? You know, the kind of surface where you could bust your head wide open or, at the very least, break a leg or crack a rib, should your makeshift rope of bed sheets not hold up! As if the details offered weren't enough for my poor little mind to absorb, he then added, "Oh, and it was raining." Recognizing that I was nearing a point of possible hyperventilation, he went on to assure me with a matter-of-fact tone of confidence, "Mom, Winston is an engineering major. He knew what he was doing when he rigged the bed sheets to the dresser." Oh, okay. I feel so much better now. Sigh.

In the book *Boys Must Be Boys*, author Meg Meeker says, "Many teenage boys live in what psychologists refer to as 'personal fable.' This is the belief that they can do anything they want to—they have a distorted sense of their own power."[4] Apparently my son and his friend were caught up in the fable of Rapunzel, minus the damsel in distress, and of course, any brain cells. Meeker further notes, "It is extremely important for young men to learn the limits of their power. It's a challenge they feel bound to confront, and it's why they climb mountains, race cars, and wrestle. It is about understanding what they have inside and how far they can take it. It's when they hit the wall that humility begins to set in."[5]

It will always be a mother's nature to want to rescue her son from those moments when he may hit the wall. Or in my son's case, a concrete sidewalk. Sometimes we will be successful in our attempts, while other times we may find ourselves eight hundred miles away in a happy state of ignorance. Oh, and for the record, I ignored the immunity offer and ended up giving my boy a stern lecture, complete with a never-ending list of what-ifs. As a bonus I googled the phrase: "boy fell from second story window" and sent him several links to real-life accounts of boys who suffered from broken bones after attempting a similar stunt. In a nutshell I probably left him *wanting* to jump out a second story window! Sadly there was no shortage of tales, which lends further evidence to the fact that boys are wired for adventure. Rick Johnson notes, "Getting hurt physically, failing, persevering, and succeeding (despite overwhelming odds) are key factors in a male's growth toward manhood."[6]

You Can't Take the Nature Out of the Boy

While walking in my neighborhood in the early evening hours on a recent summer night, I was struck by the quiet, empty cul-de-sacs. Where are the grade-school kids who should be playing tag or running through their neighbor's sprinklers on a dare? Or how about the middle-school kids who should be riding their bikes to friends' houses or playing a pickup game of horse in someone's driveway? It saddens me that today's kids are missing out on outdoor play. With the increasing load of homework at every grade level, and the lure of video games, cable TV, and the computer, empty cul-de-sacs have become the suburban norm. We've simply gotten our priorities out of order.

When I was growing up, it was a very different picture. During the school year we rushed to finish our homework each afternoon so we could head to the end of my street (a cul-de-sac) where neighbor kids of all ages gathered for a game of kickball or spud (a variation of dodgeball). We played nonstop until our mothers stepped out on the front porch and yelled down the street that dinner was ready. Some of us had dogs who would faithfully hang out near where we played and accompany us on the walk back home. When I walked through the door, I was an exhausted, sweaty mess. In Texas, the temperature can reach one hundred degrees or more, but we never seemed to notice. If we got too hot, we would duck into someone's house to cool off, have a quick snack, polish off a pitcher of Kool-Aid, and head right back out for more fun.

Boys especially suffer when outdoor play is not a common part of their day. They are missing out on the blessing of experiencing adventure in its truest form: the kind of adventure born in the great outdoors. In *Wild at Heart*, author John Eldridge notes, "In the record of our beginnings, the second chapter of Genesis makes it clear: Man was born in the outback, from the untamed part of creation. Only afterward is he brought to Eden. And ever since then boys have never been at home indoors, and men have had an insatiable longing to explore."[7]

In the book *Boys Should Be Boys*, author Meg Meeker, M.D., says, "Some scholars say that the male brain is wired to enjoy the outdoors, starting with the fact that boys are visually more attracted to movement—including, presumably, the movement of game through the woods—than girls are. Other psychologists attribute the male fascination with nature to a desire for, a memory of, freedom—boys see nature as a larger arena where they can roam and daydream, and men feel that in the outdoors they can safely express their aggressive tendencies in sports or hunting."[8]

John Eldridge notes, "Adventure, with all its requisite danger and wildness, is a deeply spiritual longing written into the soul of man. The masculine heart needs a place where nothing is prefabricated, modular, nonfat, ziplocked, franchised, on-line, microwavable. Where there are no deadlines, cell phones, or committee meetings. Where there is room for the soul. Where, finally, the geography around us corresponds to the geography of our heart."[9]

I realize some of you reading this may have sons who don't actively seek out adventure and like to play it safe. Maybe they are more timid than most other boys and gravitate toward staying in an air-conditioned house rather than hiking to the creek with their friends to fish. Or maybe they have other talents that lend themselves to a more sedentary pace. Boys are wired for adventure, but not all boys will attempt to satisfy their longing for adventure in the same way. King David is a wonderful example of a well-balanced man who was a warrior fighting battles on some days and a gentle, harp-playing composer on other days. Some boys may need more of a nudge when it comes to finding their recipe for adventure.

If your son is the more sedentary type, make it your mission to expose him to some of the more sedentary adventures like camping, hiking, fishing, rock collecting, canoeing, and other fresh-air activities. Organizations like the Boy Scouts or church mission trips are other ways to expose our sons to a wide variety of adventures. Competitive sports can be a healthy outlet for many boys and give them a sense of teamwork and satisfaction that comes from working toward a goal. In a world full of noisy distractions that bid for their constant attention, it's important to teach our boys the value of "unplugging" from technology and spending time in the outdoors.

A boy never outgrows his need for adventure. As mothers, we need to develop a healthy balance when it comes to cultivating our sons' innate sense of adventure without overprotecting them in the process or, for that matter, not protecting them at all. Whether you involve your son in competitive team sports, hunting, fishing, camping, hiking, scouting, or any other number of outdoor activities, what matters most is that you get him outside and get him outside often. The best adventures for boys occur in the open outdoors. They happen while lying zipped in sleeping bags under a canopy of twinkling stars. They happen at summer camp while roasting marshmallows by a campfire and the cologne of choice is bug repellent. They happen on dusty, Little League fields when the championship trophy is at stake and your son is playing his best friend's team. They happen on dirt piles where sword fights with sticks will determine the reigning king of the hill. They happen on fishing trips taken with Dad where they will eat their catch and come home smelling like campers. They happen in neighborhood cul-de-sacs with a pickup game of basketball or a game of flashlight tag after the sun goes down. And yes, they even happen in backyard tents where potentially rabid raccoons sneak in for a midnight snack . . . while your sons sleep soundly a few feet away.

Helicopter Moms Are Dangerous to a Boy's Health

One of the greatest threats to a boy's budding manhood and quest for adventure is the ever-present and overprotective "helicopter mom." A growing legion of hovering mothers have lined up to drink the Kool-Aid when it comes to the trend of overparenting.

Some have bubble-wrapped their children from a world of potential dangers while others micromanage their children's lives down to the tiniest detail. Innocently, many of these mothers rationalize that they are investing in the future livelihood of their children, yet in reality many of their children will lack the necessary survival skills to make it in the real world.

Consider the following list of hovering behaviors to see whether you qualify as a helicopter mom.

You might be a "helicopter mom" if you:

- Repeatedly deliver your son's lunch/backpack/gym clothes/ etc. to the school when he leaves it behind.
- Are hesitant to take the training wheels off your son's bike and he is entering middle school.
- Help manage your middle/high-schooler's calendar and keep track of his assignment/test due dates. (Bonus points if you know his last three test grades.)
- Require your son to carry hand sanitizer and lather up before/after every meal/snack and bathe in it after playing outside.
- Require your son to wear flame-retardant sleepwear to bed after age ten, as opposed to other logical alternatives: (1)The outfit he wore that day or (2) his skivvies.
- Actually followed the recommended protocol of sterilizing pacifiers/toys/bottle nipples. (Exception: You get a free pass if he was your first child; after that you're guilty.)
- Find yourself saying things like: "We are registered to take the SAT this Saturday" or "We are going to play coach-pitch baseball next year instead of tee-ball," (Key word: "we").

- Have stayed up working on a class project/paper/etc. after your son has gone to bed so he can turn it in on time and not face a late penalty.
- Have signed your son up for more than two extracurricular activities in one season. (And even two can be excessive, depending on the type of activity and time required.)
- Have contacted your son's teacher/coach to argue an injustice (such as not enough playing time in the game or a failure to make the A team rather than require your son to address the problem on his own).

Truth be told, most moms, myself included, are guilty at some level of lapsing into helicopter-mom mode on occasion. It's a mother's nature to protect our children from the dangers of the world and look for ways to help them get ahead. However, we actually do our sons more harm and we "provoke them to wrath" when we are overprotective (Eph. 6:4 KJV). The key is to find a healthy balance by being "protectors" without becoming "provokers."

Please note that I am not advocating irresponsible parenting where kids are allowed to ride their bikes without helmets, eat endless amounts of junk food for dinner, and roam the streets on the weekends with no curfew. Helicopter moms behave in a manner that is extreme in nature. They can stifle a boy's pursuit of adventure by labeling his adventurous spirit as a bad thing when, in fact, God intended it to be a good thing. A boy's sense of adventure is a necessary stepping-stone along the journey to manhood.

Consider this excerpt from an article in *Time* magazine addressing the overparenting trend (and a growing backlash):

Overparenting had been around long before Douglas MacArthur's mom Pinky moved with him to West

Point in 1899 and took an apartment near the campus, supposedly so she could watch him with a telescope to be sure he was studying. But in the 1990s something dramatic happened, and the needle went way past the red line. From peace and prosperity, there arose fear and anxiety; crime went down, yet parents stopped letting kids out of their sight; the percentage of kids walking or biking to school dropped from 41 percent in 1969 to 13 percent in 2001. Death by injury has dropped more than 50 percent since 1980, yet parents lobbied to take the jungle gyms out of playgrounds, and strollers suddenly needed the warning label "Remove Child Before Folding." Among 6-to-8-year-olds, free playtime dropped 25 percent from 1981 to '97, and homework more than doubled. Bookstores offered *Brain Foods for Kids: Over 100 Recipes to Boost Your Child's Intelligence.* The state of Georgia sent every newborn home with the CD *Build Your Baby's Brain Through the Power of Music,* after researchers claimed to have discovered that listening to Mozart could temporarily help raise IQ scores by as many as 9 points. By the time the frenzy had reached its peak, colleges were installing Hi, Mom! Web cams in common areas, and employers like Ernst & Young were creating "parent packs" for recruits to give Mom and Dad, since they were involved in negotiating salary and benefits.[10]

Patricia Somers of the University of Texas at Austin spent more than a year studying the species of helicopter parents and found there are even helicopter grandparents, who turn up with their elementary-school grandchildren for college-information sessions aimed at juniors and seniors.[11]

And speaking of college, I recall sitting in a parent/student meeting at a college orientation for incoming freshmen where an academic advisor issued a gentle yet clear warning to parents: Don't call us, we'll call you (but, probably not, so don't wait by the phone). Ouch! She then went on to share a list of common overparenting abuses during the school year that include the ever popular, "I want to check on my child's grades." Or, "How does my child go about changing majors?" There's even the ever-increasing, "My child's roommate is not a good match and we need to request a mid-semester change." Excuse me, "we"? Is mama bear sleeping on a trundle in the same room, or something?

If we were to examine a root cause of hovering, it would most likely be grounded in a need to be in control. Some mothers have a tendency to overprotect their children because they are seeking control over dangers (both real and perceived) that threaten to harm their children. Other mothers may obsess over their children's homework assignments, school schedules, and overall academic progress in order to control their destiny and, thus, provide them with future happiness. They incorrectly believe the formula: good grades = good colleges = success in the real world = happily ever after. Yet other mothers may hover when it comes to image-maintenance issues such as staying in shape, dressing attractively (or wearing name brands), having the latest gadgets, or even driving a cool car.

While at first glance, hovering helicopter moms may appear to have their child's best interests in mind, their high need for control can be classified as a form of fear-based parenting. Fear of danger. Fear their child will not find future success (a relative term). And fear their child may not be accepted among his peers if he doesn't look/perform a certain way. In a nutshell, helicopter moms, like most all moms, worry they will be to blame if their children don't "turn out well" or aren't accepted. I wonder what would happen if we replaced our perceived fears with a more rational fear that our over-parenting will leave our sons ill-equipped to survive in the real world?

For those of you who are carrying mounds of guilt over such things as a failure to go over your youngest child's math drill cards (guilty as charged!) or a failure to spend as much time reading to the youngest child (guilty as charged, again!) or even failing to know which math courses your youngest child is enrolled in (guilty yet again!), let me encourage you with this little bit of irony: My youngest son scored a perfect eight hundred on the math portion of the SAT despite the fact that I was too worn out to hover over his assignments and projects during his school years like I had with my older two children. In fact, my husband and I still laugh to this day about an early teacher conference when he was in first grade where the teacher mentioned our son's knack for math and commended us for going over his math drill cards with him in the evenings. "Huh, what math drill cards?" I responded. I found them in his backpack later that day still sealed in plastic wrap and untouched since the first day of school. If I had known then what I now know, I would have clocked out sooner and traded my helicopter for a cruise ship bound for the Caribbean.

In fact, the *Time* article I mentioned previously addresses this paradox by giving us all a little food for thought when it comes to the tendency to overparent: "We can fuss and fret and shuttle and shelter, but in the end, what we do may not matter as much as we think."[12] The article cites a finding by the authors of the popular book *Freakonomics* who analyzed a Department of Education study tracking the progress of kids through fifth grade. They found that variables such as how much parents read to their kids and how much TV kids watch, among other variables, ultimately make little difference. In an interview with *USA Today*, the authors concluded, "Frequent museum visits would seem to be no more productive than trips to the grocery store."[13] This is certainly food for thought for those of us who have put in overtime hours when it comes to managing our children's lives in an effort to protect them and help them "get ahead" in the world. So much for the expensive educational toys and Hooked on Phonics tapes! Buy yourself a latte instead and call it a day.

Mom to the Rescue!

In order to develop a healthy masculinity, boys will attempt to break away from their mothers at various stages in the growing-up journey. This is a natural occurrence that if stifled can inhibit their quest to become men. Moms who hold tightly to their boys or, worse yet, come to their rescue every time they face consequences from mistakes or irresponsible actions will breed a sense of prolonged dependency in their sons. And if there was ever a mom to come to the rescue, it's the helicopter mom. You've seen her before. She's the one zipping into a parking lot at the school, jogging into the school with a leap and bound as she delivers little Johnny's lunch to the office. Again. For the third time this month. With a sweet note written on little Johnny's napkin because that's what helicopter moms do. They rescue their sons from negative consequences because negative consequences are unpleasant.

The *Time* article I cited previously described one elementary school principal in Kansas who got so fed up with parents rescuing their children, she established a "no rescue" policy. Her breaking point came when she noticed the front-office table covered day after day with forgotten lunch boxes and notebooks, all brought in by parents. Gulp. Guilty as charged. I pulled the mom-to-the-rescue stunt more times than I'm ashamed to admit. My breakthrough finally came on my third trip in one week to the local middle school. This time I was delivering an assignment my son left behind when all of a sudden I realized there was greater value in allowing him to suffer the consequences rather than rescue him yet again and reinforce the pattern of irresponsibility.

In the book *That's My Son*, author Rick Johnson warns,

> By running too quickly to rescue their sons when things get tough, some moms are teaching their boys that the way out of hard times is to find someone to get them off the hook rather than to be accountable to the one in authority and step up to the plate. This can set patterns for boys' entire lives. A boy who avoids accountability becomes a man who is answerable to no one—a recipe for disaster.[14]

When we rescue our sons from the consequences of their irresponsible actions and mistakes, we actually hinder their progress in the journey to manhood. Let me put it to you in a more sobering fashion: When we rescue our sons from consequences, we hinder them from becoming men and encourage them to behave like little mama's boys indefinitely. Part of becoming a man is learning to accept responsibility for irresponsible actions and mistakes, learn from the experiences, and correct the behaviors before they become a habit or pattern.

I am not suggesting we have a zero-tolerance policy for mistakes and run our homes like a military boot camp. Everyone makes mistakes, and we've all been in need of a rescue from time to time. I recall an assignment my son failed to bring to school in his junior year of high school. His cumulative GPA was right on the borderline of what he needed in order to qualify for college academic scholarships. A simple ten-point grade deduction on a late assignment can serve as a punishment of sorts to me and my husband if it means missed opportunities in the way of scholarships. I made an exception but made my son do the dishes when he came home, so he didn't escape without consequences.

If we are to help our sons become men, we must be willing to employ some tough-love parenting tactics along the way. We do them no favors when we rush to their rescue time and time again and allow them to escape without consequences. Mothers who establish this pattern will be rescuing their boys for many years to come. A friend of mine recently told me about a mother from her church who sent out a churchwide e-mail soliciting employment for her grown son, who was in his thirties. My friend was appalled, as well she should be. Further, the mother attached her son's résumé and gave her e-mail address as the contact, stating she would pass along any job leads to him since he *lived at home*.

This lady isn't a mother; she's an unpaid personal assistant! It's time for mama to cut the apron strings and let her adult-aged son grow up and become a real man. This clearly isn't the first time this mom has come to her son's rescue. It probably began with a lunch that was left behind, followed by the gym clothes, a few school projects, another lunch or two, and the list goes on and on. Resist the urge to rescue your son from unpleasant consequences. If you don't, you just may find yourself working as a full-time, unpaid assistant for decades to come while your son faithfully puts in overtime on your living room sofa with a game controller in hand. Energy drinks and buffalo wings included. On your dime.

Hold on Loosely

My house is in a neighborhood that backs up to a large green-belt. We see deer year-round and always love the spring when we encounter a few fawn sightings. One particular spring I found a baby fawn abandoned along my backyard fence line. I could see it right out my back window and began to worry when a day had gone by and it was still alone. I feared it might not make it, so I did a little research on the Internet and discovered that it is perfectly normal for a doe to leave her young in the first week. If the mother stays close by, predators may pick up her scent and harm the fawn. Amazingly, fawns are odorless after they are born to help protect them from predators. I read further that the mothers do, in fact, return throughout the day to feed them and will even move them every so often if they feel the fawn may be in danger.

Much like a fawn's mother, a boy's mother knows when it's time to begin to pull away for the well-being of her son. Deep in a mother's heart, we all know that when it comes time for our sons to leave, they will leave both *physically* and *emotionally*. They will eventually turn their attention to another woman who will become the recipient of their love and adoration (if they are called to marry). Of course our sons will still love us, but their feelings won't be manifested in the same way a daughter's feelings would be toward her mother. Our role is to prepare our sons to love another, all the while, enjoying every minute of the brief season when we reign as queen in their hearts.

In the book *Teenage Guys*, author Steve Gerali comments on this awkward dance:

> As the boy begins to pull away from his mother, there is conflict between his strong need for emotional intimacy (attachment) and an equally strong need for identity (autonomy). These *attachment battles* exemplify a teenage guy's need and reluctance to connect with his mother. Mothers become aware of these attachment battles. She knows them intuitively, and she feels them acutely as they occur. This intuition or instinct is a built-in, God-designed part of mothering sons. Most mothers, unless they have some compulsive disorder, give up their sons. The greatest struggle she faces is to know when and how to let go.[15]

As a mother, whose children have flown the nest, married, and are now raising children of their own, I cannot emphasize the importance of knowing your place, especially when it comes to the mother/son relationship. Even as someone who knew these truths, it proved easier said than done in the aftermath of my sons' departures. I would be lying if I told you the letting go process was without bumps along the way. I had a particularly difficult time when my youngest son (also the "baby" of the family) left for college. When I dropped him off his freshman year, I assumed he would return home just as his older siblings had done and so saying goodbye wasn't as difficult. I rationalized he'd be back each summer, taking up residence in his childhood bedroom down the hall and I could postpone the inevitable a bit longer.

The reality is that he came home for six weeks of the summer after his freshman year and spent the remainder of his summer break as a counselor at a Christian camp. After that, he decided to stay on campus in his apartment in the summers that followed since he was in a twelve-month lease and his roommates were remaining. He was engaged to be married his senior year and began his married life upon graduation, so my expectations of having him home at least one more time went unmet. Don't get me wrong—I couldn't be more proud of my son, nor could I have picked a more wonderful girl for him to marry. I wouldn't have it any other way, but the adjustment was hard all the same because I had failed to truly "let go" when he left for college.

In processing my disappointment, God reminded me of the sobering truth that my children were only on loan to me for a time. He entrusted them to my care for the purpose of raising them to love and serve Him. When my children were in the nest, my "primary family" was me, my husband, and our three children. Once our children left the nest, my primary family transitioned to become me and my husband (and my little Yorkie, I might add!). My children have now begun their own "primary families" and will in turn, prepare their children to someday leave the nest and establish their own primary families. And so on, and so on, and so on. It is the way God intended.

One of the greatest privileges we have as mothers is to pray for our sons. In doing so, we actively release them into the care of the Lord every time we petition the Lord on their behalf. When the time comes for them to leave our care, we may feel a slight sting from their physical absence, but we will pick right back up where we left off in our prayers for them. Prayer is the link to maintaining the connection to our sons, because a boy who is prayed for by his mother always remains in his mother's heart. As Hannah prayed in 1 Samuel 1:28 when she gave up young Samuel and dedicated him to the Lord's care, we too, should pray for our sons, "So now I give him to the LORD. For his whole life he will be given over to the LORD." The most important step in launching our sons into manhood is to loosen our grip and give them over to the Lord. We are called to raise them up and let them go. The truth is, it is far easier to let go of something you knew you were never meant to keep.

Chapter 3

Masculinity Redefined

● ● ● ● ● ●

*Be on the alert, stand firm in the faith, act like men, be strong.
Let all that you do be done in love. (1 Cor. 16:13–14 NASB)*

Masculinity is experiencing a bit of an identity crisis. When it comes to the culture's portrayal of manhood, they can't seem to make up their minds. Take, for example, popular men's grooming brand Axe (owned by Unilever who brought the well-received and popular Dove campaign for beauty aimed at women). For years, Axe relied on ads featuring chiseled male models with the takeaway theme that Axe's grooming products would turn a man into an everyday chick magnet. Fast-forward to today and the release of a new ad campaign called "Find Your Magic" where they shed the one-size-fits-all approach that portrayed a rigid stereotype of manhood, and offered instead a 60-second anthem celebrating a more diverse group of men.

The ad opens with a narrator asking, "C'mon, a six-pack?" (as in chiseled abs); "Who needs a six-pack when you've got the nose?," as it shifts to a scene with a confident young man with a large nose emerging from a car. From there, the ad transitions from one scene to another highlighting a nontraditional group of men. One scene highlights a heavy-set bearded man playing with kittens, while another highlights what appears to be a trans dancer striking a pose while strutting a pair of stiletto heals. Other scenes include two male students in a dorm room exchanging affectionate glances with the innuendo of attraction and yet another scene highlights a man in a wheelchair dancing with a woman. The ad closes with the line, "Who needs some other thing when you've got your thing?"[1] The message is clear: masculinity and, more importantly, manhood can be anything you want it to be. It's up to each individual to define it.

Masculinity: The Androgynous Blurring of the Lines

Justin Sitron, a clinical assistant professor of education and human sexuality at Widener University states that "masculinity has been in a period of exploration in the last 20 to 25 years."[2] One need not look any further than advertising for evidence that the assumption of two distinct genders is a thing of the past.

While thumbing through a sales catalog advertising a line of teen furnishings, I ran across a particular image that included several teen models. A girl was sitting on a furry, neon-colored beanbag chair. Standing within a few feet of her was a guy, smiling and gesticulating as though engaged in conversation. And next to him was another guy. Or wait, was it a girl? The model had short hair and wore skinny jeans and a baggy button shirt. He/she was lanky with androgynous facial features that appeared neither overtly masculine nor feminine. I looked for any hint that might tip the scale in one direction, but I finally gave up.

Since then, Bruce Jenner has had elective surgery to become Caitlin Jenner. Covergirl named a seventeen-year-old boy to be the face for their 2017 campaign, and Facebook announced it would be expanding its gender identification options to include more than fifty choices. Should a user not be able to find an option that suits them, they also offer an additional option to self-identify.

As we stray further and further from a biblical model of manhood and womanhood, our sons (and daughters) will grow up in a world where gender-fluid is the new norm. *Gender-fluid* can be defined as "noting or relating to a person whose gender identity or gender expression is not fixed and shifts over time or depending on the situation."[3]

A recent survey found that:

- Sixty-nine percent of teens (age thirteen to eighteen) said it is acceptable to "be born one gender and feel like another."
- Thirty-three percent of teens surveyed said gender is primarily based on "what a person feels like."
- Three in ten teens surveyed reported personally knowing someone, most often a peer, who has changed his or her identity.
- One in eight teens (12 percent) describe their sexual orientation as something other than heterosexual or straight.[4]

Compare this to the approximate 3 percent of older adults who have identified with being LGBT. Why is this important? The current generation of teens (iGen or Generation Z) more than any other generation before them, considers their sexuality or gender to be central to their sense of personal identity.[5]

If we are to raise sons who are confident in their manhood, we must be aware of the outside influences that seek to undermine God's design for gender and sexuality. Genesis 1:27 reminds us that God created man in His own image. "Male and female he created them." Men and women are different because God created them to be distinctly different. It is the natural order set by our creator God and anything that suggests otherwise is a deviation from that natural order. Our sons are growing up in a day when such views are considered narrow-minded and bigoted. The gender-fluid movement has gained traction and like it or not, our sons will be exposed to this increasingly accepted deviation from God's design.

As mothers, our goal should be to teach our children the precarious balance of walking in Truth and leading with love. We need to be intentional when it comes to making sure our sons understand the creation account and God's design for manhood and, likewise, womanhood. However, we must also teach our sons to be kind and compassionate to others who don't share their same values and beliefs. Romans 3:23 reminds us, "for all have sinned and fall short of the glory of God." Rarely, do we win converts to Christianity by being combative and loudly pointing out how others fall short of God's standards.

Jesus illustrated this balance throughout His earthly ministry when He encountered those who were in sin. His goal was not to implement a moral code of behavior, but rather, to change hearts. When He encountered the Samaritan woman at a well (John 4), He didn't chastise her for having had five husbands in the past and living at the time with a man who wasn't her husband. He saw her need beneath her deeds and loved her enough to engage in a conversation and offer her living water (forgiveness of sin).

Our sons are growing up in a world where it's not uncommon for self-proclaiming Christians to compromise Truth to fit the customs of an ever-changing culture, and it's up to us to make sure our sons understand God's absolute Truth regarding gender and sexuality. As we broach these sensitive topics, it is of equal importance that they see us demonstrate an attitude of love for those who do not embrace God's Truth regarding sexuality and gender, rather than one of harsh judgment. We have the answer the world so desperately needs and it is our job to shine a spotlight on God's grace and mercy.

Lest you think this movement is not gaining traction, consider that this past year, a mother at an event where I was the speaker shared that her daughter was given in-school detention for "incorrectly stating there are only two genders." As part of her suspension, she was required to memorize a list of politically correct gender pronouns created by the school in an effort to respect the broad list of identities represented among the student body. I thought I'd heard it all when the mother added that one girl in her daughter's class has shared that she identifies as "feline." While my initial reaction to hearing her account was one of shock and even outrage that Christians would be forced to abide by a policy that enforces the ridiculous assumption that a person can identify with being anything they want to be, my anger quickly turned to compassion. How sad that so many of our children and youth are desperately searching for identity and purpose and our culture has led them down a path that will leave them even more confused and empty in the end.

If your son is struggling with gender confusion or same-sex attraction, there are many resources available to guide you. Even if you cannot personally understand or relate to his struggle, that does not mean his struggle is not real. Do not shame him by telling him he shouldn't be feeling those things. It is not a sin to have a same-sex attraction or to experience gender confusion. It is only a sin when it is acted upon. Unfortunately, the church is ill-prepared to minister to those experiencing gender confusion or same-sex attraction. I hope we will see more churches address this topic with grace and humility. The truth is, we are all fighting a battle. Colossians 3:5 calls us to "Put to death therefore what is earthly in you: sexual immorality, impurity, passion, evil desire, and covetousness, which is idolatry" (ESV). We all experience earthly temptations and therefore, we can relate to the struggle to succumb to the culture's lie that fulfilling your desires is the key to happiness. Most of us have learned the hard way that feeding the desires of the flesh can produce misery and bondage.

In 1 Peter 2:11, we are told to "abstain from the passions of the flesh, which wage war against your soul" (ESV). In order to win the battle, we must wage war against that which threatens to defeat us. Whether the battle is a temptation to view pornography, engage in pre-marital sex, have an adulterous affair, act on a same-sex attraction, or identify with a different gender, we must have a battle plan in place to protect our souls. The culture is teaching our children that "if it feels good, do it." We need to be intentional when it comes to dispelling that lie. Part of being intentional is making sure you are discussing this topic with your son so he will understand that everyone is facing a battle of some sort. Even if he is not personally experiencing the battle, it will help equip him to minister to those who are struggling from a place of compassion and love rather than judgment and shame.

The True Source of Worth

If I had to choose one topic to discuss with young people, it would be the topic of worth. The dictionary defines "worth" as "usefulness or importance, as to the world, to a person, or for a purpose."[6] At the core of our being, we all want to feel useful and important to others. We want to know we matter in this great big world we live in. Our sons are no different. Unfortunately, most of us will look for worth in all the wrong places. Most of us have subconsciously bought into the culture's lies regarding worth and rarely question their validity. It is all we know. Many of us had parents who reinforced the lies, having ignorantly believed them for themselves. So, what are the lies regarding worth?

Worth = What you look like
Worth = What you do
Worth = What others think

Not a day goes by that we don't see culture's lie, "Worth = What you look like" play out. If our children are conditioned to believe their worth is related to what they look like on the outside, we set them up for an ongoing battle. What happens when they go through a gangly awkward stage? Or their face breaks out? Or they get a bad haircut? Or they gain weight? If they have been conditioned to believe their worth is dependent on their outer appearance, they will lack worth when their reflection doesn't match their expectations.

In 1 Samuel 16:7, we are reminded that God doesn't value appearance.

> But the LORD said to Samuel, "Do not consider his appearance or his height, for I have rejected him. The LORD does not look at the things people look at. People

look at the outward appearance, but the LORD looks at
the heart."

God is clear: Worth does not equal what you look like. God
cares more about the condition of our hearts. Does your son know
that? Do you?

Another lie regarding worth is "Worth = What you do." I am the
poster child for the long-term damage that can come from believing
this lie. It has led to seasons of over-commitment and burnout in
my life when I lapse back into believing my worth is tied to what
I do rather than who I am in Christ. One tell-tale sign this is may
be a struggle for you is your calendar. Do you rush to fill empty
blocks of time in your day? Is it hard for you to sit still and relax?
Have you over-scheduled your children's lives to the point that
there is little margin left in your day or theirs, for that matter? Do
you put an unhealthy emphasis on achievement and success? There
is absolutely nothing wrong with looking for ways to cultivate your
children's natural gifts and abilities, but the problem comes when
there is an unhealthy focus on achievement to the point it begins to
define their worth.

What happens when they don't get a ribbon on their science
project? Or they fail to make the A team or first string in the sport
they have excelled in? Or they fail to make the team at all? Or
they get injured and can no longer play? What happens if they fail
a test or struggle academically in a subject? What happens if their
GPA drops and they fail to make the honor roll or maintain their
class ranking? What happens if they don't do well on their college
entrance exams and fail to get into the college of their dreams?

God has a different standard when it comes to "Worth = What
you do." In Ephesians 2:8–9, we are reminded, "God saved you by
his grace when you believed. And you can't take credit for this; it

is a gift from God. Salvation is not a reward for the good things we have done, so none of us can boast about it" (NLT). If God doesn't require good works to earn our salvation, He certainly doesn't endorse that our worth be based on our accomplishments. There is nothing wrong with striving for excellence (or for that matter, doing good works), but our worth should not be defined by our accomplishments. God never intended that we knock ourselves out like hamsters on a hamster wheel from the cradle to the grave. Life is about so much more than accomplishments and successes. Does your son know that? Do you?

Another lie regarding worth is, "Worth = What others think." Look no further than social media to see the power of this lie in play. Every picture and post invites the approval of others. Thumbs up, heart emojis, comments, a friend or follower count. Every day is a popularity contest and it never ends. Your son, by default is growing up in a culture that will let him know what they think whether he likes it or not. Who among us doesn't like approval? It can be a good thing unless our need for it becomes compulsive and our worth becomes dependent on it. The thing is, not everyone will like us and that's *okay*. Sure, sometimes it is beneficial to listen to critics if they're sincere and have our best interests in mind, but oftentimes, we allow the opinions of others to define our worth and value. The apostle Paul spoke to the people-pleasing battle in Galatians 1:10 when he said, "Am I now trying to win the approval of human beings, or of God? Or am I trying to please people? If I were still trying to please people, I would not be a servant of Christ." It poses a question for us all: Are we more focused on the approval of people, or of God?

In Psalm 139:17–18, we are reminded, "How precious to me are your thoughts, God! How vast is the sum of them! Were I to count them, they would outnumber the grains of sand." God's thoughts about you outnumber the grains of sand on the shore. Stop and think about that for a minute. We don't have to earn God's approval because He's proved His love for us by sending His Son to die for our sins "while we were still sinners" (Rom. 5:8). When the amazing reality of that sinks in, why in the world would we ever allow the opinions of others to define our worth?! Does your son know how God feels about him? Do you know how He feels about you?

If we are to refute the culture's lies regarding worth, we must focus more on the condition of our sons' hearts than their outer appearance. We must focus more on who they are in Christ rather than their successes, awards, and accomplishments. We must focus more on caring less about what others think and more about what God thinks of us. The culture will propagate the faulty worth lies and we can either support the lies or offset the damage by making sure we tell our sons the truth. For many of us (myself included), it will require a concentrated effort to shift our focus from believing the culture's lies regarding worth to believing God's truth. Old habits die hard, but the freedom that comes from seeing yourself through God's eyes is worth the effort. Do it for your son's sake, but also for your sake. You're worth it!

One of my favorite passages of Scripture is Ephesians 3:16–19. It says:

> I pray that out of his glorious riches he may strengthen
> you with power through his Spirit in your inner being, so
> that Christ may dwell in your hearts through faith. And
> I pray that you, being rooted and established in love, may
> have power, together with all the saints, to grasp how
> wide and long and high and deep is the love of Christ,
> and to know this love that surpasses knowledge—that

you may be filled to the measure of all the fullness of
God. (NIV, 1984 edition)

The Greek word for *filled* in verse 19 is: *plērōō* (play-rŏ´-o) and
it means "to make replete" or to "level up (a hollow)."[7] The passage
speaks to the hollow place we all have in our hearts and the necessity to be "rooted and established in love" and further to "grasp how
wide and long and high and deep is the love of Christ." Our tendency will be to fill that hollow place with the quick-fix solutions
offered by the world, whether it be desires, pleasures, impulses,
accomplishments, flattery, approval, or the like. While those things
may offer a temporary brand of satisfaction, they will not complete
us. The buzz will eventually wear off. The unconditional love of
God as demonstrated by the love of Christ and His willingness to
die for us, is the only thing that will fill the hollow place in our
hearts and satisfy us permanently.

If our sons are to understand their true identity and worth,
we must make sure they are rooted and established in God's love.
Better yet, we must understand it ourselves and lead by example.

What's a Mother to Do?

As mothers, we will be one of the strongest voices in our sons'
lives. First Chronicles 12:32 speaks of the men of Issachar who
"understood the temper of the times and knew the best course
for Israel to take" (TLB). We too must understand the temper of
the times and determine the best course to take when it comes to
raising our sons to be the men God intended them to be. Our best
source for determining that course is to look to the Bible and, more
specifically, the men of the Bible who sought to conform to God's
image rather than conform to the times.

Masculinity was never intended to be soft, wimpy, and feminine, nor was it intended to be hyper-aggressive and devoid of sensitivity and emotion. It seems our culture (and yes, sometimes even the church) likes to portray it as a one-size-fits-all version of one of the above extremes, when the truth is, it is neither. Jesus modeled the perfect balance of masculinity in His earthly ministry. The same man who turned the moneychangers tables over in the temple was the same man who wept with Mary and Martha over their brother's death. He was a man of courage, bravery, humility, sacrifice, sensitivity, and compassion. He walked in Truth and He led with love. When helping your son understand true masculinity and manhood, you can't go wrong by pointing him to Jesus.

Talk about It

* * * * * * * * * *

Chapter 1

Reflect on the quote I shared by E. W. Caswell (eighteenth-century hymnwriter):

> "The mother, more than any other, affects the moral and spiritual part of the children's character. She is their constant companion and teacher in formative years. The child is ever imitating and assimilating the mother's nature. It is only in after life that men gaze backward and behold how a mother's hand and heart of love molded their young lives and shaped their destiny."

Were you aware of the vital part you play in shaping your son's destiny? Share what qualities you hope to pass on to your son that he can carry with him in his journey to manhood.

What are some things you have done to pave the way for open communication between you and your son(s)?

What are your thoughts and feelings about your son pulling away from you in his adolescent years as part of his journey to manhood?

Chapter 2

What are some age-appropriate ways you can encourage independence in your son?

Is it difficult for you to find a healthy balance when it comes to cultivating your son's innate sense of adventure without overprotecting him in the process? Share about a specific adventure or occasion where you were faced with this challenge.

In what ways have you been guilty of being a "helicopter mom"?

Is it difficult for you to allow your son to suffer the consequences in an effort to teach him responsibility or is it your tendency to rescue him? Share an example that might pertain to this struggle.

Is it difficult for you to accept the idea that a mother should "hold on loosely" to her children because they are not ours to keep?

Chapter 3

If you had to define "manhood" in your own words, how would you define it? In other words, what stereotype of masculinity has most influenced your thinking?

Has your son encountered any confusing messages regarding manhood that you have had to address? If so, how did you address it?

Which of the culture's lies regarding worth do you struggle with the most? What about your son?

Worth = What you look like
Worth = What you do
Worth = What others think

What steps can you take to help your son define his worth in Christ?

Conversation 2

Guard your heart.

Chapter 4

The Tech Natives Are Restless

· · · · · ·

An evil man is held captive by his own sins; they are ropes that catch and hold him. He will die for lack of self-control; he will be lost because of his great foolishness. (Prov. 5:22–23 NLT)

I have a small collection of vintage magazines and love to thumb through them from time to time to gain a glimpse into days past. When it comes to parenting challenges, mothers over the decades past tended to worry about the same things we do today: the health and safety of their children, raising them to become independent, responsible adults, and guarding against immoral influences along the way. If you turn the clock back a century or more, you can't help but feel envious that "media" had yet to make its debut on the list of immoral influences to guard against. Consider this parenting advice given to mothers of sons in the September 1894 edition of

The Ladies' Home Journal in an article entitled "The Farmer's Wife and Her Boys":

> The farmer and the housewife are so tired with their hard day's work that they are glad to go to bed almost at dusk. What then becomes of the boys? Why, they get into the habit of spending their evenings at the country store—and very unsafe places are many of these country stores. If the farmer's wife will take time to think she will realize that in the community in which she lives there are one or two men, perhaps, that are moral plague spots on the good name of that community. She will also discover that the country store is the headquarters of these men. For this reason, if for no other, she will try and keep her boys away from that store in the evenings.[1]

If only our biggest worry was our sons cavorting at the country store in the early evening and running into a couple of unsavory men with bad morals! With technology, "moral plague spots" are only a click away and the country store is now open 24/7 and has expanded to reach every corner of their lives. They don't even have to leave the house. It will come to them whether they are looking for it or not.

Technology has completely changed the landscape of the culture in which our children are growing up. Smart phones even more so. Never before have we had so much information, whether solicited or unsolicited, at our fingertips. And while most of us can remember a time when technology and smart phones weren't a part of everyday life, our children cannot. Many of today's toddlers built their first block tower with an app on Mom's tablet and could swipe through a digital photo library before speaking in sentences. I have a few educational kids' game apps on my tablet and I've watched with amazement as my young grandsons (who have very limited amounts of screen time) know exactly where to find them and have figured out how to play them with little to no direction from me. They, like your children, are early adapters and tech natives.

I myself can't imagine having to revert back to the days of long-distance phone calls on landlines, busy signals, fold-up maps in the glove box of the car, bulky phone books, record albums, cameras with film cartridges that take twelve, twenty-four, or thirty-six pictures at a time, and encyclopedias (or card catalogs at the library!) to research a topic. As a writer, I wonder how many books would have actually been published if it required me to type them out page by page on a typewriter and correct my mistakes with Liquid Paper! Children today don't know that such a time even existed. Nor do they remember early technology and dial-up Internet that beeped and whined until it connected. If it ever did. This is their world and the challenge will be to raise them to master technology, rather than be mastered by it. But first, we must master it ourselves.

Screen Time and Mental Health

A few years ago, I experienced an intense burnout. Years of juggling back-to-back book deadlines, travel, and ministry obligations finally caught up with me and left me with an unmistakable emptiness in my soul. I knew at the time that if I didn't slow down, catch my breath, and make some necessary changes, the fallout would be immense. As part of my recovery, I had to learn to disconnect from my digital world in order to reconnect to God. As someone who had been an early adapter to technology, I realized I had been sucked into the vortex of screens bidding for my attention from morning to nightfall. Like many of our multi-tasking teens, it wasn't uncommon for me to have a laptop in my lap as I scrambled to make the latest book deadline, my phone by my side to manage my social media accounts, and oftentimes, the TV on in the background. Years of this pattern took a toll on my soul. The problem was only made worse when I would seek escape from the pressures by turning on a twenty-four-hour news show or scrolling through my social media newsfeed. It seemed mindless and innocuous, yet I could not deny that it always seemed to make me feel *worse* rather than *better.* It was just too much. It was then that I realized that at some level, I had allowed technology to master me rather than the other way around. As I began to detox and take steps to limit my media exposure, my overall mental health began to improve.

I cannot begin to imagine the impact our tech-saturated culture is having on our children, especially given that their emotional and mental capacity is immature and in a state of development. In a way, they are the guinea pigs of a social experiment where constant connectivity has replaced solitude. As true tech natives, they have no other point of reference by which to compare their lives because they have never witnessed a calmer, quieter, unplugged way of life. Most do not even know it is a possibility. Jean Twenge, a professor of psychology at San Diego State University, has devoted much of her study to the generations, past and current, and believes it is "not an exaggeration to describe iGen as being on the brink of the worst mental-health crisis in decades."[2] One of the sources she cites that led her to this conclusion is the Monitoring the Future survey, which is funded by the National Institute on Drug Abuse. The survey has asked twelfth-graders more than 1,000 questions every year since 1975 and queried eighth- and tenth-graders since 1991. The survey gauges leisure time and how it is spent and more importantly, the impact it has on their happiness. In recent years, it has taken a much closer look on screen activities such as using social media, texting, and browsing the web. Twenge claims, "The results could not be clearer: Teens who spend more time than average on screen activities are more likely to be unhappy, and those who spend more time than average on nonscreen activities are more likely to be happy. There's not a single exception. All screen activities are linked to less happiness, and all nonscreen activities are linked to more happiness."[3]

Not surprisingly, the risk of unhappiness due to social media use is the highest for the youngest teens. Eighth-graders who spent ten or more hours a week on social networking sites were 56 percent more likely to be unhappy, compared to 47 percent for tenth-graders and 20 percent for twelfth-graders.[4] Eighth-graders who are heavy users of social media increase their risk of depression by 27 percent, while those who play sports, go to religious services, or even do homework more than the average teen cut their risk significantly.[5] Even more disturbing is the finding that "teens who spend three hours a day or more on electronic devices are 35 percent more likely to have a risk factor for suicide, such as making a suicide plan."[6]

In addition to reporting record levels of unhappiness among teens, the survey also found that teens are now lonelier than at any other times since the survey began in 1991.[7] Stop and think about that for a moment. The most heavily engaged generation in social media with all their friends, followers, likes, views, and connections is proving to be the loneliest and most disconnected generation on record. If that isn't a wake-up call, I don't know what is. And it's only increasing. The survey found that "a stunning 31 percent more 8th and 10th graders felt lonely in 2015 than in 2011, along with 22 percent more 12th graders."[8] Twenge notes, "Such large changes over a short period of time are unusual, suggesting a specific cause with a big impact. Given the timing, smartphones are the most likely culprits, increasing loneliness both directly and indirectly replacing in-person social interaction."[9]

The American Freshman Survey which surveys entering college students found similar results. Twenge notes, "Every indicator of mental health issues on the survey reached all-time highs in 2016—rating emotional health below average (increasing 18 percent since 2009), feeling overwhelmed (increasing 51 percent), expecting to seek counseling (increasing 64 percent), and (perhaps most troubling) feeling depressed (increasing 95 percent, or nearly doubling), with noticeable jumps just between 2015 and 2016."[10] She goes on to say, "In 2016, for the first time, the majority of entering college students described their mental health as below average. The sudden, sharp rise in depressive symptoms occurred at almost exactly the same time that smartphones became ubiquitous and in-person interaction plummeted."[11] If you need any more proof, consider also that the National Survey on Drug Use and Health (NSDUH), which is conducted by the US Department of Health and Human Services, has screened more than 17,000 teens (ages twelve to seventeen) across the country every year for clinical-level depression since 2004. The screening results show an escalating rise in depression in a very short period of time reporting that 56 percent more teens experienced a major depressive episode in 2015 than in 2010.[12]

It is not just our teens who are at risk. Other studies have found that the more TV a child watches between the ages of one and three, the greater the likelihood that they will develop an attention problem by age seven, and six- to twelve-year-olds who spent more than two hours a day playing video games or watching TV had trouble paying attention in school and were more likely to have attention problems.[13]

Dr. Victoria Dunckley—a child psychiatrist specializing in electronic screen syndrome after having worked with countless children with psychiatric, developmental and behavioral disorders—began to take a closer look at possible underlying causes in an effort to explain the uptick in mental health disorders among children. "As she looked at the data, she saw that visits for kids diagnosed with pediatric bipolar disorder had increased 40-fold from 1994 to 2003; that between 1980 and 2007 the diagnosis of ADHD had increased by nearly 800 percent, while prescriptions for psychotropic medications given to kids had sharply increased over the past two decades."[14] As Dr. Dunckley began to parse through the data, she discovered a common denominator in play: screens.[15]

Dr. Nicholas Kardaras, an addictions expert and author of the book, *Glow Kids: How Screen Addiction Is Hijacking Our Kids*, notes that "recent brain-imaging studies conclusively show that excessive screen exposure can neurologically damage a young person's developing brain in the same way that cocaine addiction can."[16] Kardaras does an amazing job of explaining the brain science behind the compulsive nature many kids have when it comes to their screens, whether it be computers, phones, TVs, video games, or the like. Much like an electronic drug, our kids receive a dopamine blast in the reward center of their brains that keep them coming back for more and more of the same. It can be triggered by achieving the next level in a computer or video game, receiving likes or positive comments on pictures posted on social media, viewing pornography, and other technology stimulants. Some kids have a temperament or genetic influence that puts them at greater risk for addiction. Kardaras notes, "We know that having addiction in one's family can predispose a person toward that condition and that the children of addicts are eight times more likely to develop an addiction problem."[17]

Perhaps even more disturbing is that the social media and video game industries are well aware of the brain science that can lead many individuals (especially, young vulnerable children) to get "hooked" on their products and services. "Gaming companies will hire the best neurobiologists and neuroscientists to hook up electrodes to the test-gamer. If they don't elicit the blood pressure that they shoot for—typically 180 over 120 or 140 within a few minutes of playing, and if they don't show sweating and an increase in their galvanic skin responses, they go back and tweak the game to get that maximum addicting and arousing response that they're looking for."[18] Add to this that a former Facebook president recently admitted the site was built to exploit "a vulnerability in human psychology." Sean Parker admitted that when he and the team launched Facebook in the early 2000s, they were trying to figure out, "How do we consume as much of your time and conscious attention as possible?" He goes on to add, "It literally changes your relationship with society, with each other." Parker adds, "God only knows what it's doing to our children's brains."[19] Our kids may not be on Facebook much anymore (if at all), but rest assured that the latest and greatest social media platform has also figured out how to exploit the same vulnerability in human psychology.

By now, you're probably wanting to gather up all the screens in your house and use them for target practice in the backyard. It's important to remember that technology is not a bad thing. In fact, we enjoy its benefits on a daily basis and it has, on many occasions, enriched our lives. The problem lies in how we choose to utilize it. I personally have loved reconnecting with old friends (thanks to social media!) and have enjoyed many of the other benefits it has provided, such as staying in touch with friends and family members and hearing from many of the women who have read my books to name a few. I have figured out how it can best serve me rather than the other way around. As depressing as many of these findings are, I am hopeful that it will expose our desperate need for a different kind of connection. God wired our hearts for connection with Him, first and foremost. Secondly, it is His desire that we connect with others in a deep and meaningful way. Perhaps this is the wake-up call for parents to talk with their children about their deep-seated need for connection with God, so they are not as likely to fall for a false substitute.

The Spiritual Impact of a Distracted Life

In Luke chapter 10, we see a beautiful picture of the spiritual tug-of-war our souls are engaged in on a daily basis with the example of two sisters, Mary and Martha. Jesus was a guest in their home and while Mary "sat at the Lord's feet and listened to his teaching," Martha, we are told, "was distracted with much serving" (vv. 39–40 ESV). While the clear link to excessive media-consumption and mental health will compel many parents to draw limits on their children's access, Christian parents should be far more concerned with the impact it will have on the spiritual health of their children. You can't catch God on the run and expect to have a thriving, deep relationship with Him. Getting to know Christ will require silence, solitude, and stillness.

In his book, *12 Ways Your Phone Is Changing You*, author Tony Reinke proposes that we engage in digital distractions to "keep thoughts of eternity away."[20] He goes on to cite the wisdom of seventeenth-century Christian mathematician Blaise Pascal who theorized we are easily lured by distractions in an effort to avoid having to be alone with ourselves. "I have discovered that all the unhappiness of men arises from one single fact, that they cannot stay quietly in their own chamber. Hence it comes that men so much love noise and stir; hence it comes that the prison is so horrible a punishment; hence it comes that the pleasure of solitude is a thing incomprehensible."[21] How ironic that the weariness of our souls can be cured by seeking Christ and sitting at His feet and yet, much like the fickle Israelites, we choose instead to chase after our own modern-day false gods. Truth be told, this is not an issue that impacts our children. It impacts us all, regardless of age and spiritual maturity. Maybe your false gods go by different names than your children's, but the damage is the same. If they succeed in claiming your ongoing attention and more dangerously, your ongoing affection, there will be little margin left in your life to cultivate a relationship with God.

God encourages us to lay our hearts bare before Him, and yet that is the very thing many of us are trying to avoid. "Put me on trial, LORD, and cross-examine me. Test my motives and my heart" (Ps. 26:2 NLT). We are afraid to meet Him in the silence and quiet of our lives for fear of what He may show us. How ironic that the distractions we chase are false substitutes and will ultimately rob us of the One thing our hearts truly crave: intimacy with God. To know Him and be known by Him. Nothing else will do. We need to help our children recognize the emptiness that ensues in this meaningless chase and be faithful to point them to the cure. But first, we must admit our own susceptibility to the chase.

What's a Parent to Do?

Recently, while on a dinner date with my husband, I couldn't help but notice the number of people sitting at nearby tables looking at their phones rather than each other. In fact, at one table a family of four were each engaged on their own separate devices and were oblivious of one another's company. The kids couldn't have been more than ten to twelve years old, and while the older daughter was scrolling away on her phone, her younger brother had earbuds in and was playing a game on a tablet. Across from them, Mom and Dad were engaged on their own phones, tuned out to their surroundings, each other, and more importantly, their children. I couldn't help but feel a heaviness in my heart. With Mom and Dad leading by example, the kids don't stand a chance when it comes to experiencing the joy of true face-to-face friendship and intimacy. What a lonely existence and this was their "family time"!

Contrast this image to another one I witnessed later that same week when my husband and I went to lunch with a pastor and his family after I had spoken at their church on a Sunday morning. Their children were about the same age as the other children I had witnessed earlier that week, and there were no devices present. They listened to the adult conversation, politely engaged from time to time, and when they grew weary of the lingering conversation after the food had been served and consumed, they asked their parents politely if they could read their books. It had never occurred to them to beg for their parents' phones because they had clearly been taught that mealtime was a tech-free zone.

I get it. I know it's tempting to hand your kids a device to gain a little peace and quiet or have a little uninterrupted conversation with your spouse or other adults, but it should be the exception rather than the rule. Establishing tech-free zones are a good start to limiting media consumption. In addition, resist the pull to give your children devices and privileges too soon. I know this will be hard when many of their friends are allowed earlier media access or handed devices. Hold strong. Likewise, don't ban all technology out of fear and swing too far in the other direction. Ephesians 6:4 reminds us, "Fathers, do not provoke your children to anger, but bring them up in the discipline and instruction of the Lord" (ESV). *Matthew Henry's Commentary* expounds on the verse in saying, "Be not impatient; use no unreasonable severities. Deal prudently and wisely with children; convince their judgments and work upon their reason. Bring them up well; under proper and compassionate correction; and in the knowledge of the duty God requires." If you issue an all-out ban on all technology and allow your children no privileges, I can assure you it will provoke them to anger. Unreasonable severities doled out by parents oftentimes backfire. (Think here, the law of forbidden fruit.) Like it or not, technology is here to stay. The best time for your child to learn to manage it is when they are under your roof and you can guide them to use it responsibly. Expect that there will be many bumps along the way. You may extend privileges only to learn it was too soon and then have to withdraw them. You are the parent and you have that right.

I especially love the advice in the commentary above to "convince their judgments and work upon their reason." Be honest with your children from the time they are young and help them understand the link to too much media consumption and mental health, so they know the "why" behind your "wait." When you frame the conversation of media privileges as one of care and concern for their mental health and welfare, they are better able to understand why you may have rules in place that many of their friends' parents do not. Another way to "work upon their reason" is to talk to them about over-consumption of media and the link to unhappiness. For iGen children, happiness ranked as a top goal for a majority. Help them to recognize that heavy media consumption is causing an epidemic of unhappiness among their generation.

Exercising Self-Control

Our boys would be wise to learn from Paul's counsel: "'Everything is permissible for me,' but not everything is beneficial. 'Everything is permissible for me,' but I will not be mastered by anything" (1 Cor. 6:12 CSB). If our sons don't learn the godly attribute of self-control, they will be at risk of becoming "slaves to whatever has mastered them" (2 Pet. 2:19). Porn, alcohol, drugs, sex, dating relationships, video games, and other common boyhood temptations will cross their paths at some point on the journey to manhood. Sure, we need to draw reasonable boundaries in an effort to protect them (oftentimes, from themselves), but we won't always be there to guide them to make good and godly choices. We don't want to raise sons who simply behave as the result of snazzy behavior-modification tactics gleaned from the latest and greatest parenting book (whether mine or any other). Self-control is one of the fruits of the Spirit mentioned in Galatians 5:22–23 and is arguably a godly discipline that is mastered only by the indwelling of the Holy Spirit. However, parents can do certain things to introduce basic principles of self-control into their sons' lives at a young age, long before they may surrender their hearts to Christ.

In an effort to introduce the concept of self-control to even the youngest boys, I came up with a fairly simple formula that is easy to remember and provides a foundation to build on over the years: "Stop, think, pray" or for short, STP. (If they can remember "stop, drop, and roll" in school fire drills, surely they can remember this!) Let me give you a more in-depth description of the formula.

Stop

Whether your son is four years or fourteen, it's hard for him to stop and consider an action and the possible consequences related to the action. Some boys are by nature more impulsive than others, and the exercise of stopping to consider an action will prove to be difficult for them. In fact, a recent study that examined risk-taking behaviors in boys and men ranging in age from nine to thirty-five found that teenagers took the most risks compared with the other groups. The most risky behavior was seen in fourteen-year-olds. The lead author of the study went on to say that the study is a first step in determining why teenagers engage in extremely risky behaviors such as drug use and unsafe sex.[22]

This shouldn't come as a surprise as the study reveals what auto insurance companies have known for some time: Boys don't always stop to think things through and, therefore, are at higher risk than others—thus, the higher insurance premiums on teenage male drivers! Just because they are naturally more impulsive at this age doesn't mean we sit back and excuse it. It's up to us to help them make wise choices by giving them the tools to build their self-control muscles. The first step is to help them learn simply to "stop," pause, or take a breath before jumping into something that can produce a whirlwind of devastating consequences.

If our sons are to exercise their self-control muscles, they must learn to stop and regroup by bringing the scenario before God. This is a first step to training our sons to self-monitor by cultivating the daily discipline of laying their hearts bare before God. In Psalm 139:23–24, David set the example:

Search me, O God, and know my heart;

Test me and know my anxious thoughts.

Point out anything in me that offends you,

And lead me along the path of everlasting life. (NLT)

David knew firsthand the pain that can result from making impulsive decisions. If only he had asked God to "point out anything in me that offends you" in the moments that followed his witnessing Bathsheba bathing on a rooftop outside his window! Whether our boys are faced with the temptation to rudely rush to the front of the line at the church potluck, play a video game for four straight hours, succumb to peer pressure at a party and play a game of beer pong, view porn, or have sex with their girlfriend, we need to help them learn to stop and bring the temptation before God. They won't always do this (nor will we), but the key is to build the self-control muscles by moving toward the goal of cultivating a habit of exercising self-control. Every time we exercise self-control, we prove to ourselves that we can. Most important, as we look to God for guidance in making decisions, we are one step further along the "path of everlasting life." Self-control produces freedom by teaching true mastery over temptations that come. We need to help them understand that without self-control they will be prime candidates to becoming a slave to temptations that cross their path. Learning to stop before reacting is key to developing self-control.

Think

The boy brain and the girl brain have distinct differences. Dr. Francine Benes, who heads up a brain-tissue bank at Boston's McLean Hospital, notes, "The male brain is not at its full size until approximately age thirty. The female brain attains optimal size during the teenage period."[23] Steve Gerali, author of *Teenage Guys* notes, "The prefrontal cortex of a guy's brain first begins to develop during puberty. This part is responsible for discernment and judgment, something teenage guys often lack. The immaturity of his brain development may interfere with a guy's ability to accurately judge safety and the long-term effects, consequences, and implications of the risks he takes."[24]

This certainly explains the blank stares we often receive when we ask our sons, "What were you thinking?" or "Did it ever cross your mind . . . ?" Bottom line: they *weren't* thinking; and no, it likely *didn't* cross their minds. However, the delayed cognitive development in the male brain doesn't mean our sons are incapable of connecting possible consequences to certain actions. It just won't come naturally for them. Our role is to help them develop the habit. It doesn't come naturally for them to want to brush their teeth either, but for the sake of teaching them proper dental hygiene, we persevere when it comes to training them to incorporate teeth brushing into their daily routine. And for those of us who don't, we often have a hefty price to pay on down the road. The same is true with self-discipline. Even though it doesn't come naturally for our sons to stop, pause, and think things through, we persevere in the task, knowing that a lack of self-control can likewise leave them (and us) with a hefty price to pay on down the road.

Learning to stop and think are essential tools when it comes to making wise choices, but there is also a spiritual component at play. Our boys need to learn the value of leaning on God for strength. They need to develop the habit of prayer.

Pray

From an early age our sons should be taught Matthew 26:41: "Keep watch and pray, so that you will not give into temptation. For the spirit is willing, but the body is weak!" (NLT). Self-control is one of the most difficult disciplines we will learn. And I dare say, many of us (myself included) are still working on it. Our nature (or our "flesh") naturally gravitates toward instant gratification and pleasure. Our sons need to know that their desire for instant gratification is normal. However, we must give them the tools for exercising self-control lest they grow up to became impulsive, foolish adults who live from one temporary pleasure to another. Momentary, temporary pleasures do not produce an abundant and fulfilling life. They may appear to some to do so; but take a closer look behind the veil, and I can guarantee you, you will find misery. Enslavement to ungodly temptations always produces misery. True mastery over our flesh (sinful desires) is only possible with the help of Christ. Our sons must be taught to lean on Christ for guidance, wisdom, and strength when facing temptations.

Depending on your son's age, the temptation of the day may be resisting a can of sugary soda in the fridge that you said is off-limits or reining in the urge to trip his sister when she walks past him in the family room. If he's older, the temptation of the day could be saying no to a weekend party invitation where alcohol will be available. Or clicking on a link to a porn website one of his buddies told him about. Our sons need to be taught that fighting temptations in their own power will often prove futile. They need a supernatural strength that can only be found in Christ. Crying out to God in prayer and asking for Him to help them will be essential in fighting temptations that cross their paths on a daily basis.

In 2 Peter 1:6 Paul sums up the formula for self-control: ". . . knowledge with self-control, and self-control with patient endurance, and patient endurance with godliness" (NLT). Self-control is a by-product of "knowing God" and, as I mentioned earlier, a fruit of the Spirit (Gal. 5:22–23). If we want to raise sons who are self-controlled, we must first introduce them to God and the beauty of the gospel. This doesn't mean we drop them off at church each Sunday and trust that by default of being there they will develop a thriving relationship with Christ. Regular church attendance is only part of the equation. God has appointed us to be the primary disciplers of our sons, and more will be caught than taught during the years our sons spend with us.

Our priority should not be simply to teach our sons self-control but first and foremost reveal to them the grace of God. In other words, we are to live out the beauty of the gospel in front of our children. Titus 2:11–14 sums it up well:

> For the grace of God has appeared that offers salvation
> to all people. It teaches us to say "No" to ungodliness
> and worldly passions, and to live self-controlled, upright
> and godly lives in this present age, while we wait for the
> blessed hope—the appearing of the glory of our great
> God and Savior, Jesus Christ, who gave himself for us to
> redeem us from all wickedness and to purify for himself
> a people that are his very own, eager to do what is good.

To attempt to teach our sons self-control apart from the power of Christ is futile. In fact, it's not only futile but dangerous. Jesus' harshest criticism was directed at the Pharisees and their focus on "behavior modification" rather than "heart inhabitation." We all have a gluttonous, self-seeking desire to hop from one pleasure to another. Yet chasing after these desires will leave us empty in the end. When we help our sons understand this paradox, it creates a beautiful opportunity to introduce the gospel of Christ and show them their obvious need for a Savior.

Teaching Your Son to Self-Monitor

Just as you would never put a toddler on a ten-speed bike and let them loose in the bad part of town, likewise, you should never expose your child, tween, or teen to a situation they are not mature enough to manage. Just as you would help your little one on a bike with training wheels and run alongside them as they get a feel for learning to ride a bike, you should also come alongside your child when they begin engaging with technology and especially, social media. Postpone handing them devices with internet access (tablets, smart phones, gaming systems, laptops) for as long as possible, especially if you are not there to supervise them. When my children began to engage in social media, I required all of their passwords to their social media accounts and spot-checked their devices on occasion, as well as installing monitoring software on many of their devices. I'm sure they still managed to get around some of my boundaries of protection, but just knowing I was determined to be an engaged parent had to be somewhat of a deterrent. Or so I tell myself!

The truth is, if a child wants to get away with something, they will find a way to do it. We cannot monitor their behavior every minute of every day, but we can educate them about the dangers of too much media consumption and the link to mental health issues that have become all too common among children and teens. We can have open and honest conversations about our struggle with media consumption and the pull it has on our lives. Most importantly, we can expose our children to other fulfilling activities that will give them a taste for true intimacy and quality family time. Technology can be a good thing. It is not the enemy, but it can quickly become the enemy if we allow it to have too much power in our lives or the lives of our children.

Most children will not fall into the addiction category, but many if not most, will struggle with finding a healthy balance when it comes to media consumption. As parents, we must help them learn to self-monitor and recognize the warning signs of technology-induced anxiety, loneliness, and depression and take necessary steps to pull back or unplug when it gets to be too much. Most importantly, we must constantly remind them that the FOMO factor ("fear of missing out") that compels them to connect digitally whether it be mindless surfing of the web, social media, texting, online gaming, binge-watching Netflix, or any other media escape is ironically misplaced. Excess media consumption is causing them to miss out on the things that matter most.

If after reading this chapter you feel that a digital detox is in order for your child (or yourself), consider unplugging for a couple of weeks in order to prove you are not mastered by technology. You will not die. Your child will not die. In fact, it may be the very thing that enables them to begin living again. Experts recommend four to six weeks if the problem is severe, in order for the nervous system to effectively reset itself. Consider joining your child if possible. During the detox period, help your child find other activities or interests, preferably outdoors. Do what you can to expose your child to others during this time, whether it be friends or family members.

One question I've learned to ask myself on a regular basis when engaging in technology is, "Is this good for my soul?" When the answer is "no," it's up to me to do something about it. No one else is going to come along and fix the problem for me. The same is true for our children. We can draw boundaries and take steps to monitor their media consumption, but at the end of the day, they have to come to a place where they care more about the condition of their souls than we do. They will have to decide whether or not they will master the technology that influences their lives, or be mastered by it. For the sake of their mental health. For the sake of their spiritual health. For the sake of their souls.

Chapter 5

Porn: A Virtual Reality

● ● ● ● ● ●

But each one is tempted when he is carried away and enticed
by his own lust. Then when lust has conceived, it gives birth
to sin; and when sin is accomplished, it brings forth death.
(James 1:14–15 NASB)

Months before I committed to write this book, a friend contacted me to share a heartbreaking story that had recently devastated her community. A group of third-grade boys who attend a local private Christian school had been passing around an electronic device during the lunch hour during the first couple weeks of school. The school likely had rules in place regarding the use of phones and other wireless devices, but as you can imagine, it's nearly impossible for teachers and faculty to keep tabs on each and every student throughout the day to ensure they follow the rules. By the time a teacher finally noticed the boys passing around the device and took it up, the damage had been done. To the teacher's horror, the boys had been viewing a porn site.

Unfortunately the porn site the boys were viewing was not your average run-of-the-mill porn site. It was one of the largest online portals for homemade porn clips. Likely one of the boys had heard about the site from an older brother or neighbor kid. I doubt many of the parents had even had the birds-and-bees talk with their boys, given they were only eight or nine years old. They were children, far too young to even begin to process God's divine design for sex, much less the images that are now forever etched in their minds. Mind you, this could be anyone's son. Mine or yours. The sobering reality even for those of us who faithfully set up parental controls on our sons' wireless devices, is it only takes one boy in your son's peer group armed with any device that can access the Web, a little free time, and an invitation to your son to "take a look."

Mary Anne Layden, codirector of the Sexual Trauma and Psychopathology Program at the University of Pennsylvania's Center for Cognitive Therapy, called porn the "most concerning thing to psychological health that I know of existing today." She further notes, "The internet is a perfect drug delivery system because you are anonymous, aroused and have role models for these behaviors," Layden said. "To have drugs pumped into your house 24/7, free, and children know how to use it better than grown-ups know how to use it—it's a perfect delivery system if we want to have a whole generation of young addicts who will never have the drug out of their mind. . . . Pornography addicts have a more difficult time recovering from their addiction than cocaine addicts since coke users can get the drug out of their system, but pornographic images stay in the brain forever."[1]

It's Not a Matter of *If* but *When*

Before we prepare to tackle the problem of porn and talk solutions, it is first necessary to understand how widespread the problem is. By some estimations the production and sale of explicit pornography now represents the seventh-largest industry in America.[2] According to one study, researchers at the University of New Hampshire found that about 90 percent of children between the ages of eight and sixteen have looked at porn. In fact, the largest group of Internet pornography consumers are between the ages of twelve and seventeen. The study also found that most kids who watch porn weren't searching for it the first time they found it.[3]

Consider that in 1985, 92 percent of adult males had viewed a *Playboy* magazine by age fifteen as compared to today where the average age of a boy's first exposure to pornography is eleven.[4] Nearly half of boys between the third and the eighth grade have visited Internet sites with adult content.[5] Other studies have revealed that 75 percent of eighteen- to twenty-four-year-olds (late adolescent guys) visit online porn sites monthly, representing one-fourth of the visitors to all Internet porn sites. The next largest users of porn are men in their twenties and early thirties, 66 percent of whom report being regular users of porn.[6]

While porn has always been around in some form or fashion, it used to be harder for boys to get their hands on it in days past. In my generation boys were usually exposed to porn with a peek at a neighbor kid's stashed copy of Dad's back issue of *Playboy* magazine. Or if they were really desperate, the bra and panties section of the JCPenney's catalog. Today porn is accessible on the Internet, portable gaming devices, cell phones, and just about any gadget with wireless capabilities. Couple that with the fact that it offers complete anonymity and can be obtained for free, and you have a perfect storm on your hands. A boy doesn't need to go looking for it; at some point it will seem innocuous. Just like the third-grade boys who were simply passing around another boy's electronic device at lunchtime, it can happen with little or no warning.

Take, for example, Susan, whose son was exposed to pornography while working on a school laptop in high school. She contacted me several months ago to share about the painful journey they had experienced. Here is what she had to say:

> My son kept his secret for eighteen months. Although we knew something was terribly wrong, we never imagined that this was the problem. It has been a long, difficult road. We have invested much time and patience in his spiritual development to give him tools to overcome this serious addiction. I was very concerned when he went away to college this fall, but he has been faithful and by the hand of God was matched with a mentor who had struggled with the same issue and has walked a road of healing. I never expected to deal with this kind of addiction, nor did I have any idea of the long-term problems this would bring.

Another mom, Julie, also contacted me to share her account of how her son's porn habit mastered his life for several years:

> I have three sons and a daughter. My eldest son is sixteen, and he started struggling with porn around age thirteen. He told us he learned about a website from friends one day while sitting in the school cafeteria. He visited that website (which was very hardcore, by the way), and it produced a secret intrigue to see more and

more. My husband discovered his viewing history about four weeks after he first visited the site. For the most part we have dealt with it, and our son feels convicted about his actions, but there have been some slipups here and there. The scariest thing I've heard him say was, "I knew it was wrong, I told myself it was wrong, but I couldn't help it, I just had to look." I thank God that our son has come to us for support, to confess, to pray with us, etc. (and yes, we have filters on our computers). But now he faces a new challenge: He doesn't know how to be out in the world without facing the possibility of stumbling. He doesn't do church youth-group activities involving sleepovers because he says guys talk about things that make him want to visit the sites again. I catch him averting his eyes at billboards, artwork in restaurants, etc. My husband says this may be a struggle for him the rest of his life. I want him to be confident that through Christ's strength he can "be in the world, but not of the world," but it has really opened my eyes to the amount of pornographic or suggestive images that are really out there to be seen. He's just a couple years from college, and I want him to be ready to stand firm in his convictions.

Perhaps even more disturbing is the moral ambiguity about porn by teens and young adults (ages thirteen to twenty-four). According to a Barna survey, only 32 percent say, "viewing porn is wrong."[7] "The vast majority reports that conversations with their friends about porn are neutral, accepting or even encouraging. Just one in ten teens and one in twenty young adults report talking with their friends about porn in a disapproving way."[8] The Barna survey also found that when teens and young adults in the survey were asked to rank a series of actions (lying, stealing, etc.) on a five-point scale based on "always okay," "usually okay," "neither wrong nor okay," "usually wrong " and "always wrong," teens and young adults ranked "not recycling" as more immoral than viewing pornographic images. "Not recycling" ranked #4, "significant consumption of electricity or water" ranked #7, and "viewing pornographic images" was all the way down at #9.[9]

It's easy to feel like the situation is hopeless when hearing these disturbing findings. While porn is a sad reality of our times, it doesn't diminish the power of God. As mothers we will simply need to step up our game and come up with a new and improved battle plan. Our battle plan must go beyond activating parental controls and telling our sons not to look when they see it. That will not be enough. We need to take it a step further and teach our sons to guard their hearts (Prov. 4:23). Our sons are not likely to embrace the importance of monitoring and guarding their hearts in the moment unless they understand that viewing porn leads to a diminished quality of life.

The Bible Addresses Porn

In the New Testament there are twenty-six references to *porneia* (the Greek word in which our English word *porn* is derived. Porneia is translated as "fornication," "whoredom" or "sexual immorality." When spoken of in the Bible we are told that our bodies are not made for porneia (1 Cor. 6:13); we should run from it (1 Cor. 6:18); we should not seek it out (1 Cor. 7:2); and we should repent if we fall prey to it (2 Cor. 12:21). The only way to avoid the temptation of porneia is to live a life of purity; which can only be done through the process of sanctification with the help of the Holy Spirit living within us. In other words, our sons will need the power of God to stand against this temptation, and are not able to conquer it on their own mortal strength.

Because God wired our bodies for intimacy and relationship with Him first and foremost, nothing else will fill that need. Porn is a false substitute that promises intimacy in the moment, but in truth, robs the user by leaving them disabled when it comes to true intimacy in their real-life relationships. Most importantly, it robs them of spiritual intimacy with God.

Part of educating our sons to the damage and fallout of porn is making sure they understand it is a tool of the enemy to "steal, kill, and destroy" and thus, rob them of the abundant life God intended them to have (John 10:10). The world will certainly not be teaching them this truth, and it's up to us to make sure they understand that by buying into the lie that viewing porn is harmless, they have essentially been conned by the enemy. For many young men, knowledge of this truth may not be enough to ward off future temptations, but I can assure you once they have fallen into the enemy's trap, they will be aware of the emptiness that results. It should come as no surprise that existing studies have found that the "frequency of porn viewing correlates with depression, anxiety, stress and social malfunction, as well as less sexual and relationship satisfaction and altered sexual tastes, poorer quality of life and health, and real-life intimacy problems."[10] As mothers, we must speak to this emptiness, and offer our sons the hope that it's never too late to turn back to God for help and take Him up on His offer of the "abundant life."

The Trade-Offs of Viewing Porn

I cannot stress enough the importance of having regular and ongoing conversations about the long-term dangers of porn with your sons. If you feel uneasy about discussing this topic, hand the book over to your husband and let him cover the information in this chapter. What's most important is that someone cover the information with him and keep the conversation going through the years. I've highlighted three trade-offs that every young man should be made aware of when it comes to viewing porn.

1. Viewing porn rewires the brain. William M. Struthers, author of the book *Wired for Intimacy*, has written extensively on the physical dynamic that occurs in the brain when porn is viewed. "Repeated exposure to pornography creates a one-way neurological superhighway where a man's mental life is over-sexualized and narrowed." He adds, "As men fall deeper into the mental habit of fixating on these images, the exposure to them creates neural pathways and as a path is created in the woods with each successive hiker, so do the neural paths set the course for the next time an erotic image is viewed."[11] Struthers notes that experiences with pornography and pleasure hormones create new patterns in the brain's wiring and repeated experiences formalize the rewiring.[12] It certainly brings a whole new meaning to the phrase "one-track mind."

Our boys need to know that viewing porn affects the wiring of their brains. Each viewing session brings about a dose of dopamine to the brain (also known as the "feel good" or "reward" hormone), which leaves the viewer, much like an addict, craving more. "An elevated level of dopamine in the brain creates a high that the addict keeps chasing," said David Greenfield, the director of the Center for Internet Behavior and author of *Virtual Addiction*.[13] Greenfield further warns, "Sex is the most primitive, powerful, physiological force on the planet—it's wired into our DNA. We all have the potential to become addicted to it."[14]

As one viewing leads to another and yet another, a habit is developed (to get the repeated buzz or "reward"). As a habit is cultivated, neural pathways begin to develop that signal the brain to move down the same pathway over and over again. But the damage doesn't end there. Once this one-way neurological superhighway is created, it also becomes the pathway by which interaction with women is routed. "All women become potential porn stars in the minds of these men. They unknowingly have created a neurological circuit that imprisons their ability to see women rightly—as being created in God's image."[15]

Our sons are growing up in a culture that views porn as harmless fun. Porn is anything but harmless. It takes more than one victim by affecting the core of men's thinking and their view of women. Author William Struthers, in his book *Wired for Intimacy*, says, "As porn and fantasy take control of the mind, it becomes a dream theater that is transposed over the waking world. Every woman they come into contact with is objectified, undressed and evaluated as a willing (or unwilling) mental sexual partner."[16]

It is not enough simply to teach our sons not to look at porn. We need to disclose fully to them what is at stake when they make the choice to view porn. We need to help them understand that every time they practice self-control by not looking in a tempting situation, they are reinforcing a new and better neural pathway in their brain. As this pathway is developed and traveled over and over again (each time self-control is practiced), it will help create a one-way neurological superhighway that will lead them to a much better place.

William Struthers offers this hope: "Because the human brain, the source of our mental life, is such a remarkable organ, it is important to have a good understanding of how it operates. When we understand how the brain is flexible and plastic, as well as how it is unyielding and rigid, we can see not only how pornography can lead a person to a place of mental depravity, but also how hope for redemption and sanctification can be achieved."[17] In other words, even if a habit has already been developed and neural pathways established, the brain can be retrained. It won't be easy to shut down the old superhighway and establish a new one, but it is possible.

Of course, it's ideal if construction on the superhighway leading to depravity never begins in the first place, but the truth is, many boys have already begun the building process. That is why it's important to acknowledge that it's never too late to reverse the damage. When my youngest son was in high school, I candidly shared with him, "If by chance, you feel a pathway has already been established, please share that with me or your dad, so we can help you begin the deconstruction process." Let's not be naïve about this problem. Too much is at stake to live with an attitude of "ignorance is bliss."

2. Viewing porn can affect your future sex life and marriage. Our boys may not care much at this point about a warning that porn can damage a marriage relationship, but I can guarantee you their ears will perk up if you tell them viewing porn can ruin their sex life. What guy doesn't want to have amazingly good sex someday? Consider that in a Canadian sexologists' study conducted in 2014, researchers found that 53.5 percent of male teens were classified as reporting symptoms indicative of a sexual problem. Among the symptoms reported, erectile dysfunction and low desire were the most common.[18]

In his book *Boys Adrift*, author Leonard Sax, M.D., PhD says:

> In the general population, the best estimates are
> that roughly 70 percent of college-age men now use
> pornography regularly. Among those men, use of
> pornography can readily escalate from an occasional
> diversion to a daily pastime and finally, to becoming the
> preferred sexual outlet. In one Harvard study, 69 percent
> of men who sought help for sexual problems were
> experiencing "compulsive masturbation"—meaning that
> they were masturbating more than they thought they
> should be, and/or they were sometimes masturbating
> in inappropriate places or at inappropriate times. Fifty
> percent of the men in the same study were described
> as being "pornography-dependent," meaning that they
> could not achieve an erection without pornography.
> More and more boys are discovering that they prefer a
> sexy image on a computer screen to a real live woman
> with expectations, a woman who has her own agenda, a
> woman who may say things that the boy doesn't want to
> hear.[19]

I can't help but think the above information wouldn't scare a
boy half out of his wits when he hears phrases like: "compulsive
masturbation," "masturbating in inappropriate places," "pornogra-
phy-dependent," and "could not achieve an erection without pornography." Ouch. If our sons want to have amazingly good sex lives
(in the confines of marriage with their future wives), they would be
wise to resist the temptation to view porn. Of course, not every boy
who views porn will become pornography dependent, but how do

our sons know if they are among those who will? There is absolutely no way to tell. Therefore, are they willing to take a gamble?

Porn diminishes sexual fulfillment in men, the kind of sexual fulfillment God intended. In *That's My Son*, author Rick Johnson notes: "Porn users need bigger prizes—more degrading, more graphic, more explicit images . . . by viewing this material, a male is not exercising self-restraint or control. If he can't use self-control in one area of his life, he'll lack it in other areas as well. Boys who learn to govern their sexual urges grow up to be men who are able to engage in healthy sexual relations and are able to control other areas of their lives."[20] William Struthers beautifully sums it up, "Pornography is a sin that robs God of his glory in the gift of sex and sexuality. We have long known that sin takes hostages."[21]

3. Viewing porn can rob you of future happiness. If anyone ever doubted that viewing porn can act as a drug, consider the following withdrawal symptoms documented in an article in *Psychology Today* from actual porn users who were trying to break free from the habit.[22]

"Shaking w/ jitters similar to how it felt when I quit smoking."

"Intense bouts of anger leading to interpersonal difficulties, aggressive demeanor, easily stressed out, suicidal ideation."

"Bored? Masturbation. Angry? Masturbation. Sad? Masturbation. Stressed? Masturbation. I went from being the first of my class to the very bottom until I dropped out for good. . . . I fear I'll never have sex because I've learned no social skills since diving into porn eight years ago as a teen."

"I've battled a few addictions in my life, from nicotine to alcohol and other substances. I've overcome all of them, and this was by far the most difficult. Urges, crazy thoughts, sleeplessness, feelings of hopelessness, despair, worthlessness, and many more negative things were part of what I went through with this porn thing."[23]

And if anyone is left doubting that porn can diminish future happiness, consider the following quotes often heard from men in the survey:

"No matter how many orgasms I have, I never feel satisfied."

"I need extreme material that I never would have viewed before."

"I'm more anxious or depressed, and I have a strong desire to avoid other people."[24]

John 10:10 tells us, "The thief comes only to steal and kill and destroy; I have come that they may have life, and have it to the full." Let me ask you this: Do the testimonies of the men above indicate they "have life, and have it to the full"? Or do they sound like they've fallen prey to a thief who has come to "steal and kill and destroy"? We need to help our sons understand that a truly abundant life only comes by following Christ and obeying His commands. Temporary pleasures, though tempting, can rob them of the abundant life God intends for them. Ironically, porn is often argued as an individual's right to exercise his "personal freedoms," yet ironically, the end result can leave viewers imprisoned.

Warning Signs of Addiction

Our sons are growing up in a culture where viewing porn is normalized and even discussed openly among their peers with little shame. Due to the minimization of the problem, as well as the prevalence among young males, many have justified their actions and have no desire to give it up. Because they have falsely believed there is nothing wrong with viewing porn, they are not likely to approach anyone for help. I know of one Christian young man who in his early twenties began to realize he had a severe porn problem and over the course of several years, confessed it to a pastor at his church, a leader of a college ministry, and several other trusted ministry leaders only to receive a "join the club" type of response, rather than encouragement to seek professional help.

Unfortunately, most of our churches today are ill-equipped to deal with the severity of porn and/or sex addiction that is rampant among men of all ages and mistakenly offer Band-Aids to the problem in the way of Scripture memory, accountability partners, and an occasional Sunday sermon to help fight off the temptation. While this may help some men, many are already in the throws of addiction and in need of professional help to rewire the well-worn neural pathways in their brains that have been established as a result of long-term use and now create a vicious cycle of behavior.

Below are eight characteristics of porn addiction.[25] I encourage you to discuss this list with your sons on a consistent basis (along with the tradeoffs listed above), beginning at the age of twelve (and possibly sooner if you have reason to believe your son has been actively seeking out pornography). Be intentional and proactive. Don't wait until you think there may be a problem. The most important thing you can do is establish a safe and loving environment, free of shame and judgment, where your son is free to open up and share his heart.

Eight Characteristics of Porn Addiction

1. It is unmanageable. In 12-step groups, such as Alcoholics Anonymous, the first step to recovery is admitting one has a problem and is powerless over it—that the addict's life has become unmanageable. Many addicts will confess they feel like their addiction has taken over their minds, bodies, and free will. When they feel the "itch to use," they believe they cannot help themselves, but to "scratch the itch."

2. It creates a neurochemical tolerance. Viewing pornography triggers several neurochemical reactions in the brain. This produces a high feeling, which is intensified with an orgasm. This neurochemical high is also experienced when using drugs, such as cocaine or heroin. As with any other drug, a tolerance soon develops. More is needed to get the same effect. Thus, a man will spend increasing amounts of time online viewing pornography, and the type of pornography will become more extreme.

3. It is degenerative and progressive. Over time the addiction gets worse. As tolerance and dependence grow, the need for pornography grows. Instead of viewing soft porn, such as the *Sports Illustrated* Swimsuit Issue or the Victoria's Secret Catalog, the man now needs to view more deviant, hardcore pornography that is often violent and can even be illegal. Instead of spending a few minutes a week viewing pornography, he may now be viewing it for several hours every day. Ultimately the pursuit and use of pornography consumes the man's life.

4. It has negative, destructive consequences. The emotional consequences of pornography addiction include isolation, loneliness, fear, guilt, shame, anger, depression, anxiety, and low self-esteem. The most dangerous consequence of pornography addiction is the impact on one's relationship with God. Most pornography users know what they are doing is wrong and harmful to their relationship with God, yet they choose to use it anyway.

5. It is used to escape negative feelings. Here is where we most often use the term *self-medicating.* Addicts often use pornography as a coping strategy to deal with deep emotional pain. Often they don't even realize the pain is there. All they know is pornography makes them feel really good and they must go back to it over and over again. The fact that they cannot feel good without pornography indicates a deep emotional wound that they are using pornography to anesthetize.

6. It is justified by the concept of "entitlement." Many people who use pornography do so out of a sense of entitlement, which often stems from narcissism or anger. Narcissism is a great problem in our society today. People often focus on their own wants and needs with little regard to how their actions affect others.

7. It is used as a reward. Pornography addicts can also justify their pornography use by viewing it as a reward.

8. It provides a feeling of power. Using pornography gives them a sense of power. However, this false sense of power is short-lived. They don't realize that to feel a sense of control in their lives, they need to acknowledge their powerlessness and turn to God as the one true source of power.

It's not my desire to sound like a doom and gloom prophet, but given the general apathy toward the topic of viewing porn and the availability of it through Wi-Fi-enabled devices that have now been put into the hands of our children, I predict that we will see record levels of porn and sex addiction in this next generation, especially as they enter their twenties and realize the magnitude of their problem. As part of our conversations related to sexual purity in our sons' teen years, we need to include open conversations or reminders that we are willing to get our sons professional help should they need it. Additionally, we must make sure we don't attach shame to the idea of needing professional help, just as there is no shame to needing professional help regarding any other addiction. Given the brain science behind this type of addiction, we must offer our sons the hope that the damage can be reversed and they can be set free from a life of enslavement to porn. This pathway to freedom may include many hours of professional counseling and possibly even rehab, but you cannot put a price tag on freedom and their future happiness.

A Final Word to Moms

While researching for this chapter, I ran across a fabulous article in the online edition of the *Chicago Sun-Times*, encouraging mothers to warn their sons of the dangers of porn. The author offered some insightful words of wisdom to mothers that we'd be wise to take to heart: "Moms, they aren't us. Rather, I think our approach to them here should be put in the context of 'of course this interests you. This is exactly how you are designed. Don't be ashamed of that desire. You were made to find beautiful women sexually enticing, and the people making this base stuff know that. But, these images aren't good enough for you. That good desire you have will meet its greatest satisfaction with a real woman, when sex and relationship in marriage go together.'"[26]

Our boys aren't like us. As a result, it is hard for us to understand the allure of porn to our boys, but the last thing they need is to be shamed with an attitude that says, "Why would you even think about looking at that?" Of course, they're drawn to it. Any mother who believes her son is exempt from the temptation of viewing porn because he is a "good Christian boy" is being dangerously naïve. In fact, the Barna survey related to porn use found that 41 percent of "practicing Christian males, ages thirteen to twenty-four" are "frequent porn users." In fact, they represent the third highest category of "frequent porn users."[27]

If your son is age nine to eleven (or possibly younger if he has older brothers or has unmonitored access to Wi-Fi-enabled devices or sexually explicit shows through TV or streaming media), you need to broach this topic with him and begin to discuss the top three dangers above. Remember, these are only conversation starters. It's important to keep the conversations going throughout the years. Even if your son is rather innocent and less knowledgeable than other kids his age, I would consider introducing the topic like this:

> "Hey buddy. I want to talk to you about something. As
> you get older and spend more time on the computer,
> smart phone, tablet, or watching TV, you will probably
> see some stuff that God doesn't want you to see. Like
> maybe pictures or videos of girls not wearing clothes or
> even two people having sex.* Anyway, I just want you to
> know that it's important not to look if you come across
> something on the computer, phone, tablet, or TV, or if
> one of your friends wants to show you something that
> you know God wouldn't want you to look at. If that
> happens, please come tell me or your dad about it. You
> won't be in trouble because we want you to talk to us

about stuff like that. As you get older, a whole lot of your friends are going to be looking at bad stuff and may try to get you to look at bad stuff with them. Let's think of what you might say when that happens, okay?"

(*If you have not addressed the topic of what sex is and God's plan and purpose for sex, consider beginning that conversation at a basic level if you feel your son is ready. If he's ten or older, he's ready—trust me.)

Regardless of the parental controls we set up or the boundaries we put in place to protect our sons, our measures will not be foolproof. Our sons will eventually be exposed to porn on some level. As parents we must be vigilant in addressing the topic and the long-term effects of viewing porn. Over and over and over again. Our boys would be wise to follow in Job's footsteps by making "a covenant with [their] eyes not to look lustfully at a young woman" (Job 31:1). The "springs of life" await those who guard their hearts (Prov. 4:23 ESV). What boy doesn't want to experience the "good life," the kind of life God intended for him?

We must help our sons understand that decisions they make today relative to porn can impact their future happiness tomorrow. We can't be there to monitor and guard their hearts 24–7. However, we can teach them to self-monitor and examine their hearts on a regular and consistent basis. We all know someone whose marriage/life/well-being has been destroyed by porn. You may have experienced the fallout from the evils of porn and know firsthand that it leaves many victims in its wake. I feel passionately about this topic because I have personally witnessed the devastation caused by a pornography addiction in my own family. My parents divorced after thirty-nine years of marriage and a key factor was my father's long-time pornography addiction and specifically, his refusal to get help.

Having witnessed the fallout on my parents' marriage left me all the more determined to have honest and open conversations with my sons.

However, that would not be enough to spare one of my sons from experiencing the emptiness and devastation of a pornography addiction first-hand. Shortly after I agreed to update this book, my youngest son disclosed to his wife of one year that he had an addiction to pornography. This disclosure led to other disclosures that nearly cost him his marriage. Fortunately, my son recognized his need for professional help and today, he is walking in freedom from his addiction. My son would be the first to tell you that healing doesn't happen in an instant. In order to remain free, my son must be whole-heartedly and actively committed to his sobriety for the rest of his life. I praise God for my daughter-in-law who, in spite of the hurt my son's addiction caused her, remained by his side and fought for his ultimate freedom. Today, both my son and daughter-in-law share their redemptive story when needed in an effort to see other captives set free.

In the appendix, I have included a bonus conversation my son wrote to mothers of sons where he offers a couple of take-aways on how mothers can best help their sons when it comes to the lure of pornography. I wept as I read it and it is far more powerful than anything I have written in this chapter, so I encourage you to read it.

In spite of the many conversations I had with my sons regarding the dangers of pornography, my efforts would not spare one of my sons from becoming a victim. I know this may lead some of you to conclude that it is a hopeless situation. Let me remind you that as a mother, you are not responsible for the end results. You do your part and allow God to do His. I was reminded of this truth while recently rocking my grandson to sleep while my son and daughter-in-law were on an anniversary trip. I wept silent tears of joy as I held that baby boy and thought of how different this story might have looked had my son not admitted to his problem and taken steps toward recovery. Or had my daughter-in-law not remained by his side to fight the battle. Or had I not taught my son over the years that no sin is too big for the forgiveness of God. Rocking my precious grandson reminded me that no sin is wasted in God's economy. He is in the business of bringing beauty from ashes.

We must address the dangers of porn with our sons before they walk into a snare that can leave them forever entrapped with a trail of devastating fallout in its wake for years to come. Most importantly, we must remind our sons that while porn takes captives, the good news remains: Jesus came to set us free.

Chapter 6

Raising a Wise Guy

● ● ● ● ● ●

He who trusts in his own heart is a fool,
But he who walks wisely will be delivered. (Prov. 28:26 NASB)

Harvey Weinstein, Matt Lauer, Kevin Spacey, Bill Cosby, Louis C. K., Roy Moore, Al Franken, Charlie Rose, Mark Halperin, Larry Nassar, Bill Gothard, Josh Duggar, and the list goes on and on. What do these men have in common? They have all been accused of sexual misconduct, assault, or abuse. Some have lost their jobs. Some have admitted to a porn or sex addiction and sought treatment. Some are facing criminal charges. Some are in prison. Some have admitted to abuse and offered apologies.

While each of these men has had noteworthy accomplishments during the course of his life, each one is now defined by his public accusations of sexual harassment and/or sexual assault. Their past achievements have been overshadowed and replaced by tainted reputations. Some of you might be wondering, *What does this have to do with my son?* The truth is, what happened to these men can happen to any one of our sons. The scandals associated with the above-mentioned men are not the ultimate blame for their downfalls. Oh sure, the scandals triggered their *public downfalls*, but the *real downfalls* for these men began long ago, somewhere in the deep recesses of their hearts and minds.

Somewhere along the way each of these men faced a temptation and ultimately succumbed to it. Not one time or two times, but over and over again. What began as a hesitation when standing at the crossroad of temptation became second nature. Ultimately their repetition of sin bred a habit. I'm sure each one of them knew that what they were doing was wrong on some basic level, but like a drug addict in search of the next buzz, they chose to risk it all. In the end they would lose most everything. Their actions would cause untold amounts of damage to themselves, their family members, and their reputations. It would change the course of their lives forever. I bet if they could go back to the point of origin when they first stood at the crossroads of temptation, they'd slam on the brakes and rethink their decision. What they didn't conquer at the crossroads, in the end, became their master.

You don't have to be a pro athlete, politician, or charismatic church leader to suffer a downfall. Chances are, we can all think of examples of men (and women) who have been mastered by sins that, in turn, left their lives and relationships in shambles. I have a close family member who was mastered by an addiction to alcohol that nearly cost him his wife, child, and job. As it is, he lost two decades of happiness . . . all for the contents of a vodka bottle. Another couple I know has suffered the heartache of a son so addicted to heroin that he stole from them to buy drugs, was in and out of jail, and even lived on the streets for a time. Every time the doorbell or phone rang they wondered if it would be someone to notify them of their son's death. I have numerous friends who have been blind-sided by the discovery of their husbands' affairs. Some of the marriages survived and some did not. I have another friend who received a call in the middle of the night from her Sunday-school-teaching husband who was away on business. He had been arrested for soliciting a prostitute and was forced to call her so she could find him legal representation. Her world was shattered in a matter of moments. Facing criminal charges and a court date, he had no choice but to come clean with his wife about his double life. Sadly I've had far too many friends who have experienced the secondhand fallout from husbands or sons who are mastered by an addiction to porn.

Enslavement to sin always produces collateral damage. Just ask Tammy, who answered a survey question I posted on my blog where I asked mothers to share their main concerns when it comes to raising sons. She says, "My husband of fifteen years, with a nine-year old daughter and a six year-old son, one day decided he was going to abandon his family and marry another woman thirteen years younger than me. Within nine months of his leaving, he had his vasectomy reversed and was remarried. In their first year of marriage he had another child, a boy. He has had little to no interaction with our children since, in over four years. My question/concern is: How do I teach my son to be morally sound when he has been exposed to such blatant infidelity?"

I realize that many of you are like Tammy, going it alone when it comes to raising your sons to be godly men. Please don't be discouraged or give up hope. Your efforts will make a difference. By exposing your son to God's truths, the hope is that he will ultimately recognize that true freedom can only be found in Christ.

A downfall doesn't officially become a downfall when some-one leaves their spouse, is caught looking at porn, or is arrested for embezzlement. A downfall begins at the point of enslavement. While we can't control the choices our sons will make when standing at a tempting crossroad, we can educate them about the fallout that can result from being mastered by sin.

In this chapter we will address several external factors that, if addressed, can help protect our sons from enslavement by certain sins.

You may have heard the saying, "The best time to plant a tree was ten years ago. The second best time is now." Much of what we are going to discuss is most effective if introduced and implemented in the early years. I'm a big fan of taking preventative measures on the front end versus reacting to the fallout on the back end.

As we look at external factors that can better equip our sons to make godly choices, I want to focus on three primary factors: the parent factor, the friend factor, and the faith factor. As the mother of two now grown sons, I can speak firsthand to the benefits of each factor when it comes to building a foundation of godly character in their lives. When all three factors are implemented together in unison, the likelihood they will be mastered by sin is greatly reduced.

The Parent Factor

Caring, engaged parents typically raise happier and healthier children. In fact, the following findings were detailed in an article published on USAToday.com entitled, "Teens Do Better with Parents Who Set Limits."[1]

- Teens who had a bedtime of 10:00 p.m. or earlier, set by parents, got more sleep and were less likely to be depressed or consider suicide than those allowed to stay up past midnight.
- Teen drivers whose parents set and enforced rules were more likely to wear seat belts and less likely to speed, get in crashes, drink and drive, or use cell phones while driving.
- Teens whose parents set rules also smoke less, delay sex, and do better in school.

Parenting is hard work and takes tremendous amounts of time and energy. It takes time to teach and train a child. It takes time to draw up boundaries; it takes time to maintain the boundaries; and it takes time to enforce the boundaries when they are crossed.

Even if you are an engaged and attentive parent, you still must contend with parents of your child's friends who are not. Years ago my youngest son entered high school after being in private school for the preceding years. He went from an environment where we knew his friends and his friends' parents to an environment where we knew little (if anything) about his new friends. He has always made friends easily and within a few weeks was invited to watch a college football game "with a bunch of kids" over at a new friend's house (guys and girls). After the game the guys were invited to spend the night. Being an engaged parent, I called in advance to thank the parents for hosting the party and basically to make sure they were going to be there the entire time to supervise the event. Unfortunately my call was not appreciated. I began by thanking the dad for the invitation my son received and then followed with, "I just wanted to make sure you were going to be there to supervise since it sounds like most of the ninth-grade class will be there." At that moment his tone changed, and he became abrupt and rude. "Well, I can't promise you we're going to stick around the entire time, but my oldest son will be there and he's in college." Nice. He was even kind enough to offer me a bit of parenting wisdom before hanging up. "You know, you can't watch your kids 24–7. You have to let kids be kids." Sorry Pops, but if letting "kids be kids" means leaving a few dozen ninth-grade girls and guys alone in your house to engage in standard ninth-grade-kid-like behaviors, I'll pass on the invitation to the party. Perhaps the most disturbing part of the call was at the end when he admitted my call had caught him off guard because he had never received a call from a parent "checking things out" before a gathering.

The truth is, we can't protect our sons twenty-four hours a day from making foolish choices, but we *can* set up boundaries and rules to make it more difficult for them to make foolish choices. And we can certainly limit their exposure to situations where other parents are contributing to the pursuit of foolishness by failing to supervise the children in their care. There is great value in helping your son find friends who have like-minded parents. This doesn't mean you should forbid your son from hanging out with kids who don't have engaged and caring parents, but you need to find a protective balance.

The Friend Factor

He who walks with wise men will be wise, but the companion of fools will suffer harm. (Prov. 13:20 NASB)

Several months ago a friend of mine was completely caught off guard when she discovered that her good, Christian daughter had been sneaking off to smoke pot with her group of friends. She made the comment, "I just don't understand how this could happen. Every day I pray God will protect my children and help them make wise choices." My friend is a good mother and a faithful prayer warrior, but she failed to address some obvious external factors that she had dismissed as unimportant, like for example, paying a bit more attention to her daughter's peer group and limiting her daughter's contact with some of the kids who had well-known reputations for being partiers.

The type of friends your son chooses or gravitates toward can speak volumes about his developing identity. It's hard to say whether "identity determines peer group" or "peer group determines identity," but the point is really moot. Either way, when your son conforms to a peer group, it can have a positive or negative outcome on his behavior.

Benjamin Franklin once said, "He who lies down with the dogs shall rise up with fleas." If you've ever had to treat a flea-infested dog, I think you would agree that it's far better to take preventive measures on the front end than tackle the problem after the fact.

When it comes to choosing a positive peer group, one distinction we made in our home was the difference between *weekday friends* and *weekend friends*. A weekday friend might be someone my son meets at school or an after-school activity. The friendship is primarily built during school hours or during the time spent in a common activity. Any time spent after school or on weekends would be at our home in a monitored environment. A weekend friend might be someone who has similar beliefs and values as my son. I would not hesitate to have this child over on the weekends or allow my son to spend time with the friend away from our house. Obviously, the weekend friend list is a much shorter list than the weekday friend list.

Having taught our children this distinction, we had a baseline for helping them choose a positive peer group that is parent-approved. For example, if my son expressed a desire to get together with a weekday friend from school, and it was a friend we didn't know, we had the condition that the friend come to our house until we can get a better gauge on the situation. The friend may or may not transition into a weekend friend. In some situations our sons had friends they strictly saw at our home because we did not have an adequate comfort level in allowing our sons to spend time at the friend's house, like for example, the situation I mentioned earlier where my son received the invitation to a party that was going to be essentially unsupervised.

Here are some ways parents can remain vigilant about the influence of their child's peer group:

- Look beyond your child's best friend to his or her close circle and wider peer group to understand the full range of peer influence.
- Pay attention to the composition of your teen's immediate circle of friends.
- Focus more on your teen's positive friends. These are the peers who are making a difference. Helping young people sustain positive relationships with good role models is protective.
- Learn about the relationships your child's friends have with their parents. By steering your children to friends who are close to their own parents, you can help reduce risk.

Let me also add that it may be necessary in some cases to completely ban your son from high-risk associations for a season (or sometimes permanently) when boundary lines are crossed or trust is breached. Both of my sons experienced a major stand-at-the-crossroads, life-defining situation in their high school years. Keith and I have always prayed that if (when) our sons stray from the path of God, they will be caught in their sin as early as possible. Simply put, we asked God to sound the sin alarm to "Repent! Turn back!" Should our children respond by hitting the snooze button, we wanted them caught, so we could intervene in an effort to (1) address the problem at its root cause and (2) protect them from straying any farther down the path before they develop a negative habit or pattern.

In the situations where my sons were caught engaging in a sinful activity, they were immediately placed on lockdown. In addition to seizing their cell phones, laptops, and car keys (with the exception of driving to school and work), we also banned them from associating with anyone else who had been involved in the situation until we could get a better grasp on the situation. We reasoned that these "friends" were not a good influence on our sons, and our sons were in turn not a good influence on their friends.

Because a breach of trust had occurred, the burden of responsibility was placed on each of our sons to earn our trust back before privileges were reinstated. In the situations we identified certain boys who, because of a proven track record of distrust and a lack of repentance, were put on the banned friend list permanently unless they could prove otherwise. The first proverb reminds us, "My son, if sinners entice you, don't be persuaded . . . don't travel that road with them or set foot on their path, because their feet run toward evil" (Prov. 1:10, 15–16 NIV, 1984). Until our sons have the wisdom and discernment to keep a distance from those who might "entice" them or tempt them to "run toward evil," it's up to us to help them keep a distance. I know this sounds harsh but, given the power of peer influence, we have a responsibility to protect our sons, and sometimes this means drawing boundaries that would aid in protecting them from *themselves.*

The friend ban forced both of my sons to seek out new friends or make an effort to reconnect with old friends who were at least making an effort to follow Christ. In the end God provided each of our sons with a handful of solid Christian friends. Today our sons view the "friend intervention" as a much-needed wake-up call that in the end helped nudge them back to God's path.

We were fortunate that for the most part our sons made overall good choices when it came to their immediate peer group. The few bumps we experienced along the way served as tangible reminders of God's wisdom when it comes to choosing friends. Truly, "bad company corrupts good character" (1 Cor. 15:33). In spite of our time and attention invested in teaching them this truth, sometimes our sons will simply have to learn the hard way. In the meantime we can do our part by keeping tabs on their peer group and steering them to friends who share the same values and beliefs.

As social media has become more of the connecting force in our children's lives, it has become more difficult to distinguish their true friends from their virtual friends. It was much easier to monitor our children's friend groups when they were hanging out in our homes rather than online via their smartphones and tablets. That doesn't mean we give up and accept defeat. We will talk more in the next chapter about social media's impact on our children and more importantly, discuss practical ways we can monitor their expanding virtual friend circle.

The Faith Factor

In the book *Boys Should Be Boys*, author and pediatrician Meg Meeker says, "I say this not as a theologian myself, but as pediatrician, and base it on what I have seen in my clinical practice. Boys who adhere to a traditional religious practice are far more likely to be able to withstand the pressures of life, to have a sense of wholeness and purpose about themselves, than boys who have either been raised with no faith or with a formless self-directed faith."[2]

Recently, I stumbled upon some old pictures from my youngest son's senior year. Among them was a group shot of his peer group from his senior prom. Looking at their picture, I was overwhelmed with gratitude for the provision of his group of friends. Many of them grew up in the same church together, having experienced everything from preschool to VBS to youth group camps and events. They've done Wednesday night Bible studies together and traveled on weeklong mission trips. In fact, my son and three others in the picture began their friendship as port-a-crib neighbors in the church nursery. They did father-son campouts and attended one another's birthday parties over the years. A couple months prior to the prom, they spent their spring break vacation on a mission trip to Thailand.

They were a great group of kids. Not perfect, mind you, but who is? In looking back, some of them (including my own son) hit some bumps along the way in their high school and college years that knocked them off course for a season. If you asked them about those bumps in the road, they'd tell you it helped define not only *who* they are today but also *where* they are in their Christian journey. In fact, I have witnessed a neat dynamic take place with this group of young men over the past few years. If one of them strays from God's path, the others take notice and lovingly encourage their friend back into the fold. My own son has been the encourager at times, as well as the one on the receiving end of the encouragement.

If I had to come up with a list of common denominators that my son and his close childhood friends shared it would be this: (1) they were raised by committed Christian parents in the Christian faith from a young age; (2) their parents are faithful church attenders who are committed to being involved in their local church (vs. sporadic Sunday attenders); and (3) their parents were diligent in guiding them to choose friends with a like-minded set of beliefs and values. Amazingly each of the common denominators above represents the external factors we have addressed in this chapter: the parent factor, the friend factor, and the faith factor. If we are to protect our sons from being mastered by temptation and sin, we must consistently expose them to an environment that provides them with the one and only solution to the problem of sin and temptation: a close and thriving relationship with Jesus Christ. Without a foundation of faith, our sons are left without a true north to guide them through their adolescent and teen years.

The reality of the situation is that our sons will be tempted and, at times, they will fall into temptation. No amount of parent safeguards will change that fact. However, if we are diligent when it comes to being engaged parents, closely monitoring their friend group, and building a foundation of faith for them to fall back on, they are less likely to stray too far off course for long before returning to the God they love.

Talk about It

* * * * * * * * * *

Chapter 4

Were you aware of the link between excessive screen time and mental health? After reading the data, what changes do you feel led to take when it comes to your son's access to screens?

How have screens impacted your son's behavior overall? Is he able to manage his screen time in moderation or does he have a tendency to over-indulge?

Would you agree that much of our compulsion toward screens (and other distractions) is rooted in a fear of solitude? How might you teach your son that solitude is a good thing and necessary if he is to have a close, thriving relationship with Christ?

In what areas does your son lacks self-control? How might you help him implement the STP model (stop, think, pray) to help him consider consequences before he responds impulsively?

How might your tech-consumption change if you were to ask yourself on a consistent basis, "Is this good for my soul?"

Chapter 5

Were you surprised by the Barna survey findings that indicate a moral ambiguity toward porn by the youngest generation, especially the view that "not recycling" is more wrong than "viewing porn"? Why do you think that is?

Have you ever had a conversation with your son related to the dangers of viewing porn? (Assuming he is old enough.) If your son is ten or older, are you committed to discuss the "tradeoffs of viewing porn" with him on a consistent basis?

When it comes to protecting your sons from porn, do you feel you are more proactive or reactive?

Do you feel comfortable with the protection measures you have in place to reduce the likelihood your son will stumble upon porn? If not, what are some additional steps you plan to take to safeguard any electronic devices your son has access to?

Chapter 6

Have you experienced a situation where one of your son's friends had looser boundaries (due to more permissive parents) and it caused tension? Explain.

How well do you know your son's friends? Does your son currently have any "high-risk friends"? What steps might you take to guide him toward more positive friends who share your same values?

Does your son have a local church he is consistently involved in? Does he have long-time friends who share his same faith and values?

Conversation 3

Have a little sex respect.

Chapter 7

Beyond the Birds
and Bees

● ● ● ● ● ●

"Therefore a man shall leave his father and mother and hold
fast to his wife, and the two shall become one flesh. So they
are no longer two but one flesh." (Mark 10:7–8 ESV)

When my kids were young, I had a friend who was of the school of thought that private parts should always be referred to by their correct anatomical terms. I, on the other hand, could not bring myself to embrace this teaching philosophy and therefore, provided my children with nicknames for their privates. My friend would often tease me about my nickname system and tell me that my poor kids were going to be warped for life. I wondered if maybe she was right until one day when I picked up my friend's son for a play date after preschool. On the way to my house, we went over one of those big hills that can give you butterflies in your stomach. All of a sudden, her son yelled out from the backseat, "Whoa! That tickled my scrotum!" So yeah, at that point, I was sure I was on the right track, and my friend was the one warping her kids for life . . . and mine for that matter since I had to spend the next five minutes addressing my son's question that followed from the backseat.

"What's a scrotum, Mom?"

"Uh, it's a part of your body that's right by your *willy*."

Which then triggered a follow-up question from my friend's son: "What's a *willy*?"

To which I immediately replied, "Why don't you ask your mom when you get home, okay?"

My nickname system worked just fine until one day when a new family moved into our neighborhood. I had heard that they also had a six-year-old boy the same age as my older son at the time, so we stopped by one day to introduce ourselves. When the mother introduced her son to my son, Ryan, I immediately knew we had a problem. Yes, you got it—his name was *Willy*! Anyway, I shot my son a pleading look to remain silent, but by the look on his face, it was clear that we would have plenty to talk about on the way home. I'll never forget his comment as we walked away: "Mom, why would anyone name their kid Willy?" Drat. I finally had to come clean with my son. In the end the conversation was good timing because the movie *Free Willy* released a few months later. And that's certainly the last message we want to send to our sons.

Talking about sex is intimidating for many parents and even more so for mothers who attempt to broach the topic with their sons. Gone are the days when Dad worked up his nerve to have the one-time talk with his son so he could scratch it off his to-do list. Given the culture in which we live, we need all hands on deck when it comes to raising our sons to be sexually pure. We need both Mom and Dad to take advantage of teachable moments as they occur. I

know this is a difficult thought for many of you, and if you are absolutely certain you cannot bring yourself to talk with your son about
sex, hand the book over to your husband and give him the task. The
most important thing is that *at least one parent* address the topic and
continue to address it throughout the years. Even better if it's the
both of you. My husband and I viewed it as a partnership when it
came to discussing the topic of sex. In fact, truth be told, I probably
had more conversations with our sons than my husband because I
was with them more often throughout the day when many of the
teachable moments occurred.

Sex Is Good—Very, Very Good

When we are talking with our sons about sex, we need to
approach the topic with boldness and confidence rather than skit-
tishness and timidity. We also need to make sure we are balanced
in the way we present it, always remembering that sex was created
by God for His purposes (procreation) and our pleasure. In other
words, we need to leave our sons with a clear understanding that sex
in the right context (marriage) is good and something God wired us
to desire and enjoy. In the book *Hooked,* authors Joe S. McIlhaney,
M.D., and Freda McKissic Bush, M.D., say, "Sex can be considered
one of the appetites with which we are born."[1] They go on to point
out that the word "appetite" can be defined as "any of the instinctive
desires necessary to keep up organic life" or "an inherent craving."[2]
McIlhaney and Bush say, "A truth to remember is that appetites
are necessary but values-neutral. They can be used appropriately or
they can be misunderstood and misused. For example, without an
appetite for food, we wouldn't survive. Food provides energy and
fuels our bodies. Yet the misuse of this natural appetite in the forms

of overeating or eating too much of the wrong things, for example, can cause problems such as cardiovascular disease, diabetes, and many others. These health problems can dramatically change the entire course of an individual's life."[3]

As mothers, we need to be careful that we don't go overboard in our "conversations" by always emphasizing the problems associated with sex outside of marriage. If we fail to acknowledge that sex is, in fact, a gift from God and something He gave us a natural appetite for, our sons may be left with the impression that sex is shameful, even in marriage. This will be especially confusing for our sons when their sexual appetites kick in (and they will!). We need to make sure our sons understand that while their "appetite" for sex is normal and natural, it is also something that needs to be properly managed in order for them to experience optimum long-term spiritual, emotional, and physical health.

Sex on the Boy Brain

When it comes to sex being like an "appetite," we as mothers need to understand better how strong the male appetite for sex is. Because we are women, we will have a tendency to address the topic of sex from a female perspective and make assumptions based on our appetites for sex. That said, get ready. I'm about to dump some candid information on you that might make you feel a bit uneasy.

Once a boy hits adolescence, his body is undergoing changes at warp speed, and his appetite for sex kicks into overdrive. Let me put it to you this way: That same preteen boy/young teen boy who mothers commonly tell their friends is "in a growth spurt and eating them out of house and home," is also hungry for sex. Moms typically see only a boy who puts in overtime standing in front of the kitchen pantry and mumbling, "I'm staaaarrrrvvvving," but the truth is, he's also staaaarrrrvvvving for sex. I know that's an uncomfortable thought and not one you can relate to, but we must face the facts if we are to understand the challenge our boys are facing. A boy's sudden appetite for sex is fueled by a deluge of testosterone during puberty that literally floods his system. The only other time a boy experiences a testosterone wash of this nature and magnitude is when he is in utero and the embryo receives a "testosterone bath" during the sixth week of gestation, compliments of the Y chromosome delivered by his father. In their book *Raising Sons and Loving It!* Gary and Carrie Oliver write, "During this testosterone wash, the level of testosterone is ten to twenty times stronger in boys than girls. The prepubertal and adolescent boy will have between five to seven surges of testosterone per day—an increase marked by a tendency to masturbate frequently, be moody and aggressive, want more sleep, lose his temper more often, be negative and critical, act like his head is in the clouds, and have a significantly greater interest in sex."[4] I hesitate to include that during this testosterone bath his penis (a.k.a.: "willy") will increase as much as eight times in size. You probably could have lived without that last bit of information, but I share it to make the point that our sons can hardly escape the changes going on in their bodies or their appetite for sex that results.

In *Making Sense of the Men in Your Life*, Kevin Leman says, "Men reportedly think about sex an average of thirty-three times per day, or twice an hour. Some people say women think about sex only once a day—when men ask for it."[5] While that might garner a chuckle or two, stop and think about it for a moment. Try to imagine how difficult it must be for our sons (and husbands) to be sexually pure when they live in a world that is all too happy to take advantage of their sexual hunger pangs. Author Rick Johnson adds, "At the risk of perpetuating a stereotype about men, there's a distinct possibility that if women knew how and what men really think about, they would refuse to be in the same room with them (I use the term *men*, but it's interchangeable with *boys* from early adolescence on)." He goes on to say: "They'd think them perverted. Guys think about sex all the time. Men even think about sex in the most inappropriate places, such as in church or at funerals. The slightest and most innocent thing—a woman's laugh, the curve of a shapely leg, certain shoes, perfume, and thousands of other scents, sights, and sounds—can set men off. During adolescence, when hormones are raging, these stimulations are intensified."[6] For those of us who are married, it's sobering enough to associate the above information with our husbands, much less our little boys! Say it isn't so!

I was recently going through some old pictures of family vacations in an attempt to sort them into separate vacation piles. My hope was that I would someday have time to put them in albums (rather than in their gallon-size storage bags). Our family had the blessing of taking a Caribbean cruise (compliments of my in-laws) that just so happened to coincide with my youngest son's thirteenth birthday. There were plenty of pictures of him blowing out his candles during our all-inclusive five-course dinner. At the time I remember thinking he still looked very much like a little boy. Oh, I knew changes were coming right around the corner, having remembered the process with my older son, but for now he was still my little guy.

Two years later we were back on the same cruise ship, thanks to a pipe that burst and flooded our cabin on the first trip and cut the trip short. We received a complimentary cruise as compensation for our pain and suffering! The pictures from cruise two were mixed in the same slush pile of pictures from the previous cruise, only something was different this time. The boy who had officially become a teenager on that first cruise was gone. As in MIA. In his place was someone who slightly resembled that boy—same color hair, same dimples, same older brother and sister, same parents— yet he didn't look at all the same. In two short years he went from looking like a boy to a new version of that same boy—a mini-man, if you will.

It wasn't until I saw the two sets of pictures side by side that I realized how quickly he had developed from boy to young man. In two short years he had overtaken both his older sister and me in height. His face had thinned out significantly, and this new man-boy even had muscles! I thought I even spotted some hair under his arms in a pool picture! And the changes weren't just on the outside. The man-boy in the later pictures was far less interested in playing shuffleboard with his family by the poolside on the second cruise. Other things were competing for his attention at the poolside.

The short time frame where boys morph into young men is a weird and awkward season for moms. Let's be honest here. It's easier to mother a *boy* than a *man*. It's hard for us to accept that our little boys do, in fact, grow up to look and behave like men. The truth is, we need to step up our conversations during this hormonal surge in addition to stocking up the kitchen pantry with more food.

Sex 101

Sex education should begin earlier than the onset of adolescence. At the end of this chapter, I have included some suggested "sex facts" to cover through the years, beginning when our boys are young and begin to have a natural curiosity about their bodies and the differences between them and girls. When they begin to ask questions in the months or years to follow, we need to be ready to talk about the purpose of sex. I love the approach that sexual abstinence expert Pam Stenzel takes in her book *Sex Has a Price Tag: Discussions about Sexuality, Spirituality, and Self-Respect.* Here it is in a nutshell:

- Humans did not create sex. God did.
- Since God created sex, He's the one who understands it the best.
- Since God understands sex better than anyone, a person who wants to have great sex (and why would anyone want to have rotten sex?) needs to know what God says about sex.[7]

Once your son is clear on the basics regarding the purpose of sex and God's view of sex, you're ready to incorporate into your conversations some of the information we will discuss in the following two chapters, as you feel your son is ready. Break down the information into bite-size conversations rather than dumping an entire chapter's worth of information on him at one time. Continue the conversations over the years, taking advantage of teachable moments as they occur. A good rule of thumb to remember when it comes to discussing sex is to "keep the conversation simple and keep it going."

Somewhere between the ages eight and ten, children should be given a basic definition of sex by their parents before they hear otherwise from undependable sources. Some parents wait for a signal from the child before they begin the conversations about sex. This is a bit risky since some kids are quieter than others and may shy away from bringing their questions about sex to their parents. You know best when your son is showing signs of readiness, but I highly recommend that you begin initiating the conversations about sex before he enters middle school or at the first signs of adolescence, whichever comes first.

This is especially true if your son is in a public school and/or has an older brother or sister and by default has been exposed to more mature topics. However, don't let that be your only barometer. One mom recently shared a story with me about her sheltered eight-year-old son (the oldest of three children) who snuck onto the family computer and googled "what is sex?" Her husband discovered it when checking the history on the computer, and they were stunned to learn that "sex" had somehow made it onto their son's radar. When they asked their son where he first heard of sex, he matter-of-factly told them "from my friends." It's a tedious balance because we want to protect our sons' innocence for as long as possible, yet at the same time we want them to hear accurate information about sex lest they be misinformed from outside sources. Many children today are learning about sex from an Internet search engine. That should be motivation enough to take the reins and lead the charge.

When I felt it was a good time to broach the topic with my sons, I said something to the effect of, *"Hey buddy, I need to talk to you about something important. At some point in the next few years, you are going to hear things about sex from your friends or on TV or a tablet or smart phone.* (This assumes your son has been given a basic definition of the word *sex* by this point. If not, you'll need to add that to your conversation!) *Here's the deal. Some of the things you hear aren't going to be true, and I want you to know what God has to say about sex because He's the One who created it. So make me a promise. If you hear something, I want you to come and talk to me or Dad, okay? Deal?"* At that point I followed by asking my son if he had heard anything about sex and made sure he knew it was a safe topic to discuss. And yes, both of my boys admitted they had already heard something about sex at that point from other sources. Thus our conversations began.

My personal philosophy is that once boys hit middle school and are exposed to countless outside influences regarding sex, *anything* is fair game to talk about. The middle school years are also a good time to begin to discuss the topic of lust. Author Rick Johnson says, "Lust is a constant struggle, and those males who choose to live a life of sexual purity face a mighty battle. I am convinced that most women do not understand the intensity of that battle, primarily because women are not as visually stimulated as men."[8] Honestly, I cannot begin to understand the battle my sons (or husband) face when it comes to lust and their sex drive, but in becoming more aware of the challenge, I am better able to extend them grace and understanding rather than condemnation.

And when it comes to talking to our sons about sexual purity, keep in mind that your voice will be the loudest voice your son hears, even if you think he's not listening. One survey found that 88 percent of teens said it would be easier to postpone sexual activity and avoid teen pregnancy if they were able to have more open, honest conversations about sex with their parents. Interestingly, the same study found that only 32 percent of parents surveyed believe they are most influential in their teens' decisions about sex.[9] I find it sad that most parents don't realize the power they have in influencing their kids when it coming to sexual health. No doubt they will be bombarded with lies about sex on a daily basis from media and their peers. Our sons need to know the secret to having "really great sex," the kind of sex God intended. Will you tell them?

I found the following tips from the Mayo Clinic that may be helpful in breaking down the conversations according to age and level of understanding.[10]

Age 18 Months–3 Years

Children begin to learn about their own bodies. Teach your child the proper names for sex organs. Otherwise, he or she might get the idea that something is wrong with these parts of the body. *(Oops, guilty as charged here!)*

Age 3–4 Years

Take advantage of everyday opportunities to discuss sex. If there's a pregnancy in the family, for example, tell your children that babies grow in a special place inside the mother. If your children want more details on how the baby got there or how the baby will be born, tell them.

Consider these examples:

- How do babies get inside a mommy's tummy? You might say: "A mom and a dad make a baby by holding each other in a special way."
- How are babies born? For some kids it might be enough to say: "Doctors and nurses help babies who are ready to be born."
- Where do babies come from? Try to give a simple and direct response such as: "Babies grow in a special place inside the mother." As your child matures, you can add more details.

Teach your child that the parts of the body covered by a bathing suit are private and that no one should be allowed to touch them without permission.

Ages 5–7 Years

Questions about sex will become more complex as your child tries to understand the connection between sexuality and making babies. He or she may turn to friends for some of these answers. Because children can pick up faulty information about sex and reproduction, it may be best to ask what your child knows about a particular topic before you start explaining it.

Ages 8–12 Years

Children between the ages of eight and twelve worry a lot about whether they are "normal." Children of the same age mature at wildly different rates. Reassure your child that he is well within the normal range of development.

Ages 13+ Years

The American Academy of Pediatrics recommends that before they reach puberty, children should have a basic understanding of the following:[11]

- The names and functions of male and female sex organs
- What happens during puberty and what the physical changes of puberty mean—movement into young womanhood or young manhood
- The nature and purpose of the menstrual cycle
- What sexual intercourse is and how females become pregnant
- How to prevent pregnancy
- Same-sex relationships
- Masturbation
- Activities that spread sexually transmitted diseases (STDs), in particular AIDS

* Your expectations and values

Below is a chart I found in Rick Johnson's book *That's My Son* that you may also find helpful:

Discussing Sex Education with Your Children:[12]	
Age	**Topics**
Preschool	Don't punish children for touching their own genitalia. Explain what private parts are and what *privacy* means. Explain sex differences.
Grade School	Discuss issues of procreation in age-appropriate, general terms. Discuss menstruation with girls before they enter adolescence. Discuss masturbation in general terms with boys at a relatively early age.
Adolescent	Teach responsibility and self-control. Teach that sex is not just intercourse. Teach that sexual intimacy has profound consequences. Teach that it's okay to say no to sex until they're married. Teach that sex is not the most important part of a loving relationship.

Chapter 8

Play Now, Pay Later

● ● ● ● ● ●

*Flee from sexual immorality. All other sins a person
commits are outside the body, but whoever sins sexually,
sins against their own body. (1 Cor. 6:18)*

If I had to sum up the culture's message regarding sex, it would
match a customer review on Amazon for one of my books to teen
girls. Apparently my suggestion that God created sex for the confines of marriage didn't sit well with one reader who gave my book
a one star review and offered the following comments: "Ninety
percent of the world's population will have sex before they are married. . . . People will always want to have sex, it's human nature!"

Perhaps God created us with a "human nature" to want to have
sex in order that it might be enjoyed in marriage and serve as a
means to procreate the world. And perhaps 90 percent of the population has failed to follow His game plan for sex, opting instead to

write their own rules for the game. When it comes to sex, the rules of the world's game are simple: Sex is okay as long as it's mutual and protected. Go for it . . . just "be safe." Your son will hear that message over and over again, day in and day out.

When it comes to sex outside of marriage, there is some good news. Sexual intercourse among teens is on the decline. Some experts speculate this is due to the fact that so much of their social time is spent online and, as a result, they spend less time with their peers in person. One college woman offered another explanation on the decline of teen sex. "Teens are being scared into not having sex. When I was in high school the 'no sex' propaganda was strong. We watched videos of what diseased genitals looked like, and we heard all the stories about teen moms. Then that show 'Teen Mom' came out, and nobody wanted to be those girls. Their lives were sad and pathetic."[1] However, before you begin to celebrate, there is also speculation that the decline in teen sexual intercourse is due to an increase in oral sex. When Peggy Orenstein, author of the book *Girls & Sex*, interviewed teen girls, several described oral sex as "nothing . . . it's not sex" and "a step past making out with someone." Some argued it was safer and "doesn't have the repercussions that vaginal sex does. You're not losing your virginity, you can't get pregnant, you can't get STDs. So it's safer."[2] Of course, we know this is not true since you can get STDs from oral sex.

While the decline in sexual intercourse among teens is worth celebrating, we cannot minimize the impact many other behaviors are having on our sons when it comes to sexual activity. Take for example, hooking up. Many moms naïvely postpone discussing the topic of sex until their sons are in a dating relationship. The problem with that is that dating is nearly extinct. One multi-year survey of more than twenty-four thousand college students from twenty-two different US colleges and universities found that just as many students are hooking up as are dating. Sixty-two percent reported having hooked up since the beginning of their college experience, while 61 percent reported going out on a date.[3]

No doubt we have our work cut out for us when it comes to encouraging our sons to save sex for marriage. I didn't write this chapter to depress you but rather to implore you to address the seven-ton elephant that's sitting in the middle of the living room. We must have some candid and blunt conversations with our sons to arm them in the battle they face. God knew what He was doing when He created sex for the confines of marriage. It's up to us to educate our sons to the why behind His rules.

What the Media Is NOT Telling Your Son about Sex

Your son is bombarded on a daily basis with messages regarding sex. When was the last time you saw a scene on a show or movie that, after highlighting sex outside of marriage, showed one of the characters dealing with news of an unwanted pregnancy? What if the show or movie reflected the reality that teens and young adults account for 50 percent of new STIs each year?[4] What if the media portrayed the fallout from contracting an STD, like working up your nerve to tell your partner or, for that matter, your future partners? Or what if the media demonstrated the finding that two-thirds of all sexually experienced teens regret their decision to have sex and wish they had waited longer?[5]

So the lie continues to be peddled day in and day out, leaving our children with the impression that sex is nothing more than a recreational hobby. No consequences, no strings attached. But there *are* consequences, and there *are* strings attached. That's where we come in. We must be diligent in exposing the lies and counteracting them with God's truths.

In addition to ignoring the fallout from having sex outside of marriage, the media also fails to address the benefits of saving sex for marriage. Think about it. When was the last time you heard a media report announcing that those who abstain from sex outside of marriage have the best sex once they are married? Consider that one survey found that 72 percent of all married "traditionalists (those who 'strongly believe out of wedlock sex is wrong') reported a higher sexual satisfaction. 'Traditionalists' scored roughly 31 percentage points higher than the level registered by unmarried 'nontraditionalists' (those who have no or only some objection to sex outside of marriage), and 13 percentage points higher than that registered by married nontraditionalists."[6]

It gets better. A study by the National Institute for Healthcare Research found that couples who don't sleep together before marriage and who are faithful during marriage are more satisfied with their current sex life (and also with their marriages) compared to those who were involved sexually before marriage.[7] I wonder how many young people might choose to delay sex if they knew that their reward would be a higher likelihood of having a lasting, monogamous, sexually satisfying marriage.

Of course, you don't hear the media highlighting any of the above data. The culture will continue to tell our sons that sex is a natural, normal part of life. They will scream and fight to abolish abstinence-based sex education and continue to peddle the "safe sex" message ad nauseam. It is imperative that we as mothers pick up the slack and share with our sons the details that culture refuses to address.

Unless we expose the faulty thinking behind the culture's free-sex message and the fallout that has resulted from believing it, it will be impossible adequately to address the issue of sex outside of marriage with our sons. It's not enough to tell our sons to "wait because God says so." It would be nice if it were that easy. The truth is, the message that God created sex for the confines of marriage often gets drowned out by raging hormones, peer pressure, and a nonstop message coming from culture that "everyone's doing it." Our sons deserve to know all the facts before making a decision to have sex outside of marriage.

Locker Room Lies

One challenge our boys face (and mothers need to be aware of) is the attitude that "everyone's doing it" and those who aren't are actively seeking a way to shed the "virgin" label. Consider the following question a young man anonymously submitted to a secular online advice forum geared to teens and young adults: "Should I feel terrible for being a twenty-one-year-old male virgin?"

Here is a snippet from his post:

> I really want to have sex with someone I love. I can't seem to get myself to have sex with a drunk girl at a party, which is how everyone my age seems to get laid. Both of my girlfriends ended up breaking my heart after a few months, shortly after I told them I was a virgin. It was like they suddenly got uncomfortable and awkward around me. . . . I have to lie to all my friends about being a virgin. The only thing I think about is girls, girls, girls and how badly I want to make someone happy in a mutual relationship. I don't view sex as an achievement

that I want to brag about. I just want to do it because it's something I crave intensely, not just for the physical sensation but for the emotional connections. None of my guy friends understand that though, and all the girls I talk to have boyfriends or have absolutely no interest in me, sexually. . . . I feel so pathetic and like a complete loser, that I'll be terrible at sex. . . . Is it normal for me to still be a virgin at twenty-one?"[8]

I find it immensely sad that a twenty-one-year-old young man who has yet to have sex would see it as a curse rather than a blessing! Interestingly he presents an honest assessment of the "craving" he has to experience sex for the "emotional connection." Sadly our sons will be exposed at some level to the rampant mentality in our culture that male virginity garners suspicions rather than respect. In a survey of twelve hundred teen and young adult males (ages fifteen to twenty-two) conducted by *Seventeen* magazine and the National Campaign to Prevent Teen and Unplanned Pregnancy, 78 percent of those surveyed agreed there was way too much pressure from society to have sex.[9] Interestingly the survey also found that guys are not being altogether honest about their sexual experience. Among the findings:

- Sixty percent said they had lied about something related to sex.
- Thirty percent lied about how far they have gone.
- Twenty-four percent lied about their number of sexual partners.
- Twenty-three percent claimed not to be a virgin when they were.[10]

As mothers, we would be wise to inform our sons to take the locker-room banter they hear from other guys with a grain of salt. Guys who feel a need to lie in regard to their sexual experience are suffering from low self-esteem and, sadly, are trying desperately to fit in with the wrong group of guys in order to gain acceptance. Ironically, many of the guys who mock and tease other guys for being virgins aren't any more sexually experienced than the ones they're teasing! Our sons need to steer clear of guys like this and find a handful of friends who are committed to the same values and beliefs. When it comes to being teased, author Pam Stenzel shares a wonderful story in *Sex Has a Price Tag* about a college student who committed to wait to have sex until marriage. As the only guy on his football team who's still a virgin, he asked an older man what he could say to his friends when they ridiculed him or mocked his decision. The man said, "Tell them you can become just like them any time you want, but they can never again be like you. That's far more valuable than anything they've ever experienced."[11]

The Fallout from Not Saving Sex for Marriage

In this chapter I will concentrate on three areas of fallout that we will need to emphasize with our sons over and over again. Because boys today are exposed to sex at a much earlier age than in the past, I personally recommend introducing the three areas of fallout sometime between fifth and seventh grades. If your son is not exposed to older brothers or sisters, is not socially inclined, and has limited contact with television, technology, social media, and the Internet, you might be able to pull off waiting until seventh or eighth grade. If your son is younger than fifth or sixth grade, that doesn't mean you can skip this chapter! The years leading up to middle school are critical years that should be used to build a basic framework centered around God's design for sex. In other words, look at it like a building project. In the early years (pre-k to kindergarten), a foundation should be poured by addressing our sons' basic questions (e.g., Why are boys and girls different? Where do babies come from?). In the grade school years, we should begin to build the framework on that foundation by offering our sons more details to questions they may have and by developing an open line of communication (as we discussed in chapter 8). By the time they hit middle school, the prep work should be completed (the foundation and framework), so there is a support in place for the conversations that follow. In this stage nothing is off limits to talk about, and we should be ready to react to things our sons are exposed to that openly contradict God's design for sex. In addition to taking advantage of teachable moments, we will also need to initiate scheduled conversations about sex. Notice that our position needs to be proactive. We are the builder. We should not wait for our sons to come to us (most will not) and ask us to assume the role of building foreman. Nor do we hand off the role to our sons' youth ministers and assume they will take care of it. We cannot delegate the task. It is our responsibility to lay the foundation and build the framework, preferably by the time our sons leave the nest. While some boys may ultimately choose to reject our guidance and teaching, our assignment is to diligently and faithfully guide them in God's truth regarding sex.

Physical Fallout

There are about 20 million new cases of STDs each year in the United States. About half of these infections are in people between the ages of fifteen and twenty-four.[12] While we often hear of the devastating consequences that can result from an undetected STD in girls, such as cervical cancer and infertility, guys with STDs are not without consequences. The six most common STDs in men are HIV/AIDS, gonorrhea, chlamydia, herpes simplex virus-2, HPV, and syphilis. Some are known to cause inflammation of the testicles, prostate, and urethra (chlamydia); genital warts and increased risk of cancers of the penis, anus, and rectum (HPV); or damage to the brain, cardiovascular system, and many organs in the body (untreated syphilis).[13]

But STDs aren't the only possible physical consequence of sex outside of marriage. Six in ten pregnancies involving teen fathers end in a birth, which is guaranteed to change the entire trajectory of a boy's life. Author Pam Stenzel, in her book *Sex Has a Price Tag,* says, "A teen father will end up paying a total of between $50,000 and $250,000 (depending on his income) over the next 18 years" to support a child.[14] She recounts the following story involving a young man she met while doing an event at a high school event:

> A few years ago, I spoke at a high school in northern
> Minnesota. When I was done, a popular senior guy stood
> up and admitted to his classmates for the first time that
> he was a dad. The summer before he'd had sex with
> a girl whose family had been vacationing in the area.
> They'd had sex once. Neither of them thought they'd see
> the other one again. They had no plans beyond having a
> good time one night during summer break.
>
> He worked at a Burger King in town. Money was
> taken out of each paycheck to help support his baby.
> That will continue at every job he has for the next
> eighteen years.[15]

She ended by posing this question to the teen guys in the audience: "Guys, what will you say to the girl you want to marry someday if you've already got a child? 'By the way, honey, for the next ten years a chunk of my take-home pay will be used to provide for my first child, so we're going to have to stick to a tight budget.'"[16] Food for thought, and certainly something we need to share with our sons in an effort to help them better understand the long-term physical consequences of sex outside of marriage, even if sex occurs just one time.

Emotional Fallout

One of the most powerful incentives to save sex for marriage is the link between oxytocin and sexual activity. What is oxytocin, you may wonder? Oxytocin is a hormone that acts as a messenger hormone that is sent from a woman's brain to the uterus and breasts to induce labor, as well as let down milk after the baby is born to prepare for the process of nursing. But here's where it gets interesting. Oxytocin is also released during sexual activity.[17] Oxytocin is the "bonding hormone" that not only connects mother and child but also husband and wife. In addition to bonding, oxytocin increases trust.[18] The kind of trust that builds confidence that the person you have now "bonded" with will be there for you. Always and forever. Until death do you part.

Psychologist Jess Lair of Montana State University describes the bonding process that takes place during sexual intercourse in this way: "Sexual bonding includes powerful emotional, psychological, physical, and spiritual links that are so strong that the two people become one, at least for a moment. Sexual intercourse is an intense, though brief physical bonding that leaves indelible marks on the participants. . . . To believe one can walk away from a sexual experience untouched is dangerously naïve."[19]

In light of the information regarding oxytocin, now consider God's design for marriage when He says, "A man leaves his father and mother and is united to his wife, and they become one flesh" (Gen. 2:24). Other references to the act of sex bonding husband and wife as "one flesh" occur in Matthew 19:5; Mark 10:8; and Ephesians 5:31. But what if sex occurs with someone who will not become a person's spouse? Would that same act of "bonding" occur? Consider 1 Corinthians 6:16 that says, "Do you not know that he who unites himself with a prostitute is one with her in body? For it is said, 'The two will become one flesh.'" It should come as no surprise that the scientific discovery of oxytocin supports God's design for sex: It is reserved for a husband and wife in the confines of marriage. God created oxytocin as a "glue" that helps bond mother and child and husband and wife. Sex outside of marriage short-circuits God's design for sex, triggering a premature trust and bond that likely won't last. And when that bond is broken, it is sure to produce emotional fallout for all parties. Meg Meeker, pediatrician and author of *Boys Should Be Boys*, notes that boys aren't exempt from emotional fallout resulting from sex outside of marriage.

> I travel across the country speaking to groups of teenagers about sex and its medical risks. I've noticed that junior and senior boys lean forward in their seats not when I describe the dangers of sexually transmitted diseases, but when I talk about the emotional costs associated with unmarried sexual intercourse. What I've discovered is that while girls are vocal about this sense of loss, boys are not—but feel it just as deeply. But what's

more, the emotional costs of sexual intercourse are something boys didn't expect. Boys feel they were never told that sex can bring emotional hurt.[20]

In *Hooked*, authors Joe McIlhaney, M.D., and Freda McKissic Bush, M.D., note that this neuro-chemical process that takes place in males during sexual intercourse "produces a partial bond with every woman they have sex with."[21] "They do not realize that this pattern of having sex with one woman and then breaking up and then having sex with another woman limits them to experience only one form of brain activity common to humans involved sexually—the dopamine rush of sex."[22] They further say, "The individual who goes from sex partner to sex partner is causing his or her brain to mold and gel so that eventually it begins accepting that sexual pattern as normal. For most people this brain pattern seems to interfere with the development of the neurological circuits necessary for the long-term relationships that for most people result in stable marriages and family development."[23]

Given the power of oxytocin and the emotional bond it creates, it shouldn't come as a surprise that a study of sexually active adolescents found that both boys and girls who have had sex are three times more likely to be depressed than their friends who are still virgins. The girls who became sexually active were three times more likely to have attempted suicide as their virgin friends, while the sexually active boys were fully seven times more likely to have attempted suicide.[24] Sex outside of marriage can bring untold amounts of pain and heartache. When it comes to the emotional health of our sons, the healthiest path is to save sex for marriage.

Spiritual Fallout

In addition to possible physical and emotional consequences associated with having sex outside of marriage, many teens also experience spiritual consequences. Children who are raised in the church and taught God's divine plan for sex know in their hearts it's wrong to have sex outside of marriage. Yet many cave into the temptation and fall into a never-ending cycle of shame, conviction, and guilt. Many will vow to stop having sex in an effort to reconnect with God only to slip up and begin the cycle again. Before long the cycle of guilt begins to define the relationship with God. Prayer time is spent confessing and asking God for His forgiveness or begging Him for strength to endure the temptation. And if the slip-ups continue, before long a sense of defeat sets in, and it becomes more difficult to "approach God's throne of grace with confidence" (Heb. 4:16). Perhaps this is why God tells us, "The body, however, is not meant for sexual immorality but for the Lord, and the Lord for the body" (1 Cor. 6:13).

I will admit that it often feels like a losing battle when it comes to teaching our sons God's design for sex. I question why He would give our sons such strong urges in a culture that delays marriage until the late twenties. It seems like it sets them up to fail. Of course, when you consider that men used to marry much younger (especially in biblical times), waiting seems more attainable. However, we live in a different day and age where sex outside of marriage is the norm. The reality that our sons will wait is slim to none. Sorry to sound like a Debbie Downer, but the statistics confirm that reality.

We must remember, God doesn't play by the world's playbook. God wrote the playbook and His ways are higher than our ways. He never promised that abiding by His standards would be an easy task.

Does that mean we give up and hand our sons a pack of condoms? Absolutely not! We are to remain faithful to God's teachings and remember our assigned task to point our children to His standards. We are called to train our children to walk in His ways, but at the end of the day, it is up to our sons as to whether or not they will follow God or the world. Our best course is honest dialogue about the fallout from failing to follow God's design for sex, as well as the challenges associated with waiting. Acknowledge that it will be difficult to wait. Don't sugarcoat it and make it sound like a simple task, otherwise your sons will write you off early in the game as someone who is clearly out of touch with the challenges associated with waiting.

Do not be discouraged, but set forth with courage and confidence. Most importantly, pray for your sons. We greatly underestimate the power of prayer and the potential it has to change the course of a decision. Remember, as much as you love your son, God loves him (and you!) all the more. You are not alone.

Chapter 9

A New and Improved Sex Talk

● ● ● ● ● ●

"And you must commit yourselves wholeheartedly to these commands that I am giving you today. Repeat them again and again to your children. Talk about them when you are at home and when you are on the road, when you are going to bed and when you are getting up." (Deut. 6:6–7 NLT)

Years ago, I spoke to the girls in the youth group at my local church about the challenges of saving sex for marriage. Before I spoke to the girls, I handed out an informal survey for them to fill out (anonymously) and turn back in to me for a Q&A time at the end of the event. One of the questions I asked the sixty-four girls was whether or not one or both of their parents had talked to them about sex at any point over the past several years. I explained that this question included everything from formal sit-down conversations, a weekend getaway retreat, casual conversations while in the car, or a drive-by teachable moment where Mom or Dad responded or reacted to a media message about sex. It was a multiple-choice question to gauge how many conversations Mom or Dad had initiated over the years in regard to sex. I gave them the following options as answers: none, 1–3, 4–10, 10 or more. Out of sixty-four "church girls" present, only three answered "10 or more." In fact, a whopping two-thirds of the girls answered "none" or "1–3." Mind you, these girls ranged in age from seventh grade to twelfth grade and, for the most part, had parents who were consistent church attenders and highly involved in outside church activities (thus, their faithful attendance for my Saturday morning talk). Their questions on the survey also indicated that in spite of receiving little information about sex from Mom or Dad, they had heard plenty about it from outside sources. Given that moms tend to be more communicative than dads and, for the most part, more comfortable talking to their daughters about sex, I imagine the conversations with sons are scarce to nonexistent.

That is why I commend you for picking up this book, as it indicates a desire on your part to be a hands-on, engaged parent who is interested in initiating critical conversations with your sons. I realize the sex conversation can be an awkward one to introduce, especially when it comes to our sons. Please don't remain silent on this topic. Even if you are blessed to have a husband who has assumed the lead in initiating critical conversations with your son about sex, your voice is still important and much needed. It is not enough to drop your middle- or high-schooler off at a weekend retreat at the church and lean on the youth minister to educate students about God's standards regarding sex. You and your husband are the primary disciplers of your children in any and all spiritual matters.

Study after study confirms that there is a direct link between engaged, caring parents and children making wise choices. Don't ever doubt the power you have in influencing your son when it comes to sexual purity. One study indicated that teenagers in grades eight through eleven who perceive that their mother disapproves of their engaging in sexual intercourse are more likely than their peers to delay sexual activity.[1] In addition, the National Campaign to Prevent Teen Pregnancy conducted a survey that questioned a thousand young people ages twelve to nineteen and 1,008 adults age twenty and older and found that 45 percent of teens said their parents most influence their decisions about sex compared to 31 percent who said their friends are most influential. Religious leaders were only the most influential among 7 percent, while teachers and sex educators stood at 6 percent and the media at 4 percent.[2]

One study found that teenagers who "feel highly connected to their parents and report that their parents are warm, caring and supportive—are far more likely to delay sexual activity than their peers."[3] When talking to our sons about sex, Sarah Brown, director of the National Campaign to Prevent Teen Pregnancy, said that talk alone is insufficient. She further stated that what matters even more, especially among younger teenagers, is a relationship in which parents keep close tabs on them, knowing who their friends are and what they do together.[4] Amazing. Imagine that—deep down inside our sons feel more loved and cared for when they have boundaries and supervision.

Valerie F. Reyna, professor of human development and psychology at the New York State College of Human Ecology at Cornell and an author of the study, also cautions:

> Younger adolescents don't learn from consequences as
> well as older adolescents do. So rather than relying on

them to make reasoned choices or to learn from the
school of hard knocks, a better approach is to supervise
them. . . . A young teenage girl should not be left alone
in the house with her boyfriend, and responsible adults
should be omnipresent and alcohol absent when teenagers
have parties.[5]

Years ago, one of my son's college-age friends shared candidly with me that he had ended a relationship with his Christian girlfriend of over three years in an effort to maintain sexual purity after having gone too far in the relationship. He mentioned that part of their temptation was a lack of rules or boundaries on the part of her parents when he was at her home. Mind you, these are Christian parents. He shared that even while dating in high school, it was not uncommon to be left alone in the house while her parents were gone. In other words, he was stunned and amazed that her parents trusted them as much as they did. And the lesson for us in this story? Christian kids have hormones too!

A Reality Check for Parents: Church Kids Are Having Sex Too

Eighty percent of "evangelical" or "born again" teenagers think sex should be saved for marriage. Unfortunately there appears to be a huge disconnect when it comes to walking the talk. According to a study in *Forbidden Fruit: Sex & Religion in the Lives of American Teenagers* by Mark Regnerus, a professor of sociology at the University of Texas at Austin, evangelical teens are actually more likely to have lost their virginity than either mainline Protestants (denominations such as Episcopalian, Lutheran, etc.) or Catholics, and they lose their virginity at a slightly younger age—16.3, as compared to 16.7 for mainline Protestants and Catholics. In addition, they are much more likely to have had three or more sexual partners by age seventeen (13.7 percent of evangelicals versus 8.9 percent for mainline Protestants).[6]

Equally as disturbing, evangelical teens scored low on a quiz related to pregnancy and health risks. The authors of the study speculate that parents of "evangelical teens" may be talking to their kids about sex, but the conversation is more focused on the morals rather than the mechanics. In other words, we seem to have the "Don't do it until your married" part down but stop short of giving them advice based on a hypothetical "But if you do decide to have sex . . ." The article further states, "Evangelical teens don't accept themselves as people who will have sex until they've already had it."[7] And therein lies the problem: If they don't *expect* to have sex, they aren't *prepared* to address the temptation to have sex. And if we don't expect them to have sex, we don't help prepare them to resist the temptation to have sex. In fact, half of all mothers of sexually active teenagers mistakenly believe that their children are still virgins, according to a team of researchers at the University of Minnesota Adolescent Health Center.[8] Regnerus sums up our ignorance to the problem in his book *Forbidden Fruit*, "For evangelicals, sex is a 'symbolic boundary' marking a good Christian from a bad one, but in reality, the kids are always 'sneaking across enemy lines.'"[9] Certainly this is a humbling thought for well-meaning Christian parents, many of which can also relate to sneaking across enemy lines in their own teen years.

Hopefully by now you are convinced of the critical importance of talking to your son about God's design for sex and the key role you play in encouraging your son to delay sex until marriage. As our sons are exposed to the "just do it!" message by the culture that surrounds them, our job is to inform them that not everyone is "doing it." In fact, over half of high school students have not had sex, and among those who have, nearly two-thirds regret it and wish they had waited.[10] If the media is going to highlight the less than 50 percent of high school students who've had sex and paint them as the accepted norm, why don't we start highlighting the majority who aren't having sex and paint them as the new norm? In other words, our voice has to be louder than the voice of the culture. It's up to us to tell our sons the truth about sex. Not only is it God's plan to save sex for marriage, it just plain makes sense. Further, our sons need to know they are not alone in the battle to remain pure.

In an earlier chapter we discussed the delayed growth in the frontal lobe of the boy brain, which makes it difficult for our sons to connect consequences with their actions. Therefore, we shouldn't be surprised to learn that studies have found that for adolescent boys there is a lag between their bodies' capability to have sex and their minds' capacity to comprehend the negative consequences of sex.[11] Let me sum that up for you: When we tell our adolescent-aged sons, "If you have sex before you're married, you could get an STD or get a girl pregnant," their brains are not cognitively developed enough to walk down a worst-case scenario path and consider the full weight of the consequences. Their bodies are saying, "Do it," and their brains have not caught up to say, "Whoa, hold up buddy! If you do it, you might find yourself popping three pills a day for an STD or paying child support for the next eighteen years." That's where we come in. We must continue to remind our boys of the consequences that can occur from having sex outside of marriage. Or as I often told my sons, "My job is to act as the frontal lobe in your brain until yours is fully developed!"

Both of my boys would attest to the fact that I have more than made up for the developmental delay in their frontal lobes by continually reminding them of some of the possible consequences that can occur should they cave into the temptation to have sex. While I hoped my sons' primary motivation for saving sex until marriage would be rooted in a desire to please God, I wanted to make sure I gave them plenty of other reasons to save sex until marriage, should they take a spiritual detour from God's best.

Staying One Step Ahead of the Temptation

The Bible tells us to flee from sexual immorality. All other sins a man commits are outside his body, but he who sins sexually sins against his own body (1 Cor. 6:18). In addition to teaching our sons principles of self-control, we need to help them understand that the most effective way to flee temptation is first to steer clear of tempting situations and, second, come up with an escape plan in advance for times when they are caught off guard by temptation. For example, let's say your seventeen-year-old son is in a dating relationship and his girlfriend sends him a text asking him to come over and study. She then follows with another text letting him know her parents are out for a few hours. Obviously, it's much easier for your son to flee at this point (by exercising self-control and choosing not to place himself in a tempting situation) rather than head on over to his girlfriend's house and attempt to exercise self-control in the middle of a make-out session. But should the temptation come with no warning, it would be wise for our sons to think through what they might say (the escape plan) in advance. In other words, get their speech down before they find themselves in the throes of steamy passion.

It's not a bad idea to help our sons think through some of these possible scenarios before they occur (since their frontal lobes may prevent them from doing so!). Part of practicing effective self-control is learning to take the time to think in advance through possible situations that may compromise sexual purity and come up with a plan of escape. The practice of self-control begins when our sons "take captive every thought to make it obedient to Christ" (2 Cor. 10:5).

Leaving Room for the Holy Spirit

I realize by now many of you may be feeling a bit overwhelmed with the challenge we face when it comes to encouraging our sons to be sexually pure. As mothers, we like to think there is a tried and true formula that if applied faithfully and consistently will bear out a positive end result. The truth is, we can apply a formula or effective principles, but in the end we cannot control the outcome. While formulas (such as escape plans and virginity pledges) can be somewhat effective in modifying a behavior, the heart matters most. Sexual purity is not the result of a one-time pledge but rather an ongoing submission to Christ.

Mistakes will be made because our sons, like us, are sinners. When talking to youth about temptation, I often give them the analogy of coming to a four-way stop in the road. There will be times when we know that God is saying, "Go left. Left is the good and pleasing way and will keep you on My path." However, there will be times when our sons fall into temptation because "the spirit is willing, but the body is weak" (Matt. 26:41 NLT; Mark 14:38 NLT). Like us, our sons will occasionally stand at the crossroads of temptation and take a wrong turn. Once they take a wrong turn, God in

His loving patience, places U-turn sign after U-turn sign along the way to encourage them to turn back.

Most believers won't be able to head down the wrong road for long before conviction joins them on the journey. A true believer knows that a road of sin ultimately leads to a dry and dusty desert even if it is paved with momentary pleasures along the way. A true believer cannot justify and continue long-term in an action that stands opposed to God's commands. A true believer, who has chosen to take a wrong turn, will at some point along the way break down and cry out to God for help in turning back. True believers will express a sincere, godly sorrow (2 Cor. 7:10) as they reflect on the power of the cross and "that while [they] were still sinners, Christ died for [them]" (Rom. 5:8). Some believers turn back at the sign of the first U-turn while others travel down the road until they land in the dry and dusty desert. The sooner they recognize their sin, repent, and turn back, the better.

More important than employing behavior modification tactics related to sexual purity, is teaching our sons to be mindful of the condition of their hearts. If your son does not view sex outside of marriage as a sin (not many do) and, therefore, sees no problem whatsoever in heading down a path that compromises God's will, you have a bigger worry on your hands than an unexpected pregnancy or STD. A conversation about saving sex for marriage is not nearly as important as a conversation about Christ's saving man from his sins.

If You Suspect Your Son Is Already Sexually Active

Maybe as you are reading this, you suspect that your son has already had sex, and you're left wondering where to go from here.

Do not give up that battle and declare defeat. It could be that your son is having sex but desires to change. In this situation I would highly recommend that you or your husband meet with your son on a weekly basis to discuss the content we have covered in Conversation 3. Draw boundaries, supervise your son, and hold him accountable to the boundaries you have drawn. Make a point to let him know that the lines of communication are always open and nothing is off bounds to talk about. Most important, remind him that he can be forgiven of his sin if he confesses his sin and repents (Acts 2:38; 3:19). There is no need to berate our sons about their sin and shame them; that's not how God reacts, nor should we. Romans 8:1 reminds us, "There is no condemnation for those who belong to Christ Jesus" (NLT).

On the other hand, if, after discussing the matter with your son, you discover that he is unrepentant, and therefore not likely to change his behavior, persevere in continuing to remind him of the fallouts we have discussed in Conversation 3. Most important, commit to pray for your son, and ask God to change his heart. Prayer will be your most powerful force. You cannot sway your son's heart, but God can.

When talking to him, emphasize that your motive is one of concern and love. The sobering truth is that if he wants to find a way to continue having sex with his girlfriend (or hooking up), he will find a way to do it, even while living under your roof. At this point, if you suspect that he is planning to continue in sexual sin, you are caught in a precarious position. Given the high risk of STDs and pregnancy, you may need to educate him about birth control options.

An Added Conversation about Sexting

A few years ago, a mom friend of mine shared with me a harrowing tale that involved her ninth grade daughter texting her boyfriend a topless picture at his request. Before I go any further, let me vouch for her daughter in saying she is a sweet Christian girl who is actively involved in her youth group at her local church. Additionally, her mom is the kind of mom who engages in conversations and takes an active role in discipling her and her siblings (as does her father). I share this to make the point that any one of us could have been in this mother's shoes or the shoes of the boy's mother. Girls today are under immense amounts of pressure to engage in sexting as the culture has normalized it as a standard rite of passage. So, back to my story; as you probably imagined, it didn't end well. Upon breaking up, the boy sent the picture to his friends, and her daughter suffered so much embarrassment and shame, she ended up in counseling and withdrew from school to be home-schooled for the remainder of the year. She eventually returned to school but her emotional scars remain.

Studies suggest that sexting is more common than many parents might realize or want to admit. Sexting is defined as the sending or receiving of nude or seminude images or sexually explicit text messages. More than half the undergraduate students who took part in an anonymous online survey said they sexted when they were teenagers. Nearly 30 percent said they included photos in their sexts, and 61 percent were unaware that sending nude photos via text could be considered child pornography.[12] The survey also found that only 2 percent of respondents reported that they notified a parent or teacher about a sext that they received.[13] For teenagers, this scenario often happens in a dating situation or one where they like each other and one teenager (usually the female) is asked to "prove" they like the other person. That is the scenario my friend's daughter found herself in.

Sexting can also happen when one person sends a nude or semi-nude photo to another without asking for consent first. I recently had an 8th grade girl tell me that it is common for girls in her grade to receive "d*ck pics" from the boys (of themselves in an aroused state). When I asked why a boy would do that, she said it was to bait which girls might respond and in turn, agree to send nude pictures back. Noting my shock, she laughed it off and casually responded, "it's just what boys do." Boys who, no doubt, have logged many hours viewing porn and as a result, have normalized a depraved behavior to the degree that it would never occur to them that the girls in their grade were worthy of respect and honor. She went on to say that the she and her friends think it's stupid and just delete them when they get them, but some girls think it's funny and like the attention.

Why in the world would boys do this? Let me take a stab at answering that question. When you have a generation of boys, most of which have been brought up in the schoolroom of the culture—who have relentlessly been lured by the porn industry to become loyal, dependent, and life-long consumers who have in their possession a device that allows them to access that electronic drug on demand, free of charge, and with total anonymity—the fallout will be immense. Couple that with the fact that there is little shame associated with viewing porn among those in this emerging generation and that most porn centers on the theme that women are nothing more than objects who exist to satisfy the sexual urges of men. Now, add to that equation a generation of young women, most of which have been brought up in the schoolroom of the culture and bombarded with message after message through media, advertising, and the entertainment industry, that their sole purpose is to cultivate their sexuality and sensuality (long before they even know what that is, mind you) in an effort to capture the attention of the opposite sex. Add to that the lack of frontal lobe development in adolescents that often leads them to engage in high-risk behaviors with little thought of consequences. Consequences that in this case could include criminal charges, tattered reputations, and for some, a shame so immense they consider taking their lives.

Remembering the Real Prize

As we wrap up Conversation 3, know that there are many viewpoints among Christians regarding the most effective way to address sexual purity. It is oftentimes a heated topic that is fueled by much passion and good intent. There are no guarantees or foolproof formulas when it comes to raising sons who pursue sexual purity, even for those of us writing the parenting books. We can take the information presented in Conversation 3 and use it to build a case that supports God's design for sex, but in the end our sons will have to make their own decisions.

When my youngest son was in his teens, I told him, "It's your sex life, and ultimately you have to come to the conclusion that saving sex for marriage is in your personal best interest and promises the healthiest sex life possible—emotionally, physically, and spiritually speaking. Bottom line, you have to care more about your sex life and the pursuit of godly purity than I do."

Rather than focusing on saving themselves until marriage as the ultimate prize, we need to raise boys who are in the habit of laying their hearts bare before God on a daily basis. They may experience some slip-ups along the way, but their response to those slip-ups matters most to God. Just ask King David. In spite of his sexual sin with Bathsheba and subsequent orchestration of the murder of her husband, God counted him as "a man after my own heart" (Acts 13:22). When we help our sons cultivate the habit of guarding and protecting their hearts (Prov. 4:23), we address sexual purity at the root. Fewer than 10 percent of boys will make it to the altar with their sexual purity fully intact. Should your son be among the rare few, it will not be the direct result of a trendy parenting strategy, but rather the grace of God and His grace alone. Fortunately, that same grace is also available to those who slip up along the way. I, for one, am living proof that God's grace covers a multitude of sins and has the power to make all things new.

I realize the truths presented in this chapter may have left you with a heavy heart. While God's "best" when it comes to His plan and design for sex is for our sons to wait until marriage, ultimately the decision is not ours to make. Our sons possess a free will, and many will have to learn some truths the hard way. However, that doesn't mean they are beyond God's reach or, for that matter, His grace. While it's reasonable to have high expectations for our sons, we need to be careful that we don't send a message to our sons that anything less than perfection (saving sex for marriage, in this case) is ultimate failure. Sometimes, as believers, we get so caught up in peddling the "save sex until you're married" message, we lose sight of the more important issue at hand: our son's hearts. No doubt we are in desperate need of a new, upgraded sex talk. A sex talk, mind you, that focuses primarily on God's "best" design for sex (waiting until marriage) while at the same time also takes into account God's grace and redemption for times when we forfeit God's best. Where there is redemption, there is always hope.

Talk about It

* * * * * * * * * *

Chapter 7

Has the topic of sex come up with your son? How did you handle it?

What is your son's current level of understanding about sex?

If your son is on the younger end (ages 6–9), write down a script below of how you might introduce the sex topic, so your son knows you and/or your husband are the best source for information. If your son is older and you have not yet begun a conversation about sex, write down a script of what you might say.

Were you shocked to discover how strong an adolescent boy's appetite for sex is? Are you prepared to discuss that change and have some honest and open conversations about the challenges that lie ahead?

Chapter 8

Have you had a conversation with your son about physical fallout from sex such as STDs or teen pregnancy? Are you prepared to educate him as to the long-term effects of many of the common STDs and how they could affect his future? What about an unexpected pregnancy?

Have you discussed with your son the emotional fallout that can result from sex outside of marriage? How might you introduce the topic of "oxytocin" with your son in an effort to reinforce God's purpose for sex in bonding husband and wife?

Have you discussed with your son the spiritual fallout that can result from sex outside of marriage? More importantly, have you reminded him that he can always come boldly before the throne of grace?

Chapter 9

Are you comfortable with the idea of talking to your son about the fallout from having sex outside of marriage?

If he is in middle or high school, have you had conversations with him pertaining to sex? Did he initiate the conversation or did you?

Has your son been exposed to a sexting situation? Have you discussed the topic of sexting with him? (Assuming he is old enough, of course.)

When discussing the topic of sex outside of marriage with your son, do you emphasize virginity as the ultimate prize or a restored heart?

Conversation 4

Childhood is only for a season.

Chapter 10

Real Man or Peter Pan?

● ● ● ● ● ●

*When I was a child, I spoke and thought and reasoned as
a child. But when I grew up, I put away childish things.
(1 Cor. 13:11 NLT)*

In 2006 Paramount Pictures released the movie *Failure to Launch*
starring Matthew McConaughey. McConaughey played the part of
a winsome, good-looking thirty-five-year-old bachelor who lived at
home with his parents and was in no hurry to check out of Hotel
Mama's Boy. And why would he? His mother cooked his meals,
cleaned his room, and did his laundry—a sweet deal for any thirty-
five-year-old who wasn't quite ready to be a grown up in the big,
scary world. The movie was the number one movie in the U.S. for
the first three weeks after its release, grossing more than ninety million dollars. Though the movie was intended as a comedy, it seemed
to touch a raw nerve among many viewers and called attention to
the very real problem of a failure to launch among young men in

our culture today. Chances are, you know a grown-up Peter Pan or two. Whether Neverland is Mom and Dad's basement or an apartment shared with other like-minded man-boys, these adult Peter Pans share one thing in common: They are in no hurry to grow up.

Unfortunately, this problem is not just isolated to our boys. The U.S. Census Report found that in 2016 more young adults aged eighteen to thirty-four lived with parents (22.9 million) than a spouse (19.9 million). Compare this to 1975 when the reverse was true and 31.9 young adults aged eighteen to thirty-four lived with a spouse and 14.7 million lived in their parents' home.[1] The report also found that the rise in young adults living at home coincided with a decline in the economic status of young men as "more young men are falling to the bottom of the income ladder."[2] According to the U.S. Bureau of Labor Statistics, employment among males is consistently lower than employment among females, especially among young adults (ages twenty to twenty-four).[3]

If we are to launch our sons into adulthood, we must be aware of the hurdles that lie in their paths and insure we are part of the solution rather than the problem.

"Youth" Redefined

Corporations and marketers are cashing in on the failure-to-launch syndrome, having discovered that along the road of self-discovery, young men buy a lot of toys to pass the time. In fact, according to a study by a marketing demographic research firm, the traditional definition of the "youth" demographic is no longer defined by chronological age when it comes to purchasing patterns. "Contemporary youth should now be defined as 'the absence of functional and/or emotional maturity,' reflecting the fact that accepting traditional responsibilities such as mortgages, children, and developing a strong sense of self-identity/perspective is occurring later and later in life," the study concludes.[4]

The article recommends this disturbing bit of advice to corporations and marketers wishing to make a dime on this demographic shift: "As people worldwide delay the onset of adult responsibilities and stay emotionally and physically younger for longer, it is becoming more acceptable for older people to participate in youthful pursuits. To support this trend, marketers should routinely consider the often-overlooked twenty-five to thirty-four age group a part of the youth market."[5] David Morrison, president of Twentysomething Inc., a marketing consultancy based in Philadelphia, adds, "Most of their needs are taken care of by Mom and Dad, so their income is largely discretionary. [Many twentysomethings] are living at home, but if you look, you'll see flat-screen TVs in their bedrooms and brand-new cars in the driveway."[6] In a *Time* magazine article entitled "Grow Up? Not So Fast," author Lev Grossman says, "Some twixters may want to grow up, but corporations and advertisers have a real stake in keeping them in a tractable, exploitable, pre-adult state—living at home, spending their money on toys."[7]

To put the problem into perspective, imagine the outrage if churches followed suit and redefined *youth* as "the absence of functional and/or emotional maturity," rather than by chronological age. Should we take the single young men aged twenty to thirty-four who are living at home with Mom and Dad and incorporate them back into the church youth group? I'm sure many of these Peter Pans would love nothing more than to play Ping-Pong and engage in a few icebreaker games before the Bible study lesson begins on Sunday mornings. And with so few responsibilities, I'm betting they're free to pile into the fifteen-passenger youth van over the weekend for the upcoming photo scavenger hunt. They certainly ought to have the game down by age thirty-four. No wonder young adults (ages eighteen to twenty-four) are leaving the church in droves. We are no longer catering to *their needs*! What Peter Pan wants to get serious about serving Christ when his primary objective is to serve himself? Or for that matter, what Peter Pan wants to grow up, get married, and serve a wife when he can remain in the perpetual state of boyhood well into his thirties with little cultural resistance?

What's particularly confusing about this cultural shift in delayed adulthood is that national surveys reveal that an overwhelming majority of Americans, including younger adults, agree that between twenty and twenty-two, people should be finished with school, working and living on their own.[8] Yet in reality many fail to live up to their own expectations for adulthood. Which begs the question: What constitutes an official "adult"? While financial independence (no supplementary income/housing from parents) is an obvious determinant, the pursuit of marriage and parenthood were once viewed as benchmarks for adulthood. Today marriage and parenthood hardly make the radar of this budding generation of Peter Pans. (More about that in chapter 12.) Marriage is viewed as something they might start thinking seriously about after they chase their dreams, travel abroad, secure full-time jobs, and find themselves. Good luck with that! Hopefully, by the time they give you grandkids (if they ever do), you're not trying to keep up with them with a walker!

Adulting Is So Overrated

For years, many youth experts (myself included) have expressed concern over the rush for our kids to grow up. While this is true regarding exposure to mature themes due to the availability of information on demand (Internet, smart phones, technology, etc.), it is somewhat of a myth when it comes to the rush to independence and adulthood. Who among us can't recall the excitement of meeting our friends for a movie or to walk around the mall sans our parents? The first taste of freedom that comes with "hanging out" with friends is a benchmark on the road to adulthood. It is in this environment where we learn to sample the real world—out from under the protective wing of our parents. We also learn how to navigate interpersonal relationships with our friends, as well as with the opposite sex.

For today's youth, hanging out for the most part is a virtual experience. It is a group text or a social media interaction, but rarely does it involve actually going out. *Hanging out* has evolved into *hanging in* with your smart phone or tablet never far from your side. Consider that one in four teens today do not have a driver's license by the time they graduate from high school.[9] The decline in driving appears across all regions, ethnic groups, and socioeconomic classes. When I was a teen, we were begging our parents to get a hardship license so we could drive before the age of sixteen! Getting your driver's license was a major hurdle on the path to adulthood and we were counting down the days to freedom. Many teens today seem to show little urgency to get a license and seem content to have Mom or Dad chauffeur them to school and extracurricular activities for as long as possible.

Add to this the fact that fewer teens seek out summer jobs. In 1980, 70 percent of teens had a summer job as compared to 43 percent in 2010. According to the Bureau of Labor Statistics data, the decrease doesn't seem to be related to a tough job market. The number of teens who want a summer job but can't find one has stayed about the same over the years, but the number of teens who don't want a job has doubled.[10] Many parents argue that due to more stringent college requirements, their teens are unable to work due to the heavy load of homework and extracurricular activities. Author Jean Twenge found this not to be the case. In her book *iGen*, she analyzed the data and found that "high school seniors heading to college in 2015 spent four fewer hours a week on homework, paid work, volunteer work, and extracurricular activities during their last year in high school than those entering college in 1987."[11] They have more leisure time per day than Gen X'ers did. So, what exactly are they doing that takes up so much of their time? Look no further than the smart phone they are cradling in the palm of their hands. For many teens, it has filled the gap and become their new, unpaid job. Of course, we know it will come with a price.

The trend of teens not working has also led to the inability of teens to manage money. Allowance for many has become a thing of the past and paid chores are almost unheard of. Teens have come to expect that their expensive toys (electronics, etc.) and leisure activities will be financed on demand by Mom and Dad. When they have a need or want, they simply ask, or badger their parents until they wear them down into submission. Why go to the trouble of working extra hours during the week to earn money when all you have to do is hit up the First Bank of Good Ol' Mom and Dad?

Twenge noted in her study of today's children and teens (iGen or Generation Z) that "the entire developmental trajectory, from childhood to adolescence to adulthood, has slowed." "Adolescence" she claims, "is now an extension of childhood rather than the beginning of adulthood."[12] Her finding is backed by a recent study of iGen college students (versus students in the 1980s and 1990s). iGen'ers were more likely to agree with the statements, "I wish that I could return to the security of childhood" and "The happiest time in life is when you are a child." They were less likely to agree with the statements, "I would rather be an adult than a child" and "I feel happy that I am not a child anymore."[13]

To accommodate young adults (not children) who are reluctant to grow up, many college campuses have assumed the role of protective guardian and contributed to the problem of extended adolescence by offering "trigger warnings" to students who might find some lecture material emotionally distressing. I am all for offering a warning to those who have been through truly traumatic events and thus, are emotionally tender regarding subjects or discussions that might trigger a past trauma. However, there is evidence of an increasing use of trigger warnings to warn of content or an opposing viewpoint that might be upsetting to someone. In the book *Good Faith*, authors David Kinnaman and Gabe Lyons argue, "Protecting people from ideas they'd rather not hear is not only laughable, but also ultimately harmful to society. Religious liberty and freedom of speech are rights that can only be put to the test at the distressing intersection of differing ideas. If we run away from that crossroads, these freedoms are simply hypothetical."[14] Part of growing up is learning that not everyone will agree with your opinions, values, or ideals. Only in discussing and debating different schools of thought will we learn the tedious balance of introspection and weighing our personal convictions with objectivity. The irony is that today's teens and young adults pride themselves in being more tolerant than previous generations, but it appears their tolerance has limits if it requires them to tolerate an opposing viewpoint or position. This is especially true regarding the Christian faith and biblical Truth.

We have already begun to feel the fallout from a culture that now embraces a post-Christian worldview. For example, one

Pennsylvania family was ordered by their neighborhood HOA to take down a nativity scene as part of their Christmas lawn decor because a neighbor reported it as personally "offensive." The homeowner, Mark Wivell, refused to remove his nativity and responded, "People get offended by different things, but just because something offends you, doesn't mean the whole world has to change to accommodate you."[15] Wise words to a generation that has been taught otherwise. Maybe the HOA should require the Wivells to post a "trigger warning" sign in their yard in future years as a compromise. We can expect to see more stories like this emerge in the future as this generation of "snowflakes" leaves their emotionally bubble-wrapped environments and discovers to their shock that not everyone shares their same beliefs.

I don't doubt for a minute that there are some that would love to see trigger warnings applied to content in the Bible that fails to support their current worldview. In 1 Corinthians 1:18, Paul warned, "For the word of the cross is folly to those who are perishing, but to us who are being saved it is the power of God" (ESV). Be assured, the gospel will never be silenced this side of heaven, but it is already considered by many to be "offensive." In fact, in 1 Peter 2:8, Jesus is referred to as "a stone of stumbling and a rock of offense" (ESV). As I have mentioned, it has never been more important to model to our children a commitment to "walk in Truth and lead with love."

In doing so, we cannot sacrifice biblical Truth on the altar of love in an attempt to sugarcoat the message. Nor can we sacrifice love for the sake of Truth by focusing on modifying behavior rather than changing hearts. Becoming a follower of Christ requires an introspective look into our rebellion toward a holy God (sin) and own personal depravity (need for forgiveness). Doing so is not pleasant, but it is the cornerstone of the gospel message and the very thing that sets us free. What a travesty if this current generation missed the Good News of the gospel because they have been trained to avoid anything "unpleasant" or "offensive."

Another example of treating young adults as adolescents is the trend of campuses offering "safe spaces" to help students cope with anxiety before final exams or in the aftermath of upsetting current events. Such was the case in the days following the 2016 presidential election. An article entitled "Coddling Campus Crybabies" posted on FoxNews.com listed some of the universities offering "safe space" therapy:

- Cornell University recently hosted a "cry-in," complete with hot chocolate and tissues for disappointed Hillary Clinton supporters.
- University of Pennsylvania brought in a puppy and a kitten for therapeutic cuddling.
- Tufts University held arts and crafts sessions for students.
- University of Michigan Law School scheduled an event for this Friday called "Post-Election Self-Care with Food and Play" with "stress-busting self-care activities" including coloring, blowing bubbles, sculpting with Play-Doh and "positive card making."[16]

For heaven's sake, is this nursery school or college?! Ask any veteran who was shipped off to defend their country at this same age what they think about this new trend of "safe spaces" and you're sure to get an earful. If this is our future, we are in a load of trouble should we ever have to depend on this generation in times of hardship or, God forbid, a time of war. I doubt older generations are willing to pick up the pieces while a generation of kiddie-adults rushes to their safe spaces to drink hot cocoa, color, and cuddle with puppies and kittens. It's time to put an end to this nonsense and give our sons a clear launch plan from childhood to adulthood.

Better Safe Than Sorry?

Recently, I was in a conversation with other adults from my generation (older end of Gen X'ers) and we were laughing about the playgrounds we used to enjoy as children in parks and school-yards. Most were constructed of metal and coupled with a hot summer day in Texas with temperatures soaring past 100 degrees, you weren't likely to forget the back of your bare legs cooking on the slide on your way down. Not to mention, many of the slides looked more like a stairway to heaven, so you were careful to hang on tight to the rails on your way up, especially since there was no pea gravel or soft tire shredding to break your fall. If you survived the slide without a fall or 2nd degree burns, you usually made your way to the metal merry-go-round where your friends did their best to see if they could successfully eject you from the centrifugal spinning wheel of death. Bonus points if you threw up due to motion sickness. We grew up in a day and age before socket protectors, baby monitors, car seats, and mandatory seat belt laws. We walked home from school beginning in grade school and many of us were latch key kids who let ourselves in, prepared our own snacks, did our homework without parental help or supervision (usually with *Gilligan's Island* and *Brady Bunch* on in the background), and somehow, managed to survive and thrive. I'm certainly not suggesting we retreat back to the days absent of common-sense safety measures, but I can't help but wonder if we've gone a bit overboard in protecting our children.

In a recent poll, seventy percent of adults said they thought the world had become less safe for children since they were children.

REAL MAN OR PETER PAN? ❧ 173

Yet, the evidence suggests they are much safer now.[17] Teens today have fewer car accidents, get fewer tickets, and overall, take fewer risks in general. And it's not just the parents who are dedicated to the safety of their children—the children are, as well. Teen pregnancy rates are down, teens are less likely to get in a car with someone who's been drinking, and binge drinking has decreased. (Interestingly, they are just as likely to use marijuana as Millennials were because they, like the generation before them, view it is as safer than drinking.) These findings should be a huge encouragement to parents (other than the pot-smoking) and indicate children are listening to their counsel. Yet, parents are still hesitant to loosen the reins in areas where there is minimal risk. Take for example the age-old pastime of walking home from school. In 1969, 48 percent of elementary and middle school students walked or rode a bicycle to school. By 2009, only 13 percent did so. Among those who lived less than a mile from the school, 35 percent walked or rode their bicycle to school in 2009 as compared to 89 percent in 1969.[18] Many of the things we once enjoyed in our childhood years is now viewed as irresponsible or even dangerous. But why?

In a piece entitled "The Overprotected Kid," investigative journalist Hanna Rosin argued that "a preoccupation with safety has stripped childhood of independence, risk taking, and discovery—without making it safer."[19] She goes on to suggest that our safety paranoia has resulted in a "continuous and ultimately dramatic decline in children's opportunities to play and explore in their own chosen ways." In the article, she quotes several expert opinions including a Boston College psychologist, Peter Gray who authored an essay called "The Play Deficit." Gray, she says, "chronicles the fallout from the loss of the old childhood culture, and it's a familiar list of the usual ills attributed to Millennials: depression, narcissism, and a decline in empathy. In the past decade, the percentage of college-age kids taking psychiatric medication has spiked, according to a 2012 study by the American College Counseling Association." In fact, a 2011 study from the University of Tennessee at Chattanooga found that students with "hovering" or "helicopter" parents were more likely to take medication for anxiety, depression or both."[20] Rosin goes on to say in her article, "Practicing psychologists have written about the unique identity crisis this generation faces—a fear of growing up and, in the words of Brooke Donatone, a New York–based therapist, an inability 'to think for themselves.'"[21]

I believe our tendency to overprotect our children from perceived dangers of the world has clouded our judgment and produced a legion of anxious parents who in turn, have influenced a legion of anxious kids. Is it any surprise that today's children and teens suffer from fear and anxiety at a staggering rate like never seen before? It doesn't help that our newsfeeds are typically filled with links to articles about unknown dangers lurking around every corner. Button batteries, dry drowning, the brain-eating amoeba, laundry detergent pods, and the list goes on. We are exposed to more news than ever before and if we're not careful, we can come to believe these dangers are the norm, rather than the exception. I am stepping on my own toes here and I have had to limit the time I spend on news (including online and through social media) because I realized the greater my exposure, the more it began to heighten my anxiety especially when it related to potential dangers my children or grandchildren could face. I realized the direct correlation in my over-protective tendencies and the uptick in my news intake when I was recently watching some old home movies from when my children were young. I hardly recognized the mother on the videos. In addition to being a much slimmer version of myself, I was shocked to see how incredibly laid-back I was with my children. Whether it was one of my babies pulling up to a precarious and wobbly stand on a piece of furniture with sharp corners or cheering my four-year-old on as he tried the new zipline by himself for the first time from the tree house to the ground below. I audibly winced out loud at my younger mom self, yet at the same time, marveled at my calm composure. My children had not grown up in a bubble-wrapped environment free from unknown dangers because I was simply unaware. No computers, no smart phones, and no twenty-four-hour news on demand to enlighten me to the doom-and-gloom stories about the dangers my children faced. Truly, ignorance was bliss.

My transition from more of a laid-back parent to an overprotective parent occurred slowly over time, but spiked in my children's teen years when my news intake increased. In addition, I had begun writing in those years (the early 2000s) on matters of teen culture and was speaking to teen girls across the country. This was the pre-dawn era of social media where tweens and teens were flocking to MySpace.com, Internet chat rooms, engaging in instant messaging (IM'ing), and eventually text messaging (though limited at the time due to the high cost of unlimited text messaging). Many of the same parents who had worked overtime to safety-proof their children's play environments and micro-manage their lives were offering little if any supervision when it came to this new and ironically, more dangerous online world. They were, for the most part, clueless. I can't help but wonder if we contributed to the problem by scaring our kids indoors where we could more closely monitor their safety, all the while exposing them to dangers that far out-weighed a fall from a tree or riding their bikes without a helment. It is my personal belief that parents need to spend less time attempting to manage the dangers our children face in the great outdoors and more time managing the dangers they face on their electronic devices. In other words, we need to decrease screen time and increase outdoor creative play. The best way to do this is to lead by example in our own lives.

A Reminder of Your Role

Many moms today have bought into the lie that their primary parenting responsibility is to make their children's lives as safe and comfortable as possible. They have somehow equated sheltered, over-protected, isolated children to healthier, happy adults. The evidence suggests otherwise. Overly cautious children become anxious, vulnerable adults who expect Mom or Dad (or college administrators, employers, etc.) to be there to protect them at every turn from anything that might prove to be unpleasant, put them at risk, or cause them "emotional injury." The truth is, no matter how hard we try, we cannot protect our children from every physical or emotional danger they will encounter. I can't help but wonder if the pressure moms feel to be perfect in their roles as mothers has led to this unhealthy wave of over-parenting. Yet nowhere in the Bible does it endorse the idea that a mother's responsibility is to ensure her child never feels unsafe or uncomfortable. Can you imagine if the disciples' mothers had coddled them at every turn? Had they done so, they never would have agreed to follow Jesus, even unto death. The early Christian leaders we read about in the Bible were courageous and took risks for the sake of the gospel. In Matthew 9:37–38, Jesus reminds His disciples, "The harvest is plentiful, but the laborers are few; therefore pray earnestly to the Lord of the harvest to send out laborers into his harvest" (ESV). That call is still relevant for today and yet, I wonder how many of our sons (and daughters) are prepared to answer that call. Jesus didn't issue the call with a minimum age requirement or a liability release to be signed by parents. In fact, a few chapters later, He gave a more detailed description of the calling in Matthew 16:24–26: "If anyone would come after me, let him deny himself and take up his cross and follow me. For whoever would save his life will lose it, but whoever loses his life for my sake will find it. For what will it profit a man if he gains the whole world and forfeits his soul?" (ESV). There is nothing "safe" or "comfortable" about that charge. In fact, that charge requires a response from us. Is your response one of trust or fear? The spread of the gospel requires adventure and risk. Jesus offers an interesting parenting paradox: If you want your children to find life in its truest meaning and fullest sense, raise them to be radical and reckless followers of Christ rather than fragile, anxious "adultlescents" who spend decades searching for identity and purpose. On your dime—and likely, under your roof. We can parent them now or we may find ourselves stuck with the burdensome task of re-parenting them later in the years when we were looking forward to enjoying the fruits of our own hard work.

I believe one of the key reasons the current generation of children and teens is so uncertain about growing up is their declining sense of meaning and purpose. They are like ships without rudders, floating aimlessly and adrift at sea (with life preservers buckled tightly, no doubt!). Consider that among iGen (also called Gen Z) youth, just one in five is "enthusiastic about the advent of adulthood."[22] But, here is the good news: the same Barna survey found that 40 percent of engaged Christians are "very excited about becoming an adult," as compared to 16 percent of those with no faith.[23] There is a clear correlation in children raised in engaged Christian homes to a confidence in adulthood and life purpose. Identity and purpose can only be found in our creator, God. Young men who are raised to know that Jesus Christ is their one, true north have no desire to remain in the nest under the parents' wing of protection indefinitely. They have a compass to guide them into adulthood. It's up to you to teach them to use that compass.

Chapter 11

Ready, Set, Launch

● ● ● ● ● ●

Start children off on the way they should go, and even when they are old they will not turn from it. (Prov. 22:6)

Imagine for a minute that your teenage son (just pretend if yours isn't there yet!) received an invitation from NASA to join the space shuttle astronauts on their next scheduled mission to outer space. Now imagine that it just so happens this mission is due to leave the following day. Would you let him go? Obviously much preparation precedes a mission, and your son would not be prepared. As crazy as it would be for your son to go on that mission, most boys are launched into the real world with little, if any, preparation and training. Do you have a formal launch plan in place to move your son out of the nest and into the real world? Or is your boy on the self-paced program—you know, the one where he moves out to begin a new job after graduation or heads off to college with little to any training on how to live in the real world. If this is your launch plan, don't be surprised if your son shows back up on your doorstep at some point with a duffel bag in hand and a load of laundry for Mom.

As ridiculous as it sounds, the majority of parents have no formal launch plan in place for their sons. Meg Meeker, M.D., says, "The biggest mistake we make with adolescent boys is forgetting that they all need help moving out of adolescence. Millions of boys grow older, but few become men. No boy really wants to stay in the banal world of perpetual adolescence, but he needs someone to lead him out. His deepest longings pressure him toward manhood, and he needs to respond. He wants to respond but he simply doesn't know how. So help him. Be there to challenge him. Make him a little uncomfortable by stretching his intellect and demanding maturity."[1]

The truth is, our boys need help moving into manhood. Few are "growing up" and statistics support that stark reality. Consider what one modern-day single woman had to say in an article she authored for a men's magazine entitled "Babes in Boyland." The blurb reads, "Women are charging out of college, determined to take on the world—with or without a guy at their side, even when the time comes to raise a family. Are men prepared to meet the challenge?" She begins the article by reflecting on a trip to Mexico with a girlfriend. They desperately wanted their boyfriends to join them, but the author says, "They are stuck at home, short on cash—as usual. This happens a lot. Though we're hardly what you'd call fast-trackers . . . we still outearn the men we love, who are talented and smart but, let's say, motivationally challenged, career development-wise."[2] The article presents daunting statistics that reveal more women than men attend college today (fifty-six women for every forty-four men), women college graduates start working sooner than their male counterparts, and job status and security now matter more to young women than their male peers. "We're speeding along life's highway, and our men aren't even on the ramp yet . . . While you're sowing your wild oats, listening to terrible music, and letting the dishes pile up in the sink, we've begun building careers and 401(k)s. We're buying cars, applying for mortgages, and generally behaving like grown-ups."[3]

Another single woman shares her concern for the lack of male "grown-ups" with Dr. Leonard Sax, author of the book *Boys Adrift:*

> Dear Dr. Sax,
>
> As a twenty-nine-year-old woman, I'm smack in the middle of the "failure to launch" generation. I grew up in Northern Virginia. I went to my 10-year high school reunion last year. All of the girls I went to school with have moved out, gone to college, gotten real jobs, etc. Almost all the boys live at home, have menial jobs, and don't know what they want out of life.[4]

Another woman, Sharon S., writes:

> I'm newly divorced. I'm not sure I want to remarry. There just aren't any worthwhile men out there. My generation of men aren't looking for partners—they're looking for a new Mommy. I'd much rather be on my own than be with a man who can't stand on his own two feet.[5]

The Launchpad

In a fabulous column entitled, "What If There Are No Adults?," theologian R. Albert Mohler Jr. makes the following point:

> In days gone by, children learned how to be adults by living, working, and playing at the parents' side. The onset of age twelve or thirteen meant that time was running out on childhood. Traditional ceremonies like the Jewish Bar Mitzvah announced that adulthood was dawning. This point would be clearly understood by the young boy undergoing the Bar Mitzvah. By the time his body was fully formed, he would be expected to do a full day's work. He could expect to enter the ranks of full-fledged grownups soon after and marry in his late teens. Childhood was a swift passageway to adulthood, and adulthood was a much-desired state of authority and respect.[6]

We must be intentional when it comes to the task of preparing our sons for the transition from boyhood to manhood before they leave home. We must clearly verbalize the expectations that come with manhood, and we must show them what is involved in this rite of passage. In spite of the fact that our sons will grow up in a culture where women no longer count on them to provide, we must help our sons realize that God still does. And practically speaking, we must put our sons to work. It will do little good if action does not follow instruction.

Dr. Leonard Sax says, "The definition of adulthood is not how you spend your money, rent vs. ownership, and so forth. The definition of adulthood, I believe, is being independent of your parents. You can live in a tent in a forest and not pay any rent at all. But if your room and board are subsidized by your parents, you are still a child, no matter what your age. My concern is that we are seeing many more young men who seem to value being comfortable and well-fed over being independent and grown-up."[7]

As mothers, we must recognize that the most loving thing we can do for our boys is to increase their responsibilities and decrease their comforts as they get older. Boys whose mothers continue to do their laundry, cook their meals, make their haircut appointments, and manage their lives will hardly be motivated to leave the nest. What boy wants to leave the creature comforts he has grown accustomed to? Why grow up and become financially independent when you can stay up until 3:00 a.m. playing your favorite online video game and sleep 'til noon the following day, cocooned in your Spider-Man bedsheets? But the biggest argument for launching our sons into the real world is that it is *biblical*. Genesis 2:24 reminds us of the goal: "That is why a man leaves his father and mother and is united to his wife, and they become one flesh." The goal has always been to raise sons who leave and cleave. Not stay and play.

Times have changed. While age eighteen is no longer the accepted norm that signals adulthood, this doesn't mean we wholeheartedly embrace the culture's attitude regarding delayed adulthood. Opinions vary on when a boy should become a man as we've discussed earlier, but one thing is for certain: preparing them to launch is a process that begins much earlier than age eighteen. The home is the launchpad, and you and your husband (if you are married) are in charge of the mission. In a nutshell, you have eighteen to twenty-two years to launch your son into the world to become a responsible, independent member of society. In other words, you have eighteen to twenty-two years to grow your boy into a real man or you're likely to end up with a Peter Pan.

Do you have a launch plan for your son? Similar to a real launch, there are three stages that ensure a successful launch: a prelaunch phase; a test launch phase; and ultimately, a final launch phase. Even if your son is a toddler, it is not too early to think about a launch plan. Below you will find some ideas for each of the three critical phases.

Prelaunch: The stage of a boy's life from age two to fourteen should be viewed as the prelaunch phase. During this stage critical life skills should be introduced, as well as the training required over the years to help your son master life skills. Skills such as personal responsibility for belongings, money management, goal setting, time management, and a strong work ethic can be introduced at a young age and cultivated over the years. For example, my husband did an amazing job in training our children from a young age with basic money management skills. Beginning in their preschool years, he taught them to set aside money for tithing, savings, and spending. Each child had three plastic containers that served as their bank vault. To give them a sense of a strong work ethic, they were given chores from an early age that matched their level of ability. Some chores could earn them extra money while others were performed without pay to teach them the value of teamwork and doing their part to support the family. He also taught them at an early age to manage their savings by giving them each a blank check register book. (I'm sure there's a digital version of this method today!) When they received allowance or birthday/Christmas money, they put it in their register to keep track of their savings. When they spent their money, they deducted the amount. We recently stumbled upon their old check register books and got a kick out of seeing their young chicken scratch writing in some of the earlier entries. We got the biggest laugh when we saw deductions by my youngest son for penalties his father gave him such as: "not brush teeth: 50 cents;" and "left bike in rain: $1." Most of his savings was drained by penalties and what little was left was spent on candy!

Resist the urge to do everything for your sons. The real world will not cater to their every whim and desire, nor should you. Even the youngest of children can be incorporated into some of our daily tasks, whether it's meal prep, setting the table, helping with dishes or laundry, feeding the pets, watering the plants, or whatever you and your husband have on your long to-do list. Once they are able to safely carry a dish over to the sink, insist they clean up after themselves after each meal. Ditto for putting away their own laundry. With both parents working full-time in most homes today, you need every spare moment you can get. Not to mention, you do them no favors by waiting on them hand and foot. Their future roommates aren't going to pick up the slack if they leave their dishes in the sink or leave a pile of clothes in the middle of their bedroom floor. And their future wives sure won't be sending you a thank-you note. Preparing them to live independently in the real world is one of the most important jobs a parent has in raising their children. If your son has been coddled and waited on throughout his childhood, he is in for a rude awakening when he leaves home absent his maid and personal assistant.

When it comes to spiritual training, the prelaunch phase should be used to build a foundation of faith in your son's life. Teach him to love God's Word and to communicate with God through prayer. Pray with him and let him get comfortable praying out loud. Teach him basic biblical truths and reinforce that teaching by plugging into a Bible-believing local church. Attend consistently. Make it a higher priority than sports or extracurricular activities that may fall on Sundays. I cannot stress the importance of cultivating this discipline and modeling for your sons a deep reliance on gathering with a fellowship of believers. Iron sharpens iron and your sons will need all the reinforcement they can get to prepare them to live in the world without becoming of the world (Rom. 12:2).

Test Launch: The stage of a boy's life from age fourteen to eighteen should be viewed as the test launch phase. During the test launch stage, your son should be becoming more independent as he exercises the key life skills. During this stage he will have to learn some painful lessons as you begin to wean him from dependence on you and give him ownership and personal responsibility. During this time many moms have a tendency to come to the rescue of their sons and bail them out of consequences from sinful or poor decisions. Moms need to allow their sons to learn the higher lesson by refusing to rescue them from the consequences that may result. In the real world no one will rescue them from consequences that come as a result of laziness and irresponsibility. It's much less painful for them to learn the lesson while under your roof than years later when their actions can affect their entire family (spouse and children). For example, when each of my sons began driving at sixteen, my husband was clear on the expectations of car ownership. They were given used cars and told they would have to earn money for gas. We paid for the insurance, but we made clear that if they received a ticket or had an accident, they had to pay for the ticket, defensive driving course, and any amount required to repair the vehicle. But that's not all. We also told them they would have to pay any subsequent monthly increase in our insurance premium that resulted from their ticket/accident or lose the car.

My younger son (seventeen at the time) was issued a speeding ticket and experienced the pain of watching over more than one hundred dollars disappear from his savings account to pay for an online defensive driving course to cover the ticket and prevent the insurance premium from increasing. He had a minor fender-bender shortly thereafter that left his back bumper slightly dented with the paint rubbed off and he was unable to afford to have it repaired. We also did not nag or remind him about taking the online defensive driving course. If he didn't have the incentive to follow through, we were prepared to follow through by drawing the amount needed from his savings account to cover the ticket and subsequent increase in insurance.

Once your son is sixteen, if he is able to balance a part-time job, consider having him work to earn his leisure money or gas money. He is also old enough to make his own appointments whether it be for a haircut or dentist/doctor appointment. Have him fill out his own paperwork when required. Prepare him to maintain a budget and give him a few financial responsibilities. My youngest son participated in a Dave Ramsey Financial Peace program (daveramsey.com) during his high school years and I highly recommend these materials from age three and up. By the time your son reaches the test launch phase, he should be putting some of these financial disciplines into practice.

When it comes to spiritual disciplines, your son should be able to pray on his own, initiate time alone with God, and participate in projects that serve others (mission trips; community outreach projects, etc.). During this phase, some parents allow their teenagers to decide whether or not they will attend church and be involved in youth group activities. My husband and I felt strongly that as long as our children lived under our roof, they would be required to follow our guidelines and thus, attend church and be involved in the youth group, as well as take a few mission trips.

Final Launch: The stage of a boy's life from age eighteen to twenty-two should be viewed as the final launch phase. At some point during this stage a boy should become independent of his parents and become a responsible member of society. While some parents may hold the view that age eighteen signals true adulthood, others may feel it is a bit older, especially if college is a part of the plan. Regardless of whether you aim for eighteen or twenty-two, anything much older than twenty-two will increase the chances of a failure to launch. Dr. Leonard Sax notes:

> My own belief, based in part on my twenty years of medical practice, is that if parents continue to shelter their adult child after the age of twenty-one years, the parents may make it less likely that the adult child will ever be willing and able to meet the challenges of the real world. Of course one has to make reasonable distinctions. If your son has just graduated from college and he's twenty-two or twenty-three, looking for a job, I see no harm in his living at home while he's conducting his job search—provided that you and he have discussed, openly and up front, how long this situation can last before you will expect him to find some kind of part-time job to help pay his expenses. One month? Fine. One year? Too long.[8]

Prior to the final launch, parents should help their sons project the future and weigh the possibilities, all the while making the objective clear: *You need to be independent by the age of* ____ (whatever age you determine is reasonable). Some boys are not cut out for college and would perhaps do better with vocational training. In *Boys Adrift*, Dr. Sax again notes:

> Forty years ago, even thirty years ago, there was no shame in a young man choosing a career in the trades.

Beginning in the early 1980s—and particularly after publication of the *Nation at Risk* report in 1983—a consensus grew in the United States that every young person should go to college, regardless. "Vocational education" lost whatever prestige it had, and came to be viewed in some quarters very nearly as a dumping ground for the mildly retarded. Principals and superintendents began to see classes in auto mechanics or welding as expensive diversions from the school's core mission of ensuring that every student would go on to college.[9]

However, vocational training is making a comeback as society realizes that many young people lack the funds and/or ambition to attend college. In addition, there is a demand for many specialty vocations that don't require a college degree. A *Time* magazine article entitled "Grow Up? Not So Fast," that addressed the problem of delayed adulthood among men, recently reported a surge in apprenticeship programs that give high school graduates a cheaper and more practical alternative to college.

In 1996 Jack Smith, then CEO of General Motors, started Automotive Youth Educational Systems (AYES), a program that puts high school kids in shops alongside seasoned car mechanics. More than 7,800 students have tried it, and 98 percent of them have ended up working at the business where they apprenticed. "I knew this was my best way to get into a dealership," says Chris Rolando, twenty, an AYES graduate who works at one in Detroit. "My friends are still at pizza-place jobs and have no idea what to do for a living. I just bought my own house and have a career."[10]

If you recognize in advance that your son is not a candidate for college and would be better suited for a vocational career, it's not a bad idea to expose him to training opportunities by the age of sixteen, while he is still under your roof. One friend of mine who has three sons required her sons to learn a trained vocational skill in their late high school years in addition to their college education that followed. I thought this was a wonderful idea and wish I had thought to do this with my own boys, as a back-up plan to make them more marketable in a tough economy. As it stands, my sons have opted to attend college but not without clear expectations set forth as to what we expect as a return on our investment. In fact, my husband drew up a contract for each of our three children and required them to sign it before we would agree to send them to college. While we required our children to work in the summer months and earn money toward some college expenses, we were able to pay for the bulk of their college expenses and made clear that in doing so their college education is a privilege and not a right. In other words, should they not fulfill their end of the contract, the funding for college would cease.

In the contract my husband detailed what exactly we would cover over a four-year period. Should they not finish in a four-year period, they would need to secure a loan to pay for the remainder of their college education. My oldest son graduated (in four and a half years) and, as per the contract agreement, secured a loan (on his own) to pay for the last semester. He also had to cover tuition, books, and living expenses. The contract also required that each child take a minimum of fifteen hours/semester; earn a minimum GPA (determined based on each child's academic potential); remain consistently involved in a local church and Bible study while in college; and involvement in wholesome extracurricular activities, such as Christian clubs and intramural sports. Should one of our children flunk a course, the child would have to pay us back the entire amount for the course. In addition, at the end of the four-year period, a penalty fee would be required should they not meet the minimum required GPA, based on how much it fell below the pre-established goal.

I realize this may seem harsh to some reading this, but my husband and I are of the school of thought that college educations are a privilege, not a right, and college is not a season of life where young people are supposed to "sow their wild oats." For the amount we invested in their college education, we had every right to attach strings to our offer.

In addition, we made it clear that upon graduating from college, they could return home, but only as a transition to the next step in their employment time line. We likened it to a "layover" at an airport where they might need a little time at the gate (find a job, apartment, etc.) before they embark on their next flight in their journey. In other words, we can provide a stopping place, but the final destination is adulthood!

Relaunch

Every child is different, and the system my husband and I have used with our boys may not be the best system for your son(s). The main thing is to have a launch plan for your son(s) in place and let him clearly know what your expectations are. You may have to revise and tweak it along the way, but don't give in and postpone the launch indefinitely. One friend of mine has a son who experienced a "failure to launch." He went to college upon graduating from high school and came home after one year on scholastic probation. He went back for another try and flunked out completely. Back home and living in his room, he secured a part-time job and registered for a few courses at a local community college. He stayed up late at night playing video games and slept his days away. He received warning after warning from his parents, and when he flunked his courses at the community college, a tough love ultimatum was given: Get a full-time job or join the military. Your choice, but in two months your room will be converted into a home office, and you will not be able to live here any longer.

At this time his part-time job had dwindled down to less than twenty hours a week, and he took no initiative in finding additional employment. He was well on his way to becoming a grown-up Peter Pan. About one week prior to the deadline, his mother sat him down and showed him some places where he could possibly afford the rent (in an undesirable part of town). She reminded him that he would also need to pay for gas and car insurance and that his current income would not be able to cover the expenses. She then showed him the city bus routes and lovingly reminded him that the deadline to move out was fast approaching. It was the wake-up call he needed, and within days he joined the military. My friend shed many tears along the way, wondering if she had done the right thing. Today, that young man is gainfully employed, married, and raising a child of his own. His mother's tough love approach was just the nudge he needed to move from boyhood to manhood. Hopefully, your son won't require a re-launch, but should he return home unexpectedly, it may be required to aid his transition into adulthood.

Mission Accomplished

As mothers, our hearts are wired to nurture and care for our sons. When they are young and utterly dependent on us to have their needs met, we feel a sense of value and worth. It feels good to be *needed*. We must remember that our divine call as mothers is to raise up godly seed for the next generation. And part of "raising 'em up" is to "move 'em out." Or "cut the cord," so to speak. It is unbiblical to allow our sons to remain dependent on us after they reach a reasonable age of self-sufficiency. It is God's design for boys to become men while under the tutelage of their parents.

Even if you are getting a late start, I encourage you to develop a launch plan for your son. Back when this book originally released (2011), my sons were in high school and college. I guess you could say the jury was out regarding whether or not our launch plan would prove to be effective. As I write this update some eight years later, I stand in amazement at the godly young men my sons have become. Both have since graduated from college, secured full-time jobs upon graduation, married shortly after graduation, own their own homes, are financially frugal, and are now raising their own children. Most importantly, they (as well as their wives) love the Lord and are committed to raising their children to love and follow God. Their journeys have not been without some bumps along the way, but those bumps served to test their resolve and develop them into the men they are today. My husband and I could not be more proud of them. We made plenty of mistakes along the way and weren't always consistent in our training, but God more than made up for our lack.

There were times when our sons gave us a hard time about some of our rules and expectations on their journeys to manhood. I recall when my oldest son was in his first semester of his freshman year of college and my husband had very carefully explained that he was going to deposit money for his living expenses for the fall semester as a lump sum into his account. He cautioned Ryan to manage the money very carefully, so he didn't come up short before the semester was up. Well, you can guess what happened. By early November, he had drained the account and was left with a paltry sum to cover his necessities (like food!). His father refused to budge and send more money and my son subsisted off Ramen noodles for the remaining weeks. We laugh about that story now, but my son wasn't laughing at the time.

That same young man recently gave his father a card on Father's Day where he wrote the sweetest note of thanks for the time my husband invested into training him to be a man. As my husband read the card, his eyes filled with tears of gratitude. My point is, your sons may not thank you now for a tough love approach that encourages a successful launch plan, but be assured that your investment and hard work will have a return. Whether you get to hear a belated thank you or not from your son, know that God is saying, "Well done."

Chapter 12

Family Man:
An Endangered Species

● ● ● ● ● ●

He who finds a wife finds a good thing
and obtains favor from the LORD. (Prov. 18:22 ESV)

Marriage and parenthood have always been viewed as bench-marks of adulthood, so it shouldn't come as a surprise both have been on the decline for years. A report released by Demographic Intelligence, which tracks marriage and birth trends in the United States, said marriage rates are the lowest in a century and are projected to decline over the next decade.[1] In 2017, the average age of first marriages for women was 27.4 and for men, 29.5. Compare this to 1965 when it was 20.6 for women and 22.8 for men.[2] As cohabitation and having children outside of marriage have become more socially acceptable, marriage as an institution is no longer viewed as a necessity.

So, what's going on here and why do today's teens and young adults seem to have little interest in marriage and parenthood? Surveys show their priorities have shifted. Consider that in 1976, Boomer high school seniors rated "having a good marriage and family life" higher than any other life goal. By 2011, marriage and family had slipped to fourth (behind finding steady work, being successful at work, and "giving my children better opportunities than I had." Marriage and family remained at fourth in 2015, as well.[3] According to author, Jean Twenge, "marriage and children are just not as high on iGen's priority list."[4] In fact, in a recent Barna survey of today's teens and young adults (iGen/Gen Z), only 20 percent listed "getting married" as a goal they wanted to accomplish before the age of thirty. Only twelve percent desire to "become a parent" by age thirty. This was a sharp decrease from the twenty percent of Millenials who desire to "become a parent" by age thirty.[5] Should this lack of a desire to have children hold, I predict we will see many who choose not to have children at all or to have only one child. Birth rates are already on the decline supporting this likely trajectory. The trend of delayed marriage and parenthood will have a direct impact on the ever-increasing population of single adults, increased infertility issues among women, and even the role grandparents play in helping their adult children. All it takes is two generations who delay having children into their thirties to put the average age of first-time grandparents into their sixties or seventies. This is not talked about often, but as a first-time grandparent at the age of forty-eight who is now in my mid-fifties, I grieve over the devastating impact this will have on the ability of grandparents to be actively involved in their grandchildren's growing up years, as well as help their adult children during a time when they need it most. Many will not live long enough to see their grandchildren graduate from high school; much less attend their weddings. This is not just sad for a generation of grandparents, but also for the grandchildren who will miss the blessing of this relationship.

However, when it comes to the delayed marriage trend, women appear to be the biggest losers. As their biological clocks tick-tock away, their single male friends experience no external pressures to wed. The single males have their pick of a sea of women (including much younger) who are bidding for their attention. The National Marriage Project report concludes, "If this trend continues, it will not be good news for the many young women who hope to marry and bear children before they begin to face problems associated with declining fertility."[6]

Is it any wonder that the number of unmarried women between the ages of thirty and thirty-four has more than tripled during the past thirty years and that the percentage of childless women in their early forties has doubled?[7] Wendy Shalit, author of the book *Girls Gone Mild*, describes this cruel irony; "Single women approaching their late twenties become more serious about the search for a marriage partner. They've gained confidence in their capacity to 'make it on their own,' and they are ready to think about marriage. However, many say the 'men aren't there,' they're 'not on the same page,' or they're less mature."[8]

According to David Popenoe and Barbara Dafoe Whitehead, coauthors of the National Marriage Project report, "A prolonged period of single life may habituate men to the single life. . . . They have become accustomed to their own space and routines. They enjoy the freedom of not having to be responsible to anyone else."[9]

Theologian and author R. Albert Mohler Jr. offered this reminder about marriage:

Christians see marriage, first of all, as an institution made good and holy by the Creator. Its value, for us, is not established by sociology but by Scripture. We also understand that God gave us marriage for our good, for our protection, for our sanctification, and for human flourishing. In other words, the Bible compels us to see marriage as essential to human happiness, health, and infinitely more.[10]

In order to be advocates for marriage, we must first identify the primary threats that seek to undermine God's design and purpose for marriage and threaten to rob the next generation of "human happiness, health, and infinitely more." Of course, not every young man is destined to marry, but most will. It is imperative that we are intentional in teaching them God's view and intent for marriage, rather than allow the mind-set of the culture to influence their thinking. I find it ironic that studies are revealing that the current generation of children and teens are reporting record level increases in loneliness due, no doubt, to the increase in shallow, virtual relationships in place of real emotional intimacy. God created marriage to reduce man's aloneness. Yes, it requires hard work, but the payoff to having someone to share life's greatest joys with (as well as sorrows) cannot be matched by any other substitute. Marriage was intended by God to bring "health and human happiness," but our culture has perpetuated the lie that it is the very hindrance to "health and human happiness." Do your sons believe this lie?

Cheap Sex

Mark Regnerus, sociologist and author of the book *Cheap Sex: The Transformation of Men, Marriage, and Monogamy*, believes that cheap sex has doomed the institution of marriage. He claims that with porn on-demand and greater reproductive freedom, sex is a commodity that is available at any time and has left men with little motivation for marriage.[11] Women used to have leverage when they would require marriage before sex, but with the onset of sex as a free and recreational hobby, men no longer have incentive to "grow up" and get married. It brings to mind an old saying common in our grandparents' day, "Why buy the cow if you can get the milk for free?" Regnerus goes on to argue, "that men are in the driver's seat in the marriage market and are optimally positioned to navigate it in a way that privileges their (sexual) interests and preferences. It need not even be conscious behavior on their part."[12]

For the men who do go on to marry, cheap sex has also proven to have a direct impact on future marriage. Numerous studies indicate that when people have had sex before marriage, they are more likely to divorce if/when they do marry later on down the road. According to the book *Hooked: Science on How Casual Sex Is Affecting Our Children*, coauthors Joe S. McIlhaney Jr., M.D., and Freda McKissic Bush, M.D., found that individuals who have had sex before marriage are less likely to experience marital happiness, more likely to have difficulty adjusting to marriage and less likely to experience happiness, satisfaction, and love.[13]

The book further notes, "An individual who is sexually involved, then breaks up and then is sexually involved again, and who repeats this cycle again and again, is in danger of negative emotional consequences. People who behave in this manner are acting against, almost fighting against, the way they are made to function. When connectedness and bonding form and then are quickly broken and replaced with another sexual relationship, it often actually causes damage to the brain's natural connection or bonding mechanism."[14]

Even more damaging than sex outside of marriage in a steady dating relationship is the trend of sex outside of marriage in the form of "hooking up." Hooking up is when a couple decides to have sex without any promise of a future relationship. It is also commonly referred to as "friends with benefits." Hooking up is portrayed as the norm in everything from pop song lyrics to popular TV shows and movies for teens. There are even apps (ex: Tinder) to facilitate a hook-up on a moment's notice. And thanks to the sexual revolution that rallied women to pursue sex as a recreational hobby, there is no shortage of girls willing to hook up. Of course, one would hope Christian boys are different, but the truth is, they're fighting the same raging hormones as the non-Christian boys. I'm not justifying it but rather calling it to your attention as a necessary talking point. It's awfully difficult to resist something that promises instant pleasure and is free for the taking. But is it really free, or does it come with a price?

According to the book *Hooked*, "Sex is the most intimate connection we can have with another person" and "requires the integration of all we are into that sexual involvement—our love, our commitment, our integrity, our bodies, our very lives—for all of our years. If sex is less than this, it is just an animal act, and in some ways we are performing like creatures because we are not practicing it as full human beings. Sex of this type can make a person 'feel' close to their sexual partner when truly they are not close at all. Sex devoid of relationship focuses on the physical and can actually inhibit the best kind of growth in intimacy."[15] Our sons need to know that cheap sex impacts their attitudes about marriage as well as the health and well-being of their future marriages.

True Love Waits . . . but until Twenty-Nine?

As Christian mothers, we often encourage our sons to remain pure while at the same time offer the added advice not to be in a hurry to settle down and marry after they leave home and/or graduate from college. "Enjoy being single—you have your whole life ahead of you!" Sound familiar? You may not personally subscribe to that philosophy, but you can rest assured your son will be exposed to it—even by those in the church. Let's take a minute to examine the wisdom of that advice. Given that most boys begin to have sexual urges in the late adolescent/early teen years and the average age of marriage for men is now twenty-nine years old, is it really reasonable to expect our young men to fight off their sexual urges for about a decade and a half? Of course, it's *possible* to remain pure until your late twenties (or older), but is it *likely*? Further, why would God give our boys sexual urges in their teen years and then command them to keep them under wraps for a decade and a half? Something's got to give here! Could it be that we have subscribed to the culture's mind-set regarding delayed marriage rather than God's ultimate plan for marriage?

William Doherty, director of the Marriage and Family Therapy Program at the University of Minnesota, agrees that a contradictory message is being sent to our children when we preach abstinence and, at the same time, expose them to societal pressures to delay marriage. "From a traditional moral and religious standpoint, if you want to discourage premarital sex, you really need to be encouraging earlier marriage," he advises.[16] As a disclaimer, he is not endorsing teenage marriages, noting they are risky. He makes the point that "when you get into your twenties, those teen risks go away."[17]

In a thought-provoking essay addressing the problem of stunted maturity among men, author Frederica Mathewes-Green states that "God designed our bodies to desire to mate much earlier, and through most of history cultures have accommodated that desire by enabling people to wed by their late teens or early twenties. People would postpone marriage until their late twenties only in cases of economic disaster or famine—times when people had to save up in order to marry."[18] Again, I am not a proponent of teenage marriages, but I do think we need to reexamine the benefits of marrying in the early twenties. I find it ironic that many young people delay marriage in an attempt to reduce the chance of divorce, yet in reality they actually increase their chances of experiencing a failed marriage by delaying marriage. Mathewes-Green notes that "fifty years ago, when the average bride was twenty, the divorce rate was half what it is now, because the culture encouraged and sustained marriage."[19]

Can you imagine the impact on the average age of marriage if girls refused to hook up or cohabitate and rather made clear they were saving sex for marriage? As one twenty-eight-year-old man told the author of a book on marriage: "If I had to be married to have sex, I would probably be married, as would every guy I know."[20] What an interesting bit of insight over the moral mess that has resulted from hooking up and cohabitation. So much for the sexual revolution that sought to bring women the same sexual freedoms as men, with no marital strings attached. In the end, women are more beholden to men than ever as their biological clocks tick away while the men pursue free sex with no obligation to commit further. Please don't misunderstand—I am certainly not laying blame for the problems associated with delayed marriage solely on women. There is equal blame to go around. I am simply calling it to your attention in an effort to note the importance of relying on God's wisdom rather than blindly subscribing to the faulty wisdom of the world.

We have an obligation to direct our sons to seek God's perfect will over public opinion. I am certainly not saying we manipulate our sons into early marriages. The goal of this chapter is to reevaluate societal opinions about marriage in an effort to help our sons see the purpose and plan for marriage through God's lens. As it stands, marriage is hardly on the radar on a young man's mind when he leaves home (and as the latest surveys have revealed, well into his thirties). And why would it be when he's been told over and over again to "enjoy being single" and "sow your wild oats"? Of course, this puts a burden of responsibility on parents' shoulders to prepare our sons in advance for the possibility of marriage in their young to mid-twenties. It is also our responsibility to raise them to "date with marriage in mind," rather than prescribe to the culture's mind-set that dating and sex are recreational hobbies. Given the times, it may sound radical. However, few would argue that the system in place is certainly not working. Part of launching our boys into adulthood is raising them to have a more biblical mind-set about marriage.

Shacking Up

Since 1960 the number of unmarried couples who live together has increased more than tenfold.[21] What was considered immoral and unacceptable fifty years ago has now shifted to become somewhat of an expectation, especially among men. The study by the National Marriage Project found that most of the participants view cohabitation in a favorable light, and almost all the men agreed with the view that a man should not marry a woman until he has lived with her first.[22] Nearly seventy percent of those who get married lived together first.[23]

So, what is the appeal or the reasoning behind the decision to shack up? The study above sheds light on the three most common reasons cited by unmarried singles in the study above:[24]

- They hope to find out more about the habits, character, and fidelity of a partner.
- They want to test compatibility, possibly for future marriage.
- They want to live together as a way of avoiding the risks of divorce or being "trapped in an unhappy marriage."

There seems to be much confusion and miscommunication regarding any "perceived" benefits of cohabitation. Ironically cohabitation actually increases the risk that the relationship will break up before marriage. A National Marriage Project report states that "many studies have found that *those who live together before marriage have less satisfying marriages* and a considerably higher chance of eventually breaking up." One reason is that people who cohabit may be more skittish of commitment and more likely to call it quits when problems arise. Additionally the act of living together may lead to attitudes that make happy marriages more difficult. The findings of one recent study, for example, suggest, "There may be less motivation for cohabitating partners to develop their conflict resolution and support skills."[25] Those who do go on to marry have higher separation and divorce rates.[26] And whether they go on to marry their cohabitation partner or someone else, they are more likely to have extramarital affairs. When it comes to staying faithful, married partners have higher rates of loyalty every time. One study done over a five-year period, reported in *Sexual Attitudes and Lifestyles*, indicates 90 percent of married women were monogamous compared to 60 percent of cohabiting women. Statistics were even more dramatic with male faithfulness: 90 percent of married men remained true to their brides, while only 43 percent of cohabiting men stayed true to their partners.[27] Additionally those who choose cohabitation under the assumption that the sex will be better than "married" sex should take note: According to a large-scale national study, *married people have both more and better sex than do their unmarried counterparts.* Not only do they have sex more often, but they enjoy it more, both physically and emotionally.[28]

The verdict is in: living together before marriage is damaging to a person's physical, spiritual, and emotional health and can impact the health of his future marriage whether he ends up marrying the woman he lives with or someone else. Yet young men continue to buy the culture's lies, never questioning the error of their ways and the fallout it may produce in the years to come. We have a responsibility to raise our sons to be the kind of young men who view women through the eyes of God and treat them with dignity and respect. I encounter many moms who are concerned about the aggressiveness of young women, but we need to be equally concerned about the young men (including those in the church) who are happy to play along.

While many Christian parents are failing to talk with their adolescent/teenage children about the importance of saving sex for marriage, even more are failing to talk about cohabitation. For many parents it doesn't even make the radar until after their children leave home and they are faced with the reality of the situation when it occurs. Like a minister's wife I know, whose son recently dropped the bomb that he would be moving in with his girlfriend because "times have changed" and "everyone does that now." Both her son and his girlfriend had been involved in Christian ministry in their college years and even mentored high school students. They knew better, but chose to conform to the world rather than abide by God's order and design for marriage.

For this reason we must be devoted to discussing the impact of cohabitation with our children before they leave the nest. We must not be naïve to believe they will not succumb to the pressures of the day.

The Impact of Divorce on Future Marriage

Nearly half of all marriages will end up in divorce. Surprisingly the divorce statistics remain about the same for Christians as they do for non-Christians. While most every parent is somewhat familiar with that statistic, few are actually talking over the consequences of divorce with their children. Of course, when you consider that nearly half of the parents are (or have been) divorced, it is understandable that broaching the topic could be awkward and uncomfortable, to say the least. However, if we truly want our sons to experience God's best in marriage, we must educate them to the damaging consequences of divorce. I think most parents would agree that divorce is far too common in our culture today, and, due to its ready availability, many couples rush into the decision. As most of us know, every marriage will experience ups and downs. Research using a large national sample of people found that 86 percent of people who were unhappily married in the late 1980s who opted to stay in the marriage indicated when interviewed five years later that they were happier. Further, three-fifths of the formerly unhappily married couples rated their marriages as either "very happy" or "quite happy."[29] It certainly makes you wonder how many marriages could be salvaged if couples were not so quick to rush into divorce.

Far too often we hear that a couple has decided to divorce because they "are no longer in love," "are incompatible," or "have irreconcilable differences." However, in many of these cases, the marriages can still be saved with the help of counseling.

We all know of couples where one partner is willing to do whatever it takes to make the marriage work, but for whatever reasons the other partner is not. I have several friends who fall into this category, and my heart breaks for them and the pain they have experienced. They would be among the first to share that divorce produces devastating consequences for all involved. If you are reading this and have experienced divorce, I encourage you to put aside the reasons behind your own divorce and have a candid and honest discussion with your son(s) about the consequences of divorce.

A New PR Campaign for Marriage

Marriage is not doomed, but it is in danger. The good news is that 77 percent of twelfth graders in 2015 said they "expect to marry," which is exactly the same percent of Boomers who claimed the same in 1976.[30] Unfortunately our young people will hear little about the benefits of marriage. When was the last time you heard the media address the overwhelming and consistent findings by such reputable sources as *The Journal of Marriage and the Family* and the *American Journal of Sociology* that "married persons, both men and women, are on average considerably better off than all categories of unmarried persons (never married, divorced, separated, and widowed) in terms of happiness, satisfaction, physical health, longevity, and most aspects of emotional health?"[31] Given that God created marriage, should it really come as a surprise that marriage is, in fact, good for us?

Mothers, it's up to us to extol the benefits of marriage to our sons as a God-ordained union that can bring much happiness and, most important, honor to Him. The National Marriage Project states that the burden of changing attitudes about marriage rests with *parents*. "Contrary to the popular notion that the media is chiefly responsible for young people's attitudes about mating and marriage, available evidence strongly suggests that young people get many of their ideas and models of marriage from parents and the parental generation."[32] That's the good news. The bad news is that the same study also found that "many parents have had almost nothing good to say about marriage and often say nothing at all," claiming the negativism and/or silence could be due to "the parental generation's own marital problems and failures."[33]

Further, when polling young people about their attitudes regarding marriage, many in the study have unfortunately grown up with unhappily married or divorced parents. They have no baseline for determining what a healthy marriage even looks like and have therefore been left with a tainted picture. Some even described a good marriage as "the opposite of my parents."[34] Ouch. Moreover, a number of participants in the study said they received "no advice" or "mainly negative advice" about marriage from their "parents and relatives."[35] Reading that last statement should cause a collective shudder among us all. How can we break the chains of this dysfunctional cycle when many are, in fact, perpetuating and encouraging it? No doubt many reading this have experienced their fair share of hurt and pain in marriage. No one ever said marriage was easy. But can we put aside any hurt and pain we may have experienced and instead focus on God's intent for marriage? In the book *Boys Should Be Boys*, author and physician Meg Meeker notes, "The most important decision a man makes in his life (aside from ultimate questions about God) isn't choosing his college, his career, or what city he's going to live in. It's choosing his mate. If a man's marriage is good, life is good. He can lose his job, a child, a home, but if he has a solid relationship with a spouse, he draws strength from it to endure the hardships. If, on the other hand, the relationship is tumultuous and painful, life feels bad. His job leaves him feeling less satisfied, his interests in hobbies wane, and he is more likely to give up hope in all other areas of his life. One of the greatest gifts we can give our boys is preparation for marriage, if marriage is going to be part of their lives."[36]

I know this is a tricky balance and will require moms who have not experienced the kind of marriage God intended to be blatantly honest with their sons and say, "You know, honey, I realize that Dad and I haven't modeled (didn't model) the best marriage to you, but the truth is, God intended marriage to be a wonderful thing." It may mean putting pride aside and even pointing out others' healthy marriages that could perhaps serve as tangible examples to our sons. It might even be necessary to confess mistakes you may have made in an effort to dissuade your son from making the same mistakes. The problem is that too many with broken marriages are claiming marriage, in general, is the mistake. We must distinguish that God doesn't create mistakes, but people, in fact, make mistakes. Most failed marriages can be traced back to mistakes made by both spouses and a failure on the part of both spouses to adhere to God's standards of marriage. When these standards are not followed, marriages can suffer and sometimes even fail. If this is your case, can you accept responsibility for your mistakes and still speak highly about the institution of marriage when talking to your son(s)? Of course, if you are a Christian who is married to an unbeliever, you can point out to your son God's counsel for Christians not to be "unequally yoked" (2 Cor. 6:14 ESV). (This needs to be done in a manner that would not dishonor your husband.) God can heal any marriage, and prayer is an essential part of that process.

I realize others may be reading this who followed God's standards and, for whatever reason, your once godly husband chose to walk away or chase after a life of sin. I personally know several women who experienced this painful misfortune, and it is heartbreaking. Even though they have had a sour experience, they have not allowed the experience to sour their attitudes regarding marriage. They have worked hard to speak highly of marriage and make sure their sons are not left with a negative impression of marriage. This is an especially tricky balance when it comes to pointing out mistakes made by the other spouse; I caution you that if this is your situation, please refrain from sharing too many details or divulging information that could put a strain on the relationship your son has with his father.

For those of us who currently have healthy marriages, have we done our part in talking up marriage in the hearing of our sons? Do our sons know how much we value marriage? Do they see us exhibit affection and swap caring words? Do they witness positive examples of conflict/resolution and confession/forgiveness? Trust me, I am personally convicted by the weight of those words. I love being married. Sure, it's tough at times, and my husband and I have had our fair share of bumps along the way, but I wouldn't trade it for anything. Marriage is a gift from God. Moms, if we want to see a new PR campaign for marriage take place, it will start in our own homes, beginning with us.

Talk about It

● ● ● ● ● ● ● ● ● ●

Chapter 10

When you compare your children's childhood to your childhood, would you say they are more or less independent than you were?

Why do you think we are seeing a delayed adolescence among children today?

Were you surprised to find out that children are actually much safer now than in years past? Would you say you are overprotective when it comes to your children's safety?

Do you feel it's your role as a mother to ensure your child never feels unsafe or uncomfortable? If yes, how might this affect their ability to grow up?

Chapter 11

Why do you think so many young men are experiencing a "failure to launch"?

Do you have a launch plan for your son to help him transition from boyhood to manhood? Would you say he is on track?

Is your son in the prelaunch, test launch, or final launch phase? What are some steps you are currently taking to increase his level of responsibility and prepare him for the future? If you are not currently taking steps, what steps do you plan to take?

Write down below a vision for what it would look like to achieve a status of "mission accomplished" for your son and by what age.

Chapter 12

Do you speak highly of marriage and parenthood? Does your son have an overall favorable impression of marriage?

What are your thoughts about the trend of delayed marriage? Do you think it's realistic to expect young men to save themselves for marriage if they are marrying around thirty years old?

If your son is in high school, have you had conversations with him about the fallout from hooking up or shacking up?

What steps do you feel led to take to ensure that your son views marriage as a gift from God?

Conversation 5

You are who you've been becoming.

Chapter 13

Raising Up a Gentleman

● ● ● ● ● ●

He has told you, O man, what is good;
and what does the LORD require of you
but to do justice, and to love kindness,
and to walk humbly with your God? (Micah 6:8 ESV)

The traditional gentleman seems to be a lost and dying breed. The chivalrous, hat-tipping, surrender-your-seat-to-the-ladies brand of gentleman is a long-forgotten thing of the past. While I'm not suggesting we retreat back a century and start a hat-tipping revival, I do think parents need to be more purposeful when it comes to raising their sons to be gentlemen. In this chapter I want to address several key qualities that find their roots in the Bible and are necessary character qualities for every gentleman in training.

A Gentleman Values His Reputation

A good name is more desirable than great riches; to be
esteemed is better than silver or gold. (Prov. 22:1)

In my early days of ministering to teens, I would often challenge
them at events with the question, "Are you the type of person who
has a reputation?" The question makes some of them fidget a bit in
their seats. If you looked up the word *reputation* in the dictionary,
you might find this definition: "The generally accepted estimation
of somebody; character, standing, name."[1] The truth is, each of us
has a reputation, a "generally accepted estimation," as determined
by others. And that estimation can be overall good or bad.

I once heard a speaker say, "You are who you've been becoming."
Wow, what a powerful statement. Our sons need to know that you
are judged by your actions. As we discussed in Conversation 2, it is
fairly common for children and teens to have a cognitive disconnect
when it comes to making choices. In other words, it is difficult for
them to mentally walk a decision down its logical path and weigh
the possible consequences of the decision. Most of us likely can
relate to that challenge during our adolescent and teen years and
have our own fair share of negative consequences we tallied up as
a result. However, this is where we must be faithful in helping our
sons see that their actions determine their character, and their character, in turn, determines their reputation.

Socrates, the Greek philosopher from the fourth-century
BC, once said, "Regard your good name as the richest jewel that
can possibly be possessed. The way to gain a good reputation is
to endeavor to be what you desire to appear."[2] This is a difficult
challenge for our children who are growing up in an age where

the Internet and social media can record their missteps. We must be diligent in sharing the key to obtaining a good reputation with our sons. It can be found in Proverbs 3:1–4: "My son, do not forget my teaching, but keep my commands in your heart, for they will prolong your life many years and bring you prosperity. Let love and faithfulness never leave you; bind them around your neck, write them on the tablet of your heart. Then you will win favor and a good name in the sight of God and man." In order to remember God's teaching, our sons must first know God's teaching. Upon knowing it, they must tuck it away in their hearts and pull from that reserve when the need arises. This is the point of impact when God's standard goes beyond simple head knowledge and takes root in the heart. We can do our part to provide them with adequate teaching over the years, but we cannot make them treasure that teaching in their hearts. Furthermore, we cannot make them draw upon those truths and apply them to their daily lives. We can, however, pray like crazy from the sidelines.

A Gentleman Is Chivalrous

While recently trying on some jeans at a nearby store, I couldn't help but overhear a conversation between two young women in the dressing room next to me. One of them was sharing a concern with her friend about her boyfriend's lack of good manners. "He just doesn't seem to get it. He's never once opened a door for me or waited for me to enter a place in front of him. The other day we were headed into the student center, and he walked into the building right in front of me while I was digging in my purse for my student ID, and he just let the door close behind him."

By this time it was all I could do to keep from screaming, "Dump him, sister! He's a dud!" As if her plight wasn't sad enough, wait until you hear her friend's response! "Yeah, but pretty much no guy opens doors anymore. I mean, I wish they would, but we can't blame them if they're not raised that way." It certainly inspired me to sit both my boys down in the days that followed and make sure they are behaving like the gentlemen their father and I raised them to be. Clearly chivalry is on the list of endangered character qualities at risk for extinction. Author Rick Johnson says, "Boys need to be taught to respect women of all ages—girls to grandmothers. They should open doors and carry heavy items for them, not because women are weaker or incapable, but because they deserve to be honored and cherished."[3] He goes on to offer the following advice to mothers of sons: "Teach your boy at a young age to open the door for you and for his sisters. As courtesy and respect manifest themselves in other areas of his life, they will become a lifelong habit and will help create an attitude that some future young lady will greatly appreciate and praise you for."[4] I imagine my neighbors in the dressing room would have shouted out a hearty "amen!" upon hearing that bit of advice.

Chivalry is controversial given the women's movement and the residue of confusion it left in its wake. While some women may find it offensive that a man would have the nerve to hold the door for them, the majority of women still welcome the gesture of kindness. (And I doubt these feminists would dare to complain if they were on a sinking ship and a gentleman offered to give up his seat on the lifeboat to one of them.) Chivalry shouldn't be reserved for just women. Our sons should be taught to keep an eye out for anyone in need, including children and the elderly, and extend a helping hand should the opportunity arise. The wisdom of Luke 6:31 is timeless for every generation: "Do to others as you would have them do to you."

A Gentleman Respects Women

If we want to point our sons to the ultimate example of the greatest respecter and liberator of women, look no further than Jesus Christ. In a time when it was uncommon for men to even speak to or acknowledge women in public, He not only engaged with them, but also used those interactions to model a new example of how women were to be viewed and treated. When you consider that a common morning prayer among Jewish men was to thank God they were not "a gentile, a slave, or a woman," you begin to understand the power of Paul's declaration in Galatians 3:28 when he said, "There is neither Jew nor Gentile, neither slave nor free, nor is there male and female, for you are all one in Christ Jesus." With the new covenant, women were set free from the patriarchal order established in Old Testament times where men ruled over women. With this new freedom, they could equally share in the benefits of the kingdom as well as the dispensation of spiritual gifts. There was no hierarchical order of importance regarding gender, race, or status. All were equal in the eyes of God and all had equal access to the gospel of grace. Jesus cared a great deal about women and used them to further His gospel message. When He met with the Samaritan woman at the well and shared about the transforming power of "living water," she rushed back to her village to share the "good news" as a pioneer evangelist (John 4). It was women who discovered the empty tomb and whom Jesus first revealed Himself to in His resurrected state. He cared enough about women to charge them with sharing the news: "Go and tell my brothers . . ." (Matt. 28:8–10). Jesus treated women with dignity and respect in a time when they were viewed as second-class citizens or even worse, a man's property.

While much progress has been made when it comes to the respect of women, sadly, they are still often seen or treated as objects, rather than fellow image-bearers of God. Our sons are growing up in confusing times where sexual harassment and sexual assault is sometimes excused for the sake of a political position or platform, but other times, vilified by the culture at large in the wake of the #metoo movement. I don't intend for this to be a political statement, but it is especially disturbing when a candidate for the highest and most respected office in the land can brag about "grabbing a woman by the p***y," as well as be riddled by accusations of sexual assault by a dozen or more women only to have the behavior justified by many evangelicals as "locker room talk," or "fake news." This sends a dangerous message to our sons. It is never okay to treat women (by word or deed) as mere objects that exist to service men. Ever.

Dr. Russell Moore, president of the Ethics & Religious Liberty Commission of the Southern Baptist Convention, warns parents in an article entitled *How to Teach Boys to Respect Women*,

> Do not let the boys and young men around you ever,
> even for a millisecond, see you waving away or justifying
> sexual predation, misogynistic comments, or violence
> against women by a sports figure because he plays for
> your team or a politician because he belongs to your
> party or an entertainer because he makes you laugh. Your
> hypocrisy cannot only point the next generation away
> from Jesus, but may also point them toward the way of
> predation.[5]

With the #metoo movement that ushered sexual harassment and sexual abuse of women out of the shadows of shame and into the spotlight, it is necessary to address this topic with our sons. We cannot take it for granted that because they are being raised in Christian homes, they will, as a result, honor and respect women. One need only look at the #churchtoo movement that followed the #metoo movement to see that there are plenty of women who have been disrespected, harassed, sexually assaulted, and sexually abused by Christian men, many of which, sadly, are Christian leaders. Many of the women sharing their testimonies of assault and abuse have hesitated to share their stories due to the re-victimization that often occurs when women in the church come forward and church leaders rush to cover up the incident or even more disturbingly, protect the accused. It adds further insult to injury when victims are quoted Bible verses by church leaders and encouraged to "forgive and forget."

I can't help but wonder how many of these men (whether per-petrators or enablers) were raised in Christian homes or exposed to churches where lip service was given to male chivalry, but a disrespect toward women was modeled due to a skewed teaching of "male headship" that has emphasized *power over women* rather than a *mutual respect for women*. It will be difficult to teach our sons to respect women if Christians (i.e., evangelicals) are tone deaf to the problem or even worse, excuse it for a perceived "greater good." Christians should be leading the charge when it comes to zero-tolerance for the assault, abuse, and disrespect of women that has become all too common in our culture. As mothers, we must be vigilant in making sure our sons view women as fellow image-bearers and equal heirs to the gospel rather than objects for male gratification or property to be possessed.

A Gentleman Is Selfless

A true gentleman puts the needs of others before his own. Of course, this is a difficult discipline for our sons when they are exposed to a multitude of negative role models who glamorize selfish behaviors as the norm. While it's common to engage in an occasional narcissistic indulgence, for some self-indulgence becomes a year-round lifestyle. Take, for example, a recent study that found that college students are more narcissistic and self-centered than ever before. Five psychologists examined the responses of 16,475 college students nationwide who completed an evaluation called the Narcissistic Personality Inventory between 1982 and 2006 and asked for responses to such statements as: "If I ruled the world, it would be a better place," "I think I am a special person," and "I can live my life any way I want to." By 2006 the researchers found that two-thirds of the students had above-average scores, 30 percent more than in 1982.[6]

The study's lead author, Professor Jean Twenge of San Diego State University, said, "We need to stop endlessly repeating 'You're special' and having children repeat that back. . . . Kids are self-centered enough already."[7] The researchers attribute the upsurge in narcissism to the self-esteem movement that took root in the 1980s and further suggest that the effort to build self-confidence has gone too far. In the study Twenge points out that narcissists tend to lack empathy, react aggressively to criticism, and favor self-promotion over helping others. Not surprisingly, when asked to identify possible remedies to the growing problem, the researchers stated that "permissiveness seems to be a component" and that possible antidotes might include more "authoritative parenting" and "less indulgence."[8] It appears that narcissists are made rather than born.

There is nothing more unattractive than a person with entitlement issues. And yet I have to wonder how many mothers are feeding this monster, many through innocent attempts to boost their son's esteem. Oh sure, we need to cheer our children on as they discover their gifts and talents, but we go overboard if we are leaving them with the impression that they are somehow better than everyone else and deserve special favor in the world. Like when we question a coach's decision to put our son on the bench or in a position that doesn't "fully utilize his talents." Or march up to the school to fight their battles. Or allow them to sleep until noon in the summers and play video games all day without an obligation to get a job or chip in and help out around the house.

Then there are moms who feed their children the damaging lie that they can "be anything and do anything they want in the world if they just work/try hard enough." While it sounds nice in theory, it simply isn't true. Even if our sons have extraordinary talent, we need to make sure we don't build them up to the degree it lapses into an arrogant sense of entitlement. When my youngest played basketball his freshman year, a point guard on his team had amazing talent. Unfortunately the boy's parents had built him up to the degree he thought he was better than anyone else and, therefore, didn't have to play by the rules. As in, the *coach's* or *official's* rules. I remember sitting in the bleachers when an official gave him his fifth and final foul of the game. He shouted an expletive at the official before walking out of the gym (rather than back over to the bench to sit with his team). But what happened next said it all. His father flew out of the bleachers and headed for the official. The dad was up in the official's face, shouting, waving his arms, and practically foaming at the mouth over the "injustice" done to his son. Several years later, this young man had a whole host of problems: bad grades (that prohibited him from playing sports), drugs, alcohol, car accidents, numerous accounts of disciplinary actions taken at school, time spent at the alternative learning facility, and the list goes on.

A sense of entitlement doesn't just happen overnight. It is bred into a child from his earliest days. If we are to raise our sons to be gentlemen, we must nip selfish behaviors in the bud before they morph into a sense of narcissistic entitlement.

A Gentleman Is Humble

In my youngest son's junior year of high school, he and some of his football/basketball teammates started a Gentlemen's Day at their school. At one point my son referred to the group as the Junior Gentlemen's Club, but given that just about every strip club in America touts itself as a "gentlemen's club," I discouraged further use of that particular phrase! My son stated that the goal of Gentlemen's Day was to reinstate some of the old-fashioned gentlemanly qualities of days gone by. A mother could hardly argue with that. On the designated day Hayden dressed up in a button-down shirt and tie. I had visions running through my mind of these fine young men rushing to open doors for the girls, standing when their female teachers entered the room, and speaking throughout the day in standard gentleman dialect ("G'day to you, ma'am." "No please, after you." "May I carry your books to class for you, madam?")

I wasn't entirely convinced their motives in instigating a Gentlemen's Day were altogether pure. Sure enough, my suspicions were confirmed when a fellow mother of one of the Junior Gentlemen got her hands on a picture that was taken of our group of boys while they were having lunch in the cafeteria on Gentlemen's Day. She e-mailed it to me, and I literally laughed out loud. Hayden and about six of his friends, each dressed in shirt and tie (some with jackets), sat around a lunch table they had covered with a white tablecloth. On the table was a burning candle centerpiece (isn't this a fire code violation?) and a couple of bottles of sparkling grape juice. My son was wearing a fake mustache while another young man had a pipe (minus the tobacco!) perched in his mouth. But perhaps the funniest part of the picture was the young lady standing off to the side (a fellow student they had recruited), who was serenading them with violin music as they ate their chicken nugget feast from their lunch trays and sipped their grape juice from their Styrofoam cups. Missing from the group shot of the young men celebrating the first official Gentlemen's Day? A little humility!

While the boys dressed liked a gentleman, they failed to heed the biblical counsel to "young men" offered in 1 Peter 5:5 and clothe themselves with the most critical item of apparel for every gentleman in training. "All of you, clothe yourselves with humility toward one another, because 'God opposes the proud but shows favor to the humble.'" Our sons need to know that the qualities that make for a true gentleman come from a heart that is submissive to God's leading. Only by His power are we able to quench our selfish tendencies and see others as more important than ourselves. Philippians 2:3–4 reminds us: "Do nothing out of selfish ambition or vain conceit. Rather, in humility value others above yourselves, not looking to your own interests but each of you to the interests of others."

Even though true humility stems from the heart, this doesn't mean we wait for our sons to come around on their own time and terms and practice humility when they finally *feel* like it. As with the other qualities we have discussed, we teach them spiritual disciplines at an early age and reinforce them over the years until they become second nature. Our goal should be to raise our children to be Christlike. And when it comes to humility, Jesus is the ultimate example.

> In your relationships with one another, have the same mindset as Christ Jesus: Who, being in very nature God, did not consider equality with God something to be used to his own advantage; rather, he made himself nothing by taking the very nature of a servant, being made in human likeness. And being found in appearance as a man, he humbled himself by becoming obedient to death—even death on a cross! (Phil. 2:5–8)

Humility is the opposite of pride. It is a constant reminder that we are "nothing" apart from Christ. Boys who learn to practice humility are better equipped to say no to sex outside of marriage, practice integrity in school and the workplace, feed the hungry and clothe the poor, make a marriage work, and overall behave in a Christlike manner.

Perhaps the best example we can leave with our sons when it comes to behaving like the gentlemen God created them to be is not an emphasis on an established code of moral conduct, but rather, allowing them to see our own personal example of a heart surrendered to Christ. We are servants and nothing more. Everything we have (possessions, talents, health, etc.) is by God's hand and belongs to God, including the wonderful blessing of our sons. They are simply on loan to us for a season. And that is certainly a *humbling* thought.

A Few Good Role Models

If you had to guess what makes the average teen/young adult (between the ages of thirteen to twenty-four) happy, what would you say? My guess would have been "hanging out with friends," "endless amounts of freedom," or perhaps "material possessions." When 1,280 teens/young adults (between the ages of thirteen and twenty-four) were asked that open-ended question, believe it or not, the top answer was spending time with family.[9] This study, which was conducted by the Associated Press and MTV, also found that nearly three-quarters of young people say their relationships with their parents make them happy.[10] But that's not all. When asked to name their heroes, nearly half of respondents mentioned one or both of their parents. The winner, by a small margin: mom.[11] Remember that one the next time you get an eye roll from your daughter or a door slam from your son.

In the book *Teenage Guys*, Steve Gerali says, "The first and most powerfully defining context for a guy is his family. Here he learns about gender roles, social expectations, and his uniqueness."[12] No doubt, fathers are of critical importance in a boy's life. Author and psychologist Michael Thompson notes, "A boy growing up without a male role model is like an explorer without a map."[13] Boys need to see how men act on the job and at home, how they handle stress, how they balance obligations, how they get along with family members, and, most important of all, how they plan for the future.[14] But what if a boy doesn't have the blessing of a father who lives in the home and is a godly role model? While the most ideal family dynamic would be a mother and a father who are happily married, following Christ, and raising their children to do the same, that is often not the case. In fact, it has become a rarity. Take for example Amy's challenge, which she details in an e-mail she sent me:

> My son is nine. My husband is an over-the-road truck driver, and he is gone a lot. My son loves his daddy and sticks to him like glue when he's home. But his daddy

isn't a believer, and there is a shortage of positive male role models in his life. Out of a congregation of 250, only one of the men in our church is willing to work with the children on a weekly basis. What do you do when daddy isn't a believer, and there isn't a strong male influence in your son's life?

I have spoken with many mothers at my events that share heartbreaking accounts of husbands/ex-husbands who drink, swear, and/or engage in other immoral acts in the sight of their children. Please know that my heart breaks for you if you fall into that category. I cannot begin to imagine the anguish you have experienced in not having the support of a godly husband and father to your children. If you face a similar challenge and your son does not have a strong male role model in the home, please do not despair. Whether you are a single mother or you are married to a man who is not a godly role model, please know there is hope. I commend you for picking up this book. It indicates you are the kind of mom who refuses to give up. You will have to work harder to expose your son to strong male role models, but hope is not lost.

While I cannot relate to your plight, know that I have kept you in my mind (and prayers) as I have written this book. I have tried not to make general, sweeping assumptions that most of the mothers in my reading audience would have husbands who are godly men, actively engaged in the rearing of their sons. The "conversations" I have presented in this book are grounded in one assumption: that mothers will share them with their sons, regardless of whether they have a husband on board to help them in that endeavor.

With that said, I would be remiss if I didn't share the importance of exposing your sons to godly male role models. Positive male role models are an important influence in the lives of all boys, including those who have been blessed with a godly father. Author John Eldredge says, "A boy learns who he is and what he's got from a man, or the company of men. He cannot learn it from any other place. He cannot learn it from other boys, and he cannot learn it from the world of women."[15] It is not enough for mothers to engage in the necessary conversations with their sons pertaining to their becoming godly men. Mothers must actively expose their sons to godly men who are "walking their talk" and "talking their walk." Coaches, scout leaders, etc., can be strong influences in a boy's life, especially if they model godly attributes associated with biblical manhood. This is especially important if you have a husband or ex-husband who is modeling *negative* behaviors that run contrary to God's standards for biblical manhood. As your son gets older, it may be necessary for you to acknowledge to your son the situation for what it is and express sorrow that he is missing a godly father role model. Pray about whether you should take this step. If you do, be careful not to bash his father but rather address the situation with a spirit of sincere humility. If you expose your son to godly men on a regular and consistent basis, your son can't help but draw obvious conclusions when it comes to what a godly male role model looks like.

It Takes a Village

Author Steve Gerali says, "From my observations guys tend to seek out male models on their own. They just gravitate toward them—it's a part of the internal mechanism of being a guy. Therefore, instead of finding a role model for her son, a single mother may need to be more concerned with helping him screen the models he's already pursuing."[16] As mothers, our job is to expose our sons to settings with a higher than normal concentration of men who are committed Christ-followers. Send your son on church youth group or mission trips where godly male mentors are present. Look for cues your son is dropping and send the men who have made a positive impression a thank-you note. I know these men are in short supply, but I can promise you they are out there. They are in your local churches, businesses, neighborhoods, and possibly on your own family tree. Author Rick Johnson advises, "Hold up male heroes for your son; he needs to see what they look like. Heroes need not be famous, larger-than-life action figures."[17]

If your son is not gravitating toward some of these men, there is nothing wrong with pin-pointing a few men you know (or have observed) who are exhibiting godly character qualities. In fact, we'll discuss some qualities in the next chapter that can help guide you. Once you identify a candidate, pray about the possibility of approaching him with a request to mentor your son. If God gives you a green light, move forward and express your desire to expose your son to an older godly man like him and see if he's interested.

Rick Johnson says, "Older men have a responsibility to walk alongside younger men, giving them the benefit of their experience. . . . It's important that you make these men aware that your son's father is not involved in his life so they will understand their importance in your son's life."[18] Who knows, you may be the conduit God uses to challenge the man you approach to become godly mentor. Remember, the benefits of a mentoring relationship are mutual. And do not be discouraged if you approach a potential mentor for your son and he declines the invitation. Stay the course. It simply means God has someone else in mind who would be a better match for your son. Trust God's guidance in your search.

Author Leonard Sax offers this wisdom: "To become a man, a boy must see a man. But that man doesn't have to be his father. In fact, ideally, it shouldn't be only his father. Even if your son has a strong father or father figure in his life, he also needs a community of men who together can provide him with varied models of what productive adult men do."[19]

My husband and I have intentionally exposed our sons to other godly men so they may see different personality types that share an equal and unwavering devotion to Christ. Many of these men have become like second fathers to our sons and have played an active part in mentoring them along the way. A mother can teach her son about biblical manhood, but she cannot model what it looks like. I'm a big believer in the principle that "more is caught than taught." Therefore, it's crucial that our boys are exposed to godly men.

The Ultimate Role Model

Godly men are critical in our sons' lives, but the ultimate role model we should point our sons to is Jesus Christ. Even the best of human role models will make mistakes and at times disappoint, but Jesus never fails. While the trend of wearing WWJD wristbands may have expired, the question should never expire from our hearts. What would Jesus do? As our sons mature in their faith, the question needs to become a central foundation in their lives. In fact, if we followed any esteemed earthly role model for long, we would eventually become disillusioned. While our culture is quick to prop up flawed celebrities, musicians, and sports figures, our sons need to be reminded that God exalted Christ to the highest place and gave Him the name that is above every name. A day will come when every knee will bow at the name of Jesus and every tongue confess that Jesus Christ is Lord (Phil. 2:10–11).

The apostle Paul reminds us of the appropriate hierarchy when it comes to following role models: "For when one says, 'I follow Paul,' and another, 'I follow Apollos,' are you not mere men? What, after all, is Apollos? And what is Paul? Only servants, through whom you came to believe—as the Lord has assigned to each his task. I planted the seed, Apollos watered it, but God made it grow. So neither he who plants nor he who waters is anything, but only God, who makes things grow" (1 Cor. 3:4–7 NIV, 1984). A true gentleman knows his place. He is nothing more than a servant with an assigned task of pointing others in the direction of the only role model worthy of a following, Jesus Christ.

Chapter 14

Grounded for Life

● ● ● ● ● ●

For while bodily training is of some value, godliness is
of value in every way, as it holds promise for the present
life and also for the life to come. (1 Tim. 4:8 ESV)

One of my greatest blessings in life is seeing my adult children own their Christian faith. All three of my children (and their spouses) love the Lord and are actively involved in their local churches. In addition, they are raising their children to love the Lord with their heart, soul, mind, and strength. When it comes to passing down a legacy of faith to our children, parents today will face many obstacles. One LifeWay study found that seven in ten Protestants ages eighteen to thirty—both evangelical and mainline—who went to church regularly in high school said they quit attending by age twenty-three. Among those, 34 percent had not returned to church, even sporadically, by age thirty.[1] Another study estimates the exodus as even higher claiming "ninety percent of youth active in high school church programs drop out of church by the time they are sophomores on college."[2] Why are so many of our children who are raised in the church, turning their back on the faith in their young adult years? One likely factor is that we are living in a post-Christian culture where it is no longer the norm to practice the Christian faith. In fact, America's Changing Religious Landscape Study (Pew Research Center) found that over a period of just seven years (2007–2014) "the percentage of Americans who are religiously unaffiliated—describing themselves as atheist, agnostic or 'nothing in particular'—has jumped more than six points, from 16.1 percent to 22.8 percent."[3]

Another factor that is no doubt contributing to the increase among young adults leaving the church is a failure among Christian parents to instill in their children a Christian worldview. In the book *Soul Searching: The Religious and Spiritual Lives of American Teenagers*, authors Christian Smith and Melinda Lundquist found, "the de facto dominant religion among contemporary U.S. teenagers is what they call 'Moralistic Therapeutic Deism': A God exists who created and orders the world and watches over human life on earth; God wants people to be good, nice, and fair to each other, as taught in the Bible and by most world religions; the central goal of life is to be happy and to feel good about oneself; God does not need to be particularly involved in one's life except when God is needed to resolve a problem; and good people go to heaven when they die." They add that a "majority of teenagers are incredibly inarticulate about their faith, religious beliefs and practices, and its place in their lives."[4] While this news is discouraging, my prayer is that it would be a wake-up call for Christian parents to be fully engaged in grounding their children for life in the Christian faith. In years past, a parent could assume that, for the most part, their children would grow up in a culture that shared the same Christian values, but that is no longer the case. The tide has shifted and rather than stand on the banks and wring our hands as our children are swept downstream in a post-Christian tidal wave, parents need to rise up and take responsibility for the discipleship of their children.

While the news is certainly grim, I find myself feeling an undertone of excitement over the challenge that lies ahead. It will no longer be possible to coast along in our faith or rely on the local church as a spiritual filling station. Those of us who are wholeheartedly committed to living a life of purpose for the glory of God will have to double down on our efforts and be intentional on passing the torch of faith to our children. We will need all hands on deck. Parents, grandparents, aunts, uncles, children and youth pastors, teachers, coaches, neighbors and anyone who has spiritual influence over this next generation will need to band together and point our children to the God we have so faithfully followed. But that's not all. We must make sure they understand the basic tenets of the Christian faith. As parents, we are called to be the primary disciplers of our children. Local churches, Christian private schools, and other Christian organizations can assist us in the task of discipleship, but ultimately it falls on our shoulders. God entrusted our children to our care in order that we raise them to be godly seed for the next generation. If we had to sum up our divinely assigned purpose as parents it would be to raise children who love God with their hearts, souls, minds, and strength, put Christ at the center of their worship, and share Christ with a lost and dying world. It is not to raise children who live life as safely as possible and hop from pleasure to pleasure in a desperate attempt to fill the void in their hearts. It is not to raise children who make straight A's, excel in a sport, make the team, win awards, or earn college scholarships. It is not to raise children who someday excel in their careers and amass financial wealth. And believe it or not, it is not to raise children who are "happy," because happiness will not soothe the ache in their hearts for something more. That something is Jesus and it's up to us to make sure we not only tell them that, but show them with our own lives.

Study after study has shown that parents who are intentional when it comes to discipling their children are far more likely to raise solid, Christian children who grow up to be solid, Christian adults. One Barna study of Gen Z kids found that "kids whose parents are consciously, intentionally training their minds and hearts in the ways of Jerusalem are much better prepared."[5] The same Barna study concluded that Gen Z teens who fell into the category of "engaged Christians" were much more likely to hold beliefs that were consistent with the truths of the Bible. "Engaged Christians" readily identified as Christian and strongly agreed with the following: the Bible is the inspired Word of God and contains truth about the world. I have made a personal commitment to Jesus Christ that is still important in my life today. I engage with my church in more ways than just attending services. I believe that Jesus Christ was crucified and raised from the dead to conquer sin and death.[6] Additionally, four out of five engaged Christian teens agree, "I can share my honest questions, struggles and doubts with my parents" (79%), far more than any other faith segment.[7]

Sadly, when youth pastors in the same survey were given a list of thirteen common challenges they face in ministry, two-thirds (or 68%) say their biggest struggle is "parents not prioritizing their teen's spiritual growth."[8] This likely explains why the broader category of "churched teens" (as opposed to "engaged Christian teens") held beliefs and views about Christianity and the Bible that fell more in line with those of "unchurched teens." In a nutshell, parents who recognize that God has appointed them as the primary disciplers of their children are far more likely to take matters into their own hands when it comes to the spiritual training of their children rather than relying on the church to take up the task. A Sunday morning pep-talk by a Sunday school teacher or youth minister is not enough to equip our children to be "engaged Christians." Your investment in training your children to have a biblical worldview will have a direct impact on whether or not they choose to carry that faith with them in the future.

Grounded in God's Word

In the December 1948 *Ladies' Home Journal*, the following ad for Oxford Bibles can be found: "This Christmas . . . give your child the Bible. A fine Bible is the rightful inheritance of every young American. As the Pilgrims drew from it their dream that this nation might be founded in freedom . . . and Roosevelt his dream of the Four Freedoms for all the nations of the world . . . so from its pages today's young leaders will build tomorrow."[9] One of my most treasured possessions is a children's Bible my maternal grandparents gave me when I was ten years old. In my middle school and high school years, I remember retrieving the Bible off my bookshelf from time to time when I was experiencing a time of difficulty, confusion, or sadness. I would sit on my daybed, brush the dust off the cover, and open the book, somehow knowing it contained the remedy for my distress. The Bible had a very basic concordance in the back that listed helpful verses to look up in times of need. I remember being particularly comforted by Psalm 23 and memorizing it. Strangely, I was comforted by this Shepherd spoken of in the psalm, though I had yet to formally meet Him. When it came time for me to go to college, I packed that children's Bible in my suitcase just in case I needed it. I was far from God's path at the time with little interest in God, yet I sensed it might come in handy. Coincidentally, my same grandparents who had given me that Bible years prior lived a short distance from the college I attended and would be a huge influence in my decision to follow Christ several years later at the age of twenty-one.

If our sons are to build upon a firm foundation of faith, God's Word must be their treasured possession. It is our job to make sure they know the Bible is God's revelation to mankind, reliable, and relevant to today. In this digital age, many have traded their bulky leather Bibles for apps on their phones or tablets. One downside to this is that children do not witness their parents reading the Bible. Likewise, I feel it's important for our children to own an actual Bible from their earliest years. How else will they know the Bible is set apart as sacred and special if it's nothing more than just another app? Ephesians 6:17 reminds us to "take . . . the sword of the Spirit, which is the word of God." God has equipped our sons with this "sword" to battle the culture. As mothers, it will be our responsibility to teach them to arm themselves for battle with the Word of God. Most of our youth today have been indoctrinated by the popular thinking of the day concerning a moral relativism, which denies absolute standards of right and wrong behavior. In a culture that preaches moral relativism and political correctness, it is easy for even Christians to lose sight of the fact that absolute standards of right and wrong behavior are contained in God's Word. If we are to equip our sons to stand against the moral relativism they will face, we must help them become convinced that the Bible is not a book, but is the accurate revelation of God and His standards to mankind.

It is best if we can do so before seeds of doubt are planted in their minds by the culture.

The Bible contains God's words, truths, standards, and principles. It reveals His character and presents His message of love and redemption to all mankind. Paul reminds us in 2 Timothy 3:16 that "all Scripture is God-breathed." God inspired more than forty authors to write the Bible over a span of 1,500 years. If our sons fail to see the Bible as divinely inspired by God, it will become nothing more to them than just another good book containing simple suggestions brought by mere men. However, if they come to realize that God is, in fact, the Author of the Bible, they will much more easily understand and accept that the Bible is the final authority in all matters of life. The Bible trumps the popular opinions of the day brought by our culture. It changes everything. I made it a habit to tell my children that the Bible is God's love letter to each and every person. It reveals His heart to the people and unveils His eternal plan for all mankind.

It is not enough to teach our children to believe in Jesus because the "Bible says so." We must go a step further and teach them *why* we are confident the Bible was written by God through men. "The Bible says so" won't cut it as an effective argument in defending Christianity, matters of morality, or wooing someone to the Christian faith. It may have worked fifty years ago when most people accepted the Bible's divine origins without question. Today, the Bible is thought by many to be nothing more than a compilation of man-made opinions. It's not a matter of "if" our sons will be challenged in regard to their beliefs concerning the origin of the Bible, but "when." If our sons begin to doubt the reliability of the Bible, they will likely also begin to doubt the validity of the claims of Jesus, standards of right and wrong, and characteristics of God that are recorded in the Bible. Such doubt will weaken the very foundation of their Christian faith.

There is an overwhelming amount of archaeological evidence to support the validity of the Bible. Prior to the nineteenth century, there were many facts in historical accounts of the Bible that could not be confirmed. As a result, severe attacks concerning the legitimacy of the Bible were launched in the nineteenth century. It was claimed that people and places recorded in early Scripture were legend, not historical fact. Shortly after these attacks began, an explosion of archaeological finds took place. The existence of places and people described in the Old Testament was proved credible with the discoveries of ancient civilizations in Egypt, Babylonia, Palestine, and Assyria. The Bible continues to be historically verified by archaeology. It is exciting to think of the archeological finds that will occur in the years to come that will further support the validity of God's Word.

While most books have a short lifespan, the Bible has stood the test of time. To top it all off, the Bible is the best selling book of all time. When you stop and think about the longevity of the Bible, it is nothing short of a miracle. In 1 Peter, we are reminded, "The grass withers and the flowers fall, but the word of the Lord stands forever" (1 Pet. 1:24b–25a). God's principles set forth in His Word are timeless for all ages. Our sons need to know that God has left us the Bible as an instruction manual for living. J. I. Packer warns, "Disregard the study of God, and you sentence yourself to stumble and blunder through life blindfolded, as it were, with no sense of direction and no understanding of what surrounds you. This way you can waste your life and lose your soul."[10] God's standards, principles, and truths will act as a compass to steer them in the right direction (even when Mom is not there to help!) and give them the ability to filter right from wrong, good from evil, and wisdom from folly. Of course, in order for our sons to partake in this wonderful treasure, they will need to recognize its value and come to depend on it as a source of sustenance in their daily lives.

Grounded in Prayer

Prayer, simply put, is conversing with God. The more our sons converse with God, the more in touch they will be with His intended purpose for their lives. A consistent prayer life can act as a safeguard against mediocrity and a tendency toward a lukewarm Christian faith. Well-balanced "conversations" with God include both talking to God and listening to Him. After all, how good would a relationship with a friend be if our conversations always boiled down to a long to-do list for the other person. Philippians 4:6 says: "By prayer and petition, with thanksgiving, present your requests to God." There is certainly nothing wrong with asking God to do things for us, but there are other aspects of prayer that are also important. One of the simplest and best prayer models I have found that leads to a well-balanced prayer life is the ACTS model. ACTS is an acronym that stands for adoration (or praise), confession, thanksgiving, and supplication (making requests of God for others or ourselves). My husband and I taught the ACTS model to our children and utilized it as part of their bedtime ritual. We began teaching them this model of prayer when our youngest child was about four years old. By the time he was six, he could tell you what each letter stood for and give a basic definition of each word. We found the ACTS model to be very user-friendly for children of all ages.

At bedtime, my husband or I would start prayer time with our children by speaking words of adoration (praise) to God. We then allowed our child to do the same. We would go back and forth, taking turns on each aspect of ACTS. This way, it helped our kids understand what each aspect of ACTS meant and helped them put it into practice. Once they began to grasp praying the ACTS model, we had them pray it themselves. Prayer is a vital component of the Christian faith. When our children are taught to converse with God on a consistent basis, it personalizes the relationship and reminds them that God is present at all times.

A = *Adoration*

It seems only fitting that prayer to a Holy God should begin with acknowledgment to His divine characteristics and attributes. Our relationship with God is put into the proper perspective when we as the creation submit in awe and reverence to our Creator. It is an expression of faith when we take the focus off our own needs and direct our attention to the very One who promises to meet our needs. We adore God for His many attributes and just as we desire for someone to know and accept us for who we are, God desires the same from us. Scripture teaches us that God is loving, just, patient, long-suffering, everlasting, trustworthy, merciful, wise, holy, almighty, sovereign, omnipresent, forgiving, faithful, and the list goes on and on. The more we study God's Word, the more we get to know Him. (In the appendix, I have included a list of character qualities of God to use when praising Him.)

C = *Confession*

Confession is basically agreeing with God over our sin and feeling sorrow for our sin. Unless we think and feel the same way about our sin that God does, we will not repent of our sin (2 Cor. 7:10). When I would get to the confession part of prayer time with my children, I encouraged them to think of something specific that they had done or said that day, rather than make a general sweeping statement. (Ex.: "Lord, I confess that I was wrong when I spoke disrespectfully to my mom when she picked me up late from school" versus "Lord, I confess that sometimes I can be disrespectful to my parents.") If their confession involves a wrongdoing against another person, encourage them to make it right with the person by asking for forgiveness. Also, if you are taking turns going back and forth with the ACTS model, allow your son to hear you confess some specific sin that you committed that day. In doing so, we model to our sons that we (yes, even moms!) all have sinned and fall short of the glory of God (Rom. 3:23).

When our sons confess their sins on a daily basis and acknowledge God's forgiveness, it reminds them that sin is a serious matter in the eyes of God. In a world that preaches moral relativism, the discipline of confession will remind our sons that there are absolute moral standards that dictate right and wrong, and good and evil. However, we should be quick to assure our sons that no sin is too big for the forgiveness of God. First John 1:9 promises that "If we confess our sins, [God] is faithful and just and will forgive us our sins and purify us from all unrighteousness." We must help our sons recognize and respond properly to the pangs of conviction brought by the Holy Spirit over wrongdoing. We must equip them with the tools to acknowledge the conviction, confess their sins, and repent. If the habit of confession is developed early on in our sons' lives, the chances increase that when they are older, they will rush to God's throne of grace in full confidence, knowing that they will receive His mercy and grace in their time of need (Heb. 4:16).

T = Thanksgiving

When I think of the need to thank God, I am reminded of the ten lepers spoken of in Luke 17:12–18. They all cried out to Jesus to have pity on them and heal them. He responded to their cries and told them to "Go, show yourselves to the priests," and then He healed them on their way. Unfortunately, only one bothered to return and thank Him. Jesus asked the man, "Were not all ten cleansed? Where are the other nine? Has no one returned to give praise to God except this foreigner?" (v. 17). Often, I am guilty, like the nine lepers, of failing to thank God for answered prayers. As hard as it is to remember to thank God when He answers our prayers, it is even harder to thank Him when He answers, but not in a way we had hoped. Nonetheless, in 1 Thessalonians 5:18, God calls us to "give thanks in all circumstances." This is the mark of true Christian maturity.

God reminds us in Psalm 50:23 that "those who sacrifice thank offerings honor me." In addition to teaching our sons to thank God for answered prayer, we should also teach our sons to express thanks for things that they might otherwise take for granted. This would include the blessings of family, extended family, church family, a place to live, food to eat, freedom to worship, and the list goes on and on. Once again, if our sons hear us express thanks to God for our many blessings, we model what it looks like to have a heart of gratitude.

S = Supplication

Supplication is when we submit our requests or petitions to God on behalf of ourselves or others. As a reflection of the principle of putting others before ourselves, I encouraged my children to submit requests for others before praying for themselves. We can help them develop the habit of thinking of others first by gently asking them, "Is there anyone you would like to pray for tonight?" As they get older, they may want some privacy when they are praying for others or themselves. We should not take it personally, as our goal is to raise sons who are comfortable conversing one-on-one with God. As your son begins to gain independence, you might say a quick prayer for him at bedtime and then leave him to pray alone. It is no different than other areas of training. The goal is to give our sons a foundation for a healthy prayer life and assist them until they can master it on their own.

We must teach our sons early on that God is the Father of compassion and the God of all comfort who is capable of comforting them in all their troubles (2 Cor. 1:3–4). "Troubles" can range from an "owie" when they're two, a parent's divorce when they are ten, failing to make the select team at thirteen, a break-up when they are seventeen, or anything, for that matter, that leads to tears or a broken heart. Boys who learn to run to Jesus in times of sadness or suffering are less likely to turn to other unhealthy things when seeking comfort. As much as we desire to protect our sons from hurtful situations in life, it will be impossible. While it is a wonderful thing if our sons count us as trusted confidants when they are hurting, we need to be careful to show them comfort, while at the same time, pointing them in the direction of the only One who can mend a broken heart.

Hebrews 5:7 says, "During the days of Jesus' life on earth, he offered up prayers and petitions with fervent cries and tears to the one who could save him from death, and he was heard because of his reverent submission." Because Jesus had submitted to His Father's authority even before His Father had answered His prayer, He was at peace regardless of the answer. Submission to God expressed through prayer says, "Your will be done," even if it is an answer they had not expected. If our sons understand this concept, they will be less likely to question why God may choose not to answer some of their prayers in the ways they had hoped. They will understand that "no," or "wait," is as valid an answer to their prayers as "yes."

We must teach our sons that God is accessible every minute of every day. When they develop the instinct to turn to God through-out their day, whether to lift up a request or a praise to Him, they will learn the art of what it is to pray without ceasing (1 Thess. 5:17). Children who develop the habit of taking thought of and talk-ing to God throughout each day on their own initiative are much less likely to fall into tempting situations or make foolish decisions when standing at the crossroads of a difficult choice.

Grounded in Purpose

In Mark, chapter 12, Jesus was asked by one of the teachers of the law, "Of all the commandments, which is the most important?" (v. 28). Jesus answers, "The most important one," answered Jesus, "is this: 'Hear, O Israel, the Lord our God, the Lord is one. Love the Lord your God with all your heart and with all your soul and with all your mind and with all your strength.' The second is this: 'Love your neighbor as yourself.' There is no commandment greater than these" (Mark 12:29–31). In Jesus' answer, our purpose is found. The sum total of our lives is to love God and love others. And yet, we make it so complicated. As parents, we knock ourselves out trying to provide our children with all the trappings that promise future happiness. We spend ungodly amounts of money on the latest and greatest toys and gadgets and yet, they are one of the unhappiest generations on record. We invest endless amounts of time shuttling them to a plethora of extracurricular activities in the hopes it will give them a sense of worth and value, and yet, there is an epidemic of mental health issues among their generation. When we think in terms of their future, we emphasize grades, academics, and college more than Bible study, prayer, and evangelism. Sadly, even if we provide them with all of the worldly trappings above, they will still lack purpose. God wired their hearts to long for something more—Him.

As evidence points to more and more churched teens abandoning a biblical worldview and trading it for a type of moralistic therapeutic deism that is steeped in personal happiness, we must be prepared to show our sons why this will leave them empty in the end. That brand of non-faith won't rescue them from the consequences of sin and eternal separation from God. As I have said before, God has wired our hearts for His unfailing love and redemption. Nothing else will satisfy us in the end, including the futile pursuit of personal happiness. If we are faithful in exposing the lies associated with this faulty belief, we will raise sons who are not only grounded in their faith, but also prepared to minister to their peers who come up empty and are left wanting for more. In Matthew 9:37–38, Jesus reminds us that the harvest is plentiful, but the laborers are few. He tells us to pray earnestly to the Lord of the harvest to send out laborers. Never before has it been more important to raise our children to walk in Truth and lead with love. Our task is not to simply raise children who are grounded in the faith, but to also raise up laborers who are prepared to bring Jesus to an ever-increasing harvest of lost and empty souls.

Make no mistake. We are grounding our sons in *something*. There is only one foundation worth building upon. There is only one foundation that will stand the test of time. There is only one foundation that will provide our sons with the security their hearts long for. There is only one foundation that will carry them through this life and into the next. That foundation is Jesus Christ. All else is sinking sand. Is your son grounded for life?

Chapter 15

The Heart of the Matter

● ● ● ● ● ●

Whoever has the Son has life; whoever does not have
the Son of God does not have life. (1 John 5:12)

In this final chapter I want to speak to you candidly about the challenge to raise godly sons in an ungodly world. I want to come to you as a mother, not a writer with "expert opinions" (sorry, I'm not qualified!). Too often we pick up parenting books with the goal of finding some sort of tried-and-true formula for raising healthy and happy kids. You know, the kind of kids who grow up to say "please" and "thank-you," "yes ma'am" and "no sir." The kind who make their beds in the morning, share their toys with their siblings (without being told), and get gold stars on spelling tests. And when it comes to our sons, we want to raise them to be the kind of young men a mother points out to her daughter and says, "Now there's the kind of guy I hope you'll marry someday." As our sons get older, we want to hear, "That's a fine young man you're raising."

Deep in our hearts we long to see evidence that we're on the right track with this parenting thing. In school and the workplace there are six-weeks grade reports and yearly employee evaluations to review progress and make any necessary changes along the way. Not so with parenting, which is why we have a tendency to gravitate toward how-to books, depend on occasional pats on the back, or even translate our son's successes as our own personal successes. Our sons are a reflection of us, and whether we want to admit it or not, we've all been guilty of trying to ensure that everything looks neat, tidy, and pretty on the outside. Some more so than others, but alas, we all lean in that direction. And let's face it, it's just plain easier to focus on the outside, where we can see evidences of positive change . . . and so can others.

The truth is we can train our sons to be chivalrous, polite, obedient, selfless, honest, and humble, but if their behavior is not motivated by a love for Christ and a desire to follow Him, they are relying on goodness rather than godliness. Isaiah 64:6 reminds us that our righteous acts are like filthy rags. But the sternest warning comes from Christ and His harsh words to the Pharisees: "Woe to you, teachers of the law and Pharisees, you hypocrites! You clean the outside of the cup and dish, but inside they are full of greed and self-indulgence. Blind Pharisee! First clean the inside of the cup and dish, and then the outside also will be clean" (Matt. 23:25–26).

Few would argue that many of our churches are filled with Pharisees who embrace a gospel of goodness over godliness. Admittedly there have been times when I've lapsed into that frame of mind. If we want to raise sons who are not only "good guys," but more important, "godly guys," we must teach them to keep "the inside of the cup clean." In order to do that, we must not shy away from talking about sin and God's redemptive story. Sin is not merely a behavior but rather a condition. Fortunately God provides a solution for our sin. It's our job to share the good news with our sons.

Godliness Over Goodness

It's easy to focus on behavior modification strategies when it comes to training our sons in godliness. I've been guilty at times of focusing more on changing my sons' sinful behavior than encouraging them to turn to the only One who can change their hearts and their sinful behavior. And while I can manipulate my sons' behavior (at least at some level in the early years) in order to achieve a desired end result, I have no control when it comes to changing their hearts. Yet this is where true change must occur. Employing behavior modification strategies without addressing the heart does nothing more than put a Band-Aid on the problem. We must get to the heart of the matter.

Unless (or until) our sons are believers in Christ, their motivation and ability to change sinful behaviors will be rooted solely on their own human willpower. Yet for believers, true change occurs when our hearts respond to conviction of sin with a godly sorrow rather than a worldly sorrow (2 Cor. 7:10) and, as a result, turn from the sin (repent). The motivation to change is the unfailing love of God in that "while we were still sinners, Christ died for us" (Rom. 5:8). His kindness leads us toward repentance (Rom. 2:4)—the kind of kindness the father exhibited to his son in the account of the prodigal son when he ran to him and greeted him with a hug and a kiss. No one and no thing can offer our sons that brand of unfailing love.

It's easy to react to our sons' sins with a set of swift consequences that discourage a repeat of the sins. However, we need to take the time to address the sins at the heart level in an effort to offer a permanent solution. We can't make our sons experience godly sorrow or, for that matter, even repent, but we can remind them of their need for a Savior and the price that was paid. When my children were new drivers and would leave the house with car keys in hand to meet up with friends, I used to yell out a last-minute reminder to "make good choices!" When I think back on my habit of shouting out this reminder, I have to laugh. How many of our teens when faced with a tempting situation will stop, remember their mothers' sage advice, and declare to their friends, "Sorry guys, but my mom told me to 'make good choices,' so I'm going to have to pass"? It's wishful thinking on our part, but not likely to happen. Even if it did work, the motivation would be misplaced. Modifying and managing behavior won't change your heart. My husband and I were forced to realize this with our youngest son who was not respondent to our familiar behavior modification parenting strategies. Only when we began to shift our attention to his heart rather than his behavior did we begin to see change. When he would leave the house with car keys in hand, I would yell out, "Hayden, remember the cross!" Reflecting on the sacrifice Christ made on the cross is far more likely to evoke a change in behavior than a parent pep talk.

One of the verses I often share when speaking at events is Psalm 26:2–3, "Test me, O LORD, and try me, examine my heart and my mind; for your love is ever before me, and I walk continually in your truth" (NIV, 1984). We must teach our sons to lay their hearts bare before God on a regular and consistent basis. They are more likely to "walk continually in His truth" when they are in the habit of looking to God for an honest appraisal concerning the motives of their hearts. And of course, their motivation to stay on God's path is found in keeping His amazing, unfailing love ever before them.

Even Good Guys Do Ungodly Things

Some months ago I received an e-mail from a mother who was distraught to learn that her daughter, whom she described as a "good, Christian girl" had had sex. Her daughter was a junior in college and dating a "good, Christian guy" who was in his first year of seminary. Her daughter was living at home, and the mother stumbled upon a note from GCG (good, Christian guy) that indicated they had had sex. She was devastated that this "future pastor in training robbed her daughter of her virginity." Her purpose for writing me was to ask if she should come clean and tell her daughter about finding the note and encourage her to break up with GCG. She included excerpts from the note as evidence that they had clearly had sex. And based on her report, it was clear her daughter was a willing party.

Strangely, when I read it, I walked away with a completely different impression of GCG. I was most struck by the sincere regret he expressed in the note that they had "slipped up." His purpose for writing was to let her know he had experienced tremendous conviction and, after spending time in prayer over their sin, had felt led to take steps "to guard and protect her heart in the future." Some of the steps he listed included weekly accountability to an older, godly man, not spending time alone together in their apartments when their roommates were gone, and spending some time reading God's Word together and praying. But what really struck me was the godly sorrow he expressed in the note over what had happened and, more important, his desire to get back on track in his relationship with God, both for his sake and for his girlfriend's sake.

So in a nutshell there was a sin (a wrong turn at the crossroads); there was conviction over the sin, ownership of the sin (on the boyfriend's part), and godly sorrow that followed; there was an immediate U-turn and new direction; and there was a plan in place (as a result of his initiative) to hold him further accountable in the future in order that he might "protect and guard her heart." And this mother wants her daughter to break up with this guy? Through her hurt and disappointment over the loss of her daughter's virginity (by her daughter's own choice), this mother had failed to see that even though this good, Christian guy did a not-so-good thing, he chose to respond in a good and, more important, *godly* manner. Because that's how good, Christian guys behave when they love Jesus and are doing their best to follow Him on a daily basis. Mom failed to see that sometimes good Christian guys and good Christian girls do, in fact, make mistakes. In the end it's the heart that matters most.

When my youngest son was in high school, my husband and I experienced a situation when our son (also "a good Christian guy") made a foolish choice with some of his "good Christian guy" friends from school. Suffice it to say, they got off track in their walk with the Lord. I know some of you mothers with younger children may not want to hear that good Christian kids do, in fact, sin because, like me, maybe you imagined that if you did all the right things (read the latest and greatest parenting book; take them to church every Sunday; raise them on VeggieTales; sign them up for VBS every summer; involve them in youth group at church; send them to Christian camps and events; sign them up for mission trips; etc.) that somehow you can protect them from making some of the same foolish choices you may have made. Sorry to be the one to burst your bubble. Those are all wonderful things; and, no doubt, you are making "holy deposits" along the way. However, your sons will not be exempt from saying yes to temptations and straying from God's path. I know this because I was once you. And when my children strayed, I would somehow manage to blame *myself*.

Given our own sin nature, why are we always so surprised when our sons (who don't have our maturity or fully developed frontal lobes!) choose to sin? This question weighed heavy on my heart as Keith and I dealt with our son's situation. We worked hard to get to the root of the real issue: the why behind his decision to sin and, more important, the condition of his heart. Oh sure, there were consequences and privileges revoked, but we invested most of our time in helping our son better understand the principle of godly sorrow and true repentance. We reminded him of God's patient and enduring love for him, even when he behaves in ways that are unbecoming. And then Keith and I prayed that he would react with brokenness and godly sorrow. We knew that without brokenness and godly sorrow the root of the sin would not be addressed. We might be able to modify our son's behavior with stern consequences, but it would only solve the problem temporarily.

In the end God used the situation to grow our son spiritually. He later admitted it was a wake-up call to get his attention before he strayed too far from God's path. We witnessed evidence of positive change on the outside; but, more importantly, we knew God was at work in our son's heart. In spite of our best efforts, our sons (yes, even the good Christian ones) are going to sin at times. Just as we do. Part of being a good parent is to teach our children how to get back up when they fall down. Not pretend they never will or, even worse, pick them up and give them a quick brush-off before the neighbors see them. It's far more difficult to raise a *godly guy* than a *good guy*. And if we're honest, we also know it's far more difficult to be a *godly mom* than a *good mom*.

Final Thoughts

When I penned my final thoughts in the original version of this book back in 2011, the timing was strangely ironic. It coincided with my oldest son's graduation from college and my youngest son's final months in the nest before graduating from high school. Needless to say, I wrote the book with a certain sense of urgency as the clock ticked louder and louder in the background of my own parenting journey, signaling the close of one chapter and the beginning of another. My youngest son's exit from the nest would mark my official entrance into the empty-nest years.

As I have mentioned at multiple points in this book, it has been an interesting experience to update this book in the aftermath of my sons' transitions into adulthood. It's been eight years since I wrote the original version of this book. I guess you could say the jury was still out when I wrote the original book regarding the effectiveness of the conversations. If I could leave you with a final word of encouragement, it would be this: Your diligence and persistence in raising your sons to be godly men will be worth it. However, the end goal in having these necessary conversations with your sons should not be to raise perfectly well-behaved sons who never slip up or deviate from God's path. (Good luck with that one!) Both my boys made many mistakes along the way. They didn't always follow their parents' teaching or, for that matter, embrace the wisdom offered at the time in the conversations I had with them. Sometimes, the most valuable lesson was learning the hard way, by way of personal experience. It was hard to witness at the time, but now that I'm able to look back on my parenting journey, I see God's hand in every detail. I recognize the value of missteps along the way and how it's contributed to the godly young men they are today.

There were times when I wondered, "Why bother?" It would have been far easier to be a lazy, carefree parent who did little to nothing when it came to preparing her children to leave the nest. I said before and I still believe it, "There is no foolproof formula when it comes to raising our children." There is a chance you could pour your entire being into raising your sons to be godly men only to have little fruit to show for it in the way of results. I hope that is not the case, but I want you to know that had it been the case with my sons, I would have no regrets. At the end of the day, I don't answer to anyone but God. He trusted me with the stewardship of my sons while they were in my nest and I did what I could to honor Him in the task and raise them to, in turn, bring honor to Him. I am not responsible for the results. I can rest in knowing I performed my job (though not perfectly) as best I could for God's glory and leave the results to Him.

Recently, while talking to my youngest son on the phone, he said something that will encourage any mother who is striving to impact her children in a meaningful way. As a background, my youngest son is leading a group of young men at his church in a Bible study and was expressing his frustration that many of the men have a hard time opening up about their sin and weaknesses. One of the reasons my son is leading the group is because he has faced his own fair share of demons along the way and has emerged from the battle victorious. As a result, he is passionate about seeing other men find the same freedom in order that they, too, might live a life that would honor God. My son knows that true freedom is not possible unless you are willing to lay your heart bare before God and be honest about the sin in your life. My son can relate to the story of the prodigal son, even though at the time of his wandering, many would not have known he was a prodigal. He continued to go through the motions of being a faithful Christian—church: check. Bible study: check. Counselor at a Christian camp: check. Young Life leader: check. To many (including his parents), all looked well on the outside. But all was not well, and at some point, living with a divided heart caught up with him. Let me also add that had my son listened to my counsel in the conversations laid out in this book, he could have been spared this battle. So, what were his encouraging words on the phone that day? They weren't a "Thanks, Mom, for having all those conversations with me and investing so much time into raising me to be a godly man." Nope. It wasn't an acknowledgment of all my biblical wisdom and knowledge that I tried to pass along. Nope. He said, "Mom, I realized it's not hard for me to be honest about the messy parts of my life because when I was growing up, you weren't afraid to tell me that you were a mess too." The conversations I had with my son over the years mattered, but my honesty and transparency about my own need for Christ every minute of every day spoke louder than any wise words I could offer.

As we close, I want to encourage you to let yourself off the hook for being a perfect mom. At the end of the day, my son didn't thank me for being a perfect mom, but rather, an imperfect sinner who has been forgiven by a perfect God. The conversations in this book are valuable, but they will have a far greater impact if they are presented by a mother who is not afraid to acknowledge that she, too, is a work in progress.

In the closing pages of the original book, I said this and it bears repeating:

> Take the time to talk to your son . . . and keep talking
> through the years. I promise you, he's listening. Remind
> him that you aren't expecting him to be perfect and have
> the guts to tell him that you're not perfect either. Model

that a relationship with Christ and a life lived in response to what He did on the cross is where true contentment and joy are found. Tell him God is more concerned with his heart and having a relationship with him than merely his good deeds. And tell him that no matter what, you will never, ever cease to pray for him.

Your job as a mother, will never end. Your job description will change over the years, but you will always be your son's mother. Enjoy the fleeting years when your sons are in your nest and under your care. Trust me, they are fleeting. But take it from this mother, who is now looking back in the rearview mirror—give it everything you've got and don't forget to enjoy the ride along the way.

Talk about It

• • • • • • • • • •

Chapter 13

In what ways are you raising your son to be chivalrous?

In what ways are you raising your son to respect and honor women?

In what ways are you encouraging humility in your son?

Who are some positive role models in your son's life? If he doesn't currently have godly role models, who might you consider pointing him to?

Chapter 14

In what ways have you been intentional when it comes to training your son to embrace a biblical worldview?

Does your son view the Bible as the inerrant Word of God and his instruction manual for life?

Do you make it a regular habit to pray with your son? How comfortable is your son praying?

Chapter 15

Is it your tendency to emphasize godliness or goodness when parenting your sons?

How might you emphasize heart examination over behavior modification?

Have you taught your son how to get back up when falling down (as a result of sin)?

Is it hard for you to trust God for the results when it comes to raising your sons or do you feel responsible for the outcome?

Appendix

Talk Sheets

● ● ● ● ● ●

Conversation 2

● ● ● ● ● ● ● ● ● ● ● ● ●

Bonus Conversation: Pornography and Sex Addiction

One Conversation a Son Had with His Mother

By: Hayden Courtney

Sometime in the spring of 2017, I (Hayden) had a conversation with my mom (Vicki) where finally, I was the one giving the advice. At the time, I was a newly married young adult. I remember her asking me through her tears, "Was there anything I could have done differently to avoid this?" Now, the "this" she was speaking of involves enough pain and hope to justify an entirely separate book. It's hard to write about "this" in such few words, but I will do my best.

"This" was referring to the extreme pain I brought on my wife, Becca, in October of 2016, when I told her that I had a severe "struggle with pornography" and had been lying to her about it for as long as she had known me. "This" was about Christmas Eve a few months later, and how I woke my parents up in the middle of the night to tell them Becca and I had to leave, and that I wasn't sure if we were going to stay married. "This" was about the further pain and trauma I brought on Becca during a three-day, couples counseling intensive, where it became abundantly clear that my problem, and my behaviors, were far more severe than a "struggle with pornography." "This" involved twenty-eight days of in-patient treatment that gave me a foundation for recovery from sex addiction. In summary, when my mom asked me, "Was there anything I could have done differently to avoid this," she was referring to the pain I put her, my family, and most of all, my wife Becca through, because of my selfish and secretive behaviors.

Even in light of "this," before my mom could finish asking her question, I knew my answer.

"No."

She gave some push-back, clearly feeling responsible for "this."

"Mom, I said no," I replied.

She wasn't having it. She couldn't shake the feeling that "this" was somehow, at least partially her fault. Recognizing that my previous emphatic responses were not taking effect, I elaborated.

"Mom, your job as my mother was never to keep me from falling into sin, but to show me how to respond when I did. And you did exactly that."

This seemed to sink in, but she still needed more convincing. She brought up the fact that she had not only had specific conversations with me on the dangers of sexual sin, but had literally written an entire conversation about it in a book for mothers of sons.

I asked her, "Did you pray for me?"

"Of course I prayed for you," she answered.

"Then no. My answer is still no. There is not anything in this world you could have done to help prevent this."

Finally, it seemed that she was understanding. The conversation (dramatic effect added) went on further, but it lead me to two take-aways that I think are vital for every mother to hear.

First, just as I told my mom, understand that your job as a mother is not to protect your son from sinning. News flash: he is going to sin, and sin often. Your job, rather, is to show him how to respond to his sin. Notice I said "show" him how to respond to his sin. I didn't say "tell him" (although you should do that as well). Take it from a son who has only recently left the nest; I can remember very little of what my mother *told* me. (Disclaimer: the things I do remember were extremely important and helpful to me in my walk, such as these five conversations, so you are not off the hook there!) The point is that much of who I am today is because of what my mother *showed* me. I am walking in freedom from my addiction today not because of factual evidence that my mom shared with me about the dangers of pornography when I was thirteen years old, but because I saw my mother *own* her sin and take it to the cross. Mothers, please *tell* your sons as much as you possibly can, but don't neglect to *show* them what it looks like to follow Jesus.

Second, pray for your sons. Pray that they would respond to their sin by running to Jesus. Pray that they will be vulnerable about their sin, even the dark and shameful sins. Pray that the Lord would surround them with a few, genuine brothers in Christ who will be vulnerable with him. Lastly, pray for yourself. Pray that the Lord would give you peace, a heart of surrender, and trust that He is in control.

Mothers: I tell this story not to scare anyone, but to bring hope. Hope not rooted in your abilities as a mother, or even in the ever-so-important conversations in this book, but a hope in the goodness and faithfulness of our God. If you can remember one thing, remember this:

These five conversations that you will have with your son must never take priority over your own countless and continuous conversations with the Son.

Signs Your Child Might Be Addicted

Early research on screen addiction has found that the amount of time spent on media consumption is not the biggest determinant of addiction, but rather, if it "causes problems in other areas of life or has become an all-consuming activity."[1]

Based on a key study related to technology and addiction among children, here are some warning signs that could indicate your child's media consumption has lapsed into a compulsive addiction:[2]

Unsuccessful Control: It is hard for my child to stop using screen media.

Loss of Interest: Screen media is the only thing that seems to motivate my child.

Preoccupation: Screen media is all my child seems to think about.

Psychosocial Consequences: My child's screen media use interferes with family activities.

Serious Problems Due to Use: My child's screen media use causes problems for the family.

Withdrawal: My child becomes frustrated when he/she cannot use screen media.

Tolerance: The amount of time my child wants to use screen media keeps increasing.

Deception: My child sneaks using screen media.

Escape/Relieve Mood: When my child has had a bad day, screen media seems to be the only thing that helps him/her feel better.

Conversation 3

STD Fact Sheet[3]

What are sexually transmitted diseases (STDs)?

STDs are diseases that are passed from one person to another through sexual contact. These include chlamydia, gonorrhea, genital herpes, human papillomavirus (HPV), syphilis, and HIV. Many of these STDs do not show symptoms for a long time. Even without symptoms, they can still be harmful and passed on during sex.

How are STDs spread?

You can get an STD by having vaginal, anal, or oral sex with someone who has an STD. Anyone who is sexually active can get an STD. You don't even have to "go all the way" (have anal or vaginal sex) to get an STD. This is because some STDs, like herpes and HPV, are spread by skin-to-skin contact.

How common are STDs?

STDs are common, especially among young people. There are about 20 million new cases of STDs each year in the United States. About half of these infections are in people between the ages of 15 and 24.

Young people are at greater risk of getting an STD for several reasons:

- Young women's bodies are biologically more prone to STDs.
- Some young people do not get the recommended STD tests.
- Many young people are hesitant to talk openly and honestly with a doctor or nurse about their sex lives.
- Not having insurance or transportation can make it more difficult for young people to access STD testing.
- Some young people have more than one sex partner.

What can I do to protect myself?

- The surest way to protect yourself against STDs is to not have sex. That means not having any vaginal, anal, or oral sex ("abstinence"). There are many things to consider before having sex. It's okay to say "no" if you don't want to have sex.
- If you do decide to have sex, you and your partner should get tested for STDs beforehand. Make sure that you and your partner use a condom from start to finish every time you have oral, anal, or vaginal sex. Know where to get condoms and how to use them correctly. It is not safe

to stop using condoms unless you've both been tested
for STDs, know your results, and are in a mutually
monogamous relationship.

- Mutual monogamy means that you and your partner both
  agree to only have sexual contact with each other. This
  can help protect against STDs, as long as you've both been
  tested and know you're STD-free.

- Before you have sex, talk with your partner about how
  you will prevent STDs and pregnancy. If you think you're
  ready to have sex, you need to be ready to protect your
  body. You should also talk to your partner ahead of time
  about what you will and will not do sexually. Your partner
  should always respect your right to say no to anything that
  doesn't feel right.

- Make sure you get the health care you need. Ask a doctor
  or nurse about STD testing and about vaccines against
  HPV and hepatitis B.

- Girls and young women may have extra needs to protect
  their reproductive health. Talk to your doctor or nurse
  about regular cervical cancer screening, and chlamydia
  and gonorrhea testing. You may also want to discuss
  unintended pregnancy and birth control.

- Avoid mixing alcohol and/or recreational drugs with sex.
  If you use alcohol and drugs, you are more likely to take
  risks, like not using a condom or having sex with someone
  you normally wouldn't have sex with.

If I get an STD, how will I know?

Many STDs don't cause any symptoms that you would notice.
The only way to know for sure if you have an STD is to get tested.

You can get an STD from having sex with someone who has no symptoms. Just like you, that person might not even know he or she has an STD.

Where can I get tested?

There are places that offer teen-friendly, confidential, and free STD tests. This means that no one has to find out you've been tested. Visit gettested.cdc.gov to find an STD testing location near you.

Can STDs be treated?

Your doctor can prescribe medicine to cure some STDs, like chlamydia and gonorrhea. Other STDs, like herpes, can't be cured, but you can take medicine to help with the symptoms. If you are ever treated for an STD, be sure to finish all of your medicine, even if you feel better before you finish it all. Ask the doctor or nurse about testing and treatment for your partner, too. You and your partner should avoid having sex until you've both been treated. Otherwise, you may continue to pass the STD back and forth. It is possible to get an STD again (after you've been treated) if you have sex with someone who has an STD.

What happens if I don't treat an STD?

Some curable STDs can be dangerous if they aren't treated. For example, if left untreated, chlamydia and gonorrhea can make it difficult—or even impossible—for a woman to get pregnant. You also increase your chances of getting HIV if you have an untreated STD. Some STDs, like HIV, can be fatal if left untreated.

What if my partner or I have an incurable STD?

Some STDs, like herpes and HIV, aren't curable, but a doctor can prescribe medicine to treat the symptoms.

If you are living with an STD, it's important to tell your partner before you have sex. Although it may be uncomfortable to talk about your STD, open and honest conversation can help your partner make informed decisions to protect his or her health.

If I have questions, who can answer them?

If you have questions, talk to a parent or other trusted adult. Don't be afraid to be open and honest with them about your concerns. If you're ever confused or need advice, they're the first place to start. After all, they were young once, too.

Talking about sex with a parent or another adult doesn't need to be a one-time conversation. It's best to leave the door open for conversations in the future.

It's also important to talk honestly with a doctor or nurse. Ask which STD tests and vaccines they recommend for you.

Sexting Fact Sheet[4]

Start the Discussion Early

Start the conversation with your child by asking broad questions such as, "Have you heard of sexting? Tell me what you think it is." You can then frame your conversation around how much your child does or does not know. Seeing a story in the news, community, or at your child's school is a good prompt to check in again. Emphasize the consequences of sexting as shown by situations in the news where it has gone badly.

Use Examples Appropriate for Your Child's Age

For tweens with cell phones, let them know that text messages should never include images of anyone without clothes. For teenagers, be specific about what sexting is and that it can lead to serious consequences. For all ages, remind them that once an image is sent, it is no longer in their control and they cannot get it back. What is online or sent via text can exist forever and be sent to others.

Remind Your Teenager of Their Own Worth

Let your child know that being pressured to send a sext is not okay, nor is it a way to "prove" their love or show attraction. Let your child know you understand it is hard to be pressured or dared to do something but that they have the power to stand up for themselves. Remind your teenager that they are worthy of respect.

Sexual Assault Fact Sheet[5]

Sexual assault is any type of sexual activity or contact that you do not consent to.

Sexual assault can happen through physical force or threats of force or if the attacker gave the victim drugs or alcohol as part of the assault. Sexual assault includes rape and sexual coercion. In the United States, one in three women has experienced some type of sexual violence. If you have been sexually assaulted, it is not your fault, regardless of the circumstances.

What is sexual assault?

Sexual assault is any type of sexual activity or contact, including rape, that happens without your consent. Sexual assault can include non-contact activities, such as someone "flashing" you (exposing themselves to you) or forcing you to look at sexual images.

Sexual assault is also called sexual violence or abuse. Legal definitions of sexual assault and other crimes of sexual violence can vary slightly from state to state. If you've been assaulted, it is never your fault.

What does sexual assault include?

- Any type of sexual contact with someone who **cannot** consent, such as someone who is underage (as defined by state laws), has an intellectual disability, or is passed out (such as from drugs or alcohol) or unable to respond (such as from sleeping)
- Any type of sexual contact with someone who **does not** consent
- Rape
- Attempted rape
- Sexual coercion
- Sexual contact with a child
- Fondling or unwanted touching above or under clothes

Sexual assault can also be verbal, visual, or noncontact. It is anything that forces a person to join in unwanted sexual activities or attention. Other examples can include:

- Voyeurism, or peeping (when someone watches private sexual acts without consent)
- Exhibitionism (when someone exposes himself or herself in public)
- Sexual harassment or threats
- Forcing someone to pose for sexual pictures

* Sending someone unwanted texts or "sexts" (texting sexual photos or messages)

What does "consent" mean?

Consent is a clear "yes" to sexual activity. Not saying "no" does not mean you have given consent. Sexual contact without consent is sexual assault or rape.

Your consent means:

* You know and understand what is going on (you are not unconscious, blacked out, asleep, underage, or have an intellectual disability).
* You know what you want to do.
* You are able to say what you want to do or don't want to do.
* You are aware that you are giving consent (and are not impaired by alcohol or drugs).

Sometimes you cannot give legal consent to sexual activity or contact—for example, if you are:

* Threatened, forced, coerced, or manipulated into agreeing
* Not physically able to (you are drunk, high, drugged, passed out, or asleep)
* Not mentally able to (due to illness or disability)
* Under the age of legal consent, which varies by state

Remember:

* **Consent is an ongoing process,** not a one-time question. If you consent to sexual activity, you can change your mind and choose to stop at any time, even after sexual activity has started.

- **Past consent does not mean future consent.** Giving consent in the *past* to sexual activity does not mean your past consent applies *now* or in the *future*.
- **Saying "yes" to a sexual activity is not consent for all types of sexual activity.** If you consent to sexual activity, it is only for types of sexual activities that you are comfortable with at that time with that partner. For example, giving consent for kissing does not mean you are giving consent for someone to remove your clothes.

What is NOT considered consent in sexual activity?

- **Silence.** Just because someone does not say "no" doesn't mean she is saying "yes."
- **Having consented before.** Just because someone said "yes" in the past does not mean she is saying "yes" now. Consent must be part of every sexual activity, every time.
- **Being in a relationship.** Being married, dating, or having sexual contact with someone before does not mean that there is consent now.
- **Being drunk or high.** Read more about alcohol, drugs, and sexual assault.
- **Not fighting back.** Not putting up a physical fight does not mean that there is consent.
- **Sexy clothing, dancing, or flirting.** What a woman or girl wears or how she behaves does not show consent for sexual activity. Only a verbal "yes" means "yes" to sexual activity.

Who commits sexual assault?

Sexual assault is most often committed by someone the victim knows. This may be a friend, an acquaintance, an ex, a relative, a date, or a partner. Less often, a stranger commits sexual assault. Women and men commit sexual assault, but more than 90 percent of people who commit sexual violence against women are men.

What is the average age a woman is sexually assaulted?

Four of every five women who are raped are raped before age twenty-five. About 40 percent of women who have been raped, or two in every five, were assaulted before age eighteen.

Conversation 5

● ● ● ● ● ● ● ● ● ● ● ● ● ●

Chapter 14: Characteristics of God (for ACTS prayer model)

Father/personal God

Love—unlimited and unconditional

Grace

Mercy

Holy

Righteous/perfect

Hates sin and unrighteousness (but loves sinners)

Just

Omniscient (all knowing)

All wise

Omnipotent (all powerful)

Sovereign

Omnipresent (everywhere at the same time)

Immutable (does not change)

Eternal (no beginning and no ending)

Infinite (not constrained by time or space)

Creator

Sustainer

Comforter

Patient

Faithful

Is Truth

Compassionate

Protector

Provider

Notes

● ● ● ● ● ●

Chapter 1: A Time for Everything

1. Meg Meeker, M.D., *Boys Should Be Boys—7 Secrets to Raising Healthy Sons* (New York: Ballantine Books, 2008), 122–23.

2. Ibid., 91.

3. Ibid., 123–24.

4. 2010 FLOTV—"Injury Report" Sneak Peek, http://superbowl-ads.com/article_archive/2010/02/06/2010-flotv-injury-report-sneak-peek, posted on February 6, 2010.

5. "Dockers 'Men Without Pants' March to Super Bowl," https://www.adweek.com/brand-marketing/dockers-men-without-pants-march-super-bowl-101378/, posted on January 21, 2010.

6. James Poniewozik, "Dodge Charger, 'Man's Last Stand,'" http://content.time.com/time/specials/packages/article/0,28804,1960734_1960750_1960769,00.html, posted on February 7, 2010.

7. Peg Tyre, *The Trouble with Boys* (New York: Crown Publishing Group, 2009).

8. https://www.theatlantic.com/education/archive/2017/08/why-men-are-the-new-college-minority/536103/

9. Albert Mohler, "Where Are the Young Men?" http://www.albertmohler.com/2010/02/09/newsnote-where-are-the-young-men, posted on February 10, 2010.

10. Rick Johnson, *That's My Son* (Grand Rapids, MI: Revell, 2005).

11. Study explores why boys are falling behind girls in school, http://www.physorg.com/news66925169.html, posted on May 15, 2006.

12. Ibid.

13. Polly Leider, "Why Boys Are Falling Behind; Doctors and Educators Pinpoint Reasons for Gender Gap in Schools," http://www.cbsnews.com/stories/2006/01/23/earlyshow/leisure/books/main1231713.shtml, posted on January 23, 2006.

14. Ibid.

15. Peg Tyre, *The Trouble with Boys* (New York: Crown Publishing Group, 2009), 181–82.

16. https://www.today.com/parents/want-kids-listen-more-fidget-less-try-more-recess-school-t65536

17. http://www.foxnews.com/opinion/2016/08/22/parents-vs-schools-war-on-recess.html

18. Stephen James and David Thomas, *Wild Things: The Art of Nurturing Boys* (Carol Stream, IL: Tyndale House Publishers, 2009), 125.

Chapter 2: Wired for Adventure

1. Rick Johnson, *That's My Son* (Grand Rapids, MI: Revell, 2005), 49.

2. Stephen James and David Thomas, *Wild Things: The Art of Nurturing Boys* (Carol Stream, IL: Tyndale House Publishers, 2009), 119.

3. John Eldredge, *Wild at Heart* (Nashville, TN: Thomas Nelson Publishers, 2001), 13.

4. Meg Meeker, M.D., *Boys Should Be Boys—7 Secrets to Raising Healthy Sons* (New York: Ballantine Books, 2008), 46.

5. Ibid., 49.

6. Rick Johnson, *That's My Son*, 49.

7. John Eldredge, *Wild at Heart*, 4.

8. Meg Meeker, M.D., *Boys Should Be Boys*, 33.

9. John Eldredge, *Wild at Heart*, 5.

10. Nancy Gibbs, *The Growing Backlash Against Overparenting*, http://www.time.com/time/nation/article/0,8599,1940395,00.html, posted on November 20, 2009.

11. Ibid.

12. Ibid.

13. Ibid.

14. Rick Johnson, *That's My Son*, 105.

15. Steve Gerali, *Teenage Guys* (Grand Rapids, MI: Zondervan, 2006), 208.

Chapter 3: Masculinity Redefined

1. http://www.adweek.com/brand-marketing/ad-day-axe-gets-inclusive-remarkable-ad-thats-really-pretty-magical-168996/

2. Lini S. Kadaba, "Manning up; As the testosterone turns: The new retrosexual gets that strong and gallant guy thing going again," *Philadelphia Inquirer* (March 7, 2010).

3. gender-fluid. Dictionary.com. *Dictionary.com Unabridged* (Random House, Inc.) http://www.dictionary.com/browse/gender-fluid, accessed May 22, 2018.

4. "Gen Z: The Culture, Beliefs and Motivations Shaping the Next Generation," Barna Group, January 23, 2018.

5. Ibid.

6. worth. Dictionary.com. *Dictionary.com Unabridged* (Random House, Inc.), http://www.dictionary.com/browse/worth (accessed: May 22, 2018).

7. James Strong, *A Concise Dictionary of the Words in the Greek Testament and The Hebrew Bible*, Vol. 1 (2009), 58.

Chapter 4: The Tech Natives Are Restless

1. "The Farmer's Wife and Her Boys," *Ladies' Home Journal* (September 1894).

2. Jean M. Twenge, "Have Smartphones Destroyed a Generation?" September 2017, https://www.theatlantic.com/magazine/archive/2017/09/has-the-smartphone-destroyed-a-generation/534198/.

3. *Ibid.*

4. Jean M. Twenge, PhD, *iGen: Why Today's Super-Connected Kids Are Growing Up Less Rebellious, More Tolerant, Less Happy—and Completely Unprepared for Adulthood—and What That Means for the Rest of Us* (New York: Atria Books, 2017), 79.

5. Twenge, "Have Smartphones Destroyed a Generation?"

6. Ibid.

7. Twenge, *iGen*, 97.

8. Ibid.

9. Ibid., 98.

10. Ibid., 103–104.

11. Ibid.

12. Ibid., 108.

13. Nicholas Kardaras, *Glow Kids: How Screen Addiction Is Hijacking Our Kids—and How to Break the Trance* (New York: St. Martin's Press, 2017), 123.

14. Ibid., 114–16.

15. Ibid.

16. Ibid., 3.

17. Ibid., 59.

18. Ibid., 22.

19. "Facebook Is Addictive Because It 'Exploits a Vulnerability in People's Brains," cofounder Sean Parker says by Julia Glum on November 10, 2017, http://www.newsweek.com/russia-facebook-trump-sean-parker-707964.

20. Tony Reinke, *12 Ways Your Phone Is Changing You* (Wheaton, IL: Crossway, 2017), 44: Blaise Pascal, *Thoughts, Letters, and Minor Works*, ed. Charles W. Eliot, trans. W. F. Trotter, M. L. Booth, and O. W. Wight (New York: P.F. Collier & Son, 1910).

21. Ibid., 63.

22. "Teenagers Programmed to Take Risks; Risk-Taking Peaks in Adolescence, According to Scientists at UCL," http://www.eurekalert.org/pub_releases/2010-03/ucl-tpt032310.php, posted on March 24, 2010.

23. Peg Tyre, *The Trouble with Boys* (New York: Crown Publishing Group, 2009), 181.

24. Steve Gerali, *Teenage Guys* (Grand Rapids, MI: Zondervan, 2006), 170.

Chapter 5: Porn: A Virtual Reality

1. Ryan Singel, "Internet Porn: Worse than Crack?" http://www.wired.com/science/discoveries/news/2004/11/65772, posted on November 19, 2004.

2. "Hijacking the Brain—How Pornography Works," https://www.christianheadlines.com/news/hijacking-the-brain-%E2%80%94-how-pornography-works-11625757.html, posted on February 1, 2010.

3. Paul Knight, "Teen Porn 101," http://www.houstonpress.com/2010-02-18/news/teen-porn-101, posted on February 18, 2010.

4. Patricia M. Greenfield, "Inadvertent Exposure to Pornography on the Internet: Implications of Peer-to-Peer File-Sharing Networks for Child Development and Families," *Applied Developmental Psychology* 25 (2004), 745–46, as cited in Meg Meeker, M.D., *Boys Should Be Boys—7 Secrets to Raising Healthy Sons* (New York: Ballantine Books, 2008), 65–66.

5. Ibid.

6. R. Albert Mohler Jr., "Pornified American—The Culture of Pornography," *Commentary by R. Albert Mohler Jr.*, August 22, 2005, as cited in Steve Gerali, *Teenage Guys* (Grand Rapids, MI: Zondervan, 2006), 88.

7. https://www.barna.com/research/porn-in-the-digital-age-new-research-reveals-10-trends/

8. Ibid.

9. Ibid.

10. William M. Struthers, "This Is Your Brain on Porn," Youthworker journal.com.

11. Ibid.

12. "Hijacking the Brain—How Pornography Works," www.AlbertMohler.com, posted on February 1, 2010.

13. JUJU Chang and Vanessa Weber, "Hiding a Porn Habit Is Part of the Thrill for Many Addicts," Abcnews.com, posted on September 8, 2008.

14. Ibid.

15. Struthers, "This Is Your Brain on Porn," Youthworkerjournal.com.

16. William Struthers, *Wired for Intimacy* (Downers Grove, IL: InterVarsity Press, 2009), 45.

17. Struthers, "This Is Your Brain on Porn," Youthworkerjournal.com.

18. *Your Brain on Porn*, Location 602–603.

19. Leonard Sax, M.D., Ph.D., Boys Adrift (New York: Basic Books, 2009), 132.

20. Rick Johnson, *That's My Son* (Grand Rapids, MI: Revell, 2005), 73.

21. "Hijacking the Brain—How Pornography Works," https://www.christianheadlines.com/news/hijacking-the-brain-%E2%80%94-how-pornography-works-11625757.html, posted on February 1, 2010.

22. Marnia Robinson, "Unexpected Lessons from Porn Users," www.PsychologyToday.com, posted on October 7, 2009.

23. *Your Brain on Porn*; Location: 383–84.

24. Marnia Robinson, "Unexpected Lessons from Porn Users."

25. http://www.covenanteyes.com/2015/11/17/8-characteristics-of -porn-addiction/

26. Betsy Hart, "Give Sons a 'Porno Pep Talk,'" http://jewishworld review.com/cols/hart033010.php3#.W-8I33pKi9Y, posted on March 30, 2010.

27. https://www.barna.com/research/porn-in-the-digital-age-new -research-reveals-10-trends/

Chapter 6: Raising a Wise Guy

1. Kim Painter, "Your Health: Teens Do Better with Parents Who Set Limits," *USA Today*, http://www.usatoday.com/news/health/painter /2010-02-08-yourhealth08_ST_N.htm, updated February 7, 2010.

2. Meg Meeker, M.D., *Boys Should Be Boys—7 Secrets to Raising Healthy Sons* (New York: Ballantine Books, 2008), 190–91.

Chapter 7: Beyond the Birds and the Bees

1. Joe S. McIlhaney, M.D. and Freda McKissic Bush, M.D., *Hooked* (Chicago, IL: Northfield Publishing, 2008).

2. Ibid.

3. Ibid.

4. Gary and Carrie Oliver, *Raising Sons and Loving It!* (Grand Rapids, MI: Zondervan, 2000, 66, as cited in Rick Johnson, That's My Son (Grand Rapids, MI: Revell, 2005), 27.

5. Kevin Leman, *Making Sense of the Men in Your Life* (Nashville: Thomas Nelson, 2001), 130, as cited in Johnson, *That's My Son*, 68.

6. Johnson, *That's My Son*, 66.

7. Pam Stenzel, *Sex Has a Price Tag: Discussions about Sexuality, Spirituality, and Self-Respect* (Grand Rapids, MI: Zondervan, 2003).

8. Johnson, *That's My Son*, 68.

9. "Two-thirds of teens who had sex wish they had waited," http:// www.bpnews.net/bpnews.asp?ID=17294, posted on December 18, 2003.

10. "Sex Education: Start Discussions Early," MayoClinic.com, http://www.mayoclinic.com/health/sex-education/HQ00547.

11. Kristen Zolten, M.A., and Nicholas Long, Ph.D., "Talking to Children about Sex," Center for Effective Parenting, 1997, http:// parenting-ed.org/wp-content/themes/parenting-ed/files/handouts /sex.pdf, as cited in Johnson, *That's My Son*.

12. Johnson, *That's My Son*, 71.

Chapter 8: Play Now, Pay Later

1. Jean M. Twenge, PhD, *iGen: Why Today's Super-Connected Kids Are Growing Up Less Rebellious, More Tolerant, Less Happy-and*

Completely Unprepared for Adulthood-and What That Means for the Rest of Us (New York: Atria Books, 2017), 209.

2. Ibid.

3. *A Practical Guide to Culture: Helping the Next Generation Navigate Today's World*; Location 1824.

4. https://www.cdc.gov/std/products/youth-sti-infographic.pdf

5. The National Campaign survey questioned 1,000 young people ages twelve to nineteen and 1,008 adults age twenty and older, according to the news release. The telephone surveys were conducted by International Communications Research in August and September 2003. Founded in 1996, National Campaign is a private nonprofit organization with the goal of reducing the teen pregnancy rate by one-third between 1996 and 2005, www.teenpregnancy.org.

6. David Larson and Mary Ann Mayo, "Believe Well, Live Well," Family Research Council (1994).

7. David B. Larson, M.D., NMSPH, et al, "The Costly Consequences of Divorce: Assessing the Clinical, Economic, and Public Health Impact of Marital Disruption in the United States" (Rockville, MD: National Institute for Healthcare Research, 1994), 84–85.

8. See http://www.girlsaskguys.com/Sexuality-Questions/248240 -should-i-feel-terrible-for-being-a-21-year-old.html.

9. Sharon Jayson, "Truth about Sex: 60% of Young Men, Teen Boys Lie about It," *USA Today*, January 26, 2010. Survey originally in *Seventeen* magazine.

10. Ibid.

11. Pam Stenzel, *Sex Has a Price Tag: Discussions About Sexuality, Spirituality, and Self-Respect* (Grand Rapids, MI: Zondervan, 2003), 36–37.

12. https://www.cdc.gov/std/life-stages-populations/YouthandSTDs -Dec-2017.pdf

13. Peter Jaret, "The 6 Most Common STDs in Men," http://live healthyandlaugh.com/the-6-most-common-stds-in-men/.

14. Pam Stenzel, *Sex Has a Price Tag: Discussions about Sexuality, Spirituality, and Self-Respect* (Grand Rapids, MI: Zondervan, 2003), 51.

15. Ibid.

16. Ibid.

17. K. Christensson et al., "Effect of Nipple Stimulation on Uterine Activity and on Plasma Levels of Oxytocin in Full Term, Healthy, Pregnant Women," *Acta Obstetricia at Gynecologica Scandinavia* 68 (1989): 205–10; Larry J. Young and Zuoxin Wang, "The Neurobiology of Pair Bonding," *Nature Neuroscience* 7, no. 10. (October 2004): 1048–54; K. M. Kendrick, "Oxytocin, Motherhood, and Bonding," *Experimental Physiology* 85 (March 2000): 111S–124S, as cited in "Unprotected: A Campus Psychiatrist Reveals How Political Correctness in Her Profession Endangers Every Student."

18. Michael Kosfeld, et al., "Oxytocin Increases Trust in Humans," *Nature* 435 (June 2005): 673.

19. "The Benefits of Chastity before Marriage," https://forever families.byu.edu/pages/benefits-chastity.

20. Meg Meeker, M.D., *Boys Should Be Boys—7 Secrets to Raising Healthy Sons* (New York: Ballantine Books, 2008), 67.

21. Joe S. McIlhaney, M.D., and Freda McKissic Bush, M.D., *Hooked* (Chicago, IL: Northfield Publishing, 2008).

22. A. Aron, H. Fisher, et al., (2005), "Reward, Motivation, and Emotional Systems Associated with Early-Stage Intense Romantic Love," *Journal of Neurophysiology* 94 (1): 327–37.

23. J. R. Kahn, K. A. London, "Premarital Sex and the Risk of Divorce," *Journal of Marriage and the Family* 53 (November 1991): 845–55. T. B. Heaton, "Factors Contributing the Increasing Marital Stability in the United States," *Journal of Family Issues*, vol. 23 no. 3, April 2002, 392–409.

24. McIlhaney and Bush, *Hooked*.

Chapter 9: A New and Improved Sex Talk

1. Alan Guttmacher Institute in New York.

2. The National Campaign to Prevent Teen Pregnancy.

3. Neil Howe, William Strauss, and R. J. Matson, *Millennials Rising: The Next Great Generation* (New York: Vintage Books, 2000), 200.

4. Diana Jean Schemo, "Mothers of Sex-Active Youths Often Think They're Virgins," the *New York Times*, http://www.nytimes .com/2002/09/05/national/05SEX.html.

5. 6. Jane E. Brody, "Teenage Risks, and How to Avoid Them," http://www.nytimes.com/2007/12/18/health/18brod.html?page-wanted=1&_r=1&ref=science?_r, posted on December 18, 2007.

6. Hanna Rosin, "Even Evangelical Teens Do It: How Religious Beliefs Do and Don't Influence Sexual Behavior," http://www.slate .com/id/2167293, posted May 30, 2007. (From the original study *Forbidden Fruit: Sex & Religion in the Lives of American Teenagers* by Mark Regnerus, a professor of sociology at the University of Texas at Austin. The book is a serious work of sociology based on several comprehensive surveys of young adults, coupled with in-depth interviews.

7. Ibid.

8. Diana Jean Schemo, "Mothers of Sex-Active Youths Often Think They're Virgins," http://www.nytimes.com/2002/09/05/national /05SEX.html.

9. Rosin, "Even Evangelical Teens Do It," http://www.slate.com /id/2167293, posted on May 30, 2007.

10. "It's Better on TV: Does Television Set Teenagers Up for Regret Following Sexual Initiation?" https://www.guttmacher.org/journals/ psrh/2009/06/its-better-tv-does-television-set-teenagers-regret-fol-lowing-sexual-initiation, first published online: June 4, 2009.

11. Joan Jacobs Brumberg, *The Body Project: An Intimate History of American Girls* (New York: Vintage Books, 1998), 204.

12. https://www.cnn.com/2014/11/18/living/teens-sexting-what -parents-can-do/index.html; Sources original study: http://drexel.edu /now/archive/2014/June/Sexting-Study/

13. Ibid.

Chapter 10: Real Man or Peter Pan?

1. https://www.census.gov/content/dam/Census/library/publications/2017/demo/p20-579.pdf

2. Ibid.

3. "Gen Z: The Culture, Beliefs and Motivations Shaping the Next Generation," Barna Group, January 23, 2018, 52.

4. "Youth No Longer Defined by Chronological Age; Consumers Stay 'Younger' Longer," "Golden Age of Youth" study from Viacom Brand Solutions International (VBSI), http://www.marketingcharts.com/topics/asia-pacific/youth-no-longer-defined-by-chronological-age-35-is-new-18-6530.

5. Ibid.

6. https://www.therebelution.com/blog/2005/09/kidults-part-2-peter-pans-that-shave/; Kidults: "Peter Pans That Shave."

7. Lev Grossman, "Grow Up? Not So Fast," http://content.time.com/time/magazine/article/0,9171,1018089,00.html, posted on January 16, 2005.

8. Jean M. Twenge, PhD, *iGen: Why Today's Super-Connected Kids Are Growing Up Less Rebellious, More Tolerant, Less Happy-and Completely Unprepared for Adulthood-and What That Means for the Rest of Us* (New York: Atria Books: 2017).

9. Ibid.

10. Ibid.

11. Ibid.

12. Ibid.

13. "Gen Z: The Culture, Beliefs and Motivations Shaping the Next Generation," Barna Group, January 23, 2018.

14. "Gen Z: The Culture, Beliefs and Motivations Shaping the Next Generation," Barna Group, January 23, 2018, 28. Original source: *Good Faith: Being a Christian When Society Thinks You're Irrelevant and Extreme*, by David Kinnaman and Gabe Lyons.

15. http://www.foxnews.com/us/2017/12/23/pennsylvania-family-ordered-to-take-down-jesus-christmas-display-after-neighbor-said-it-was-offensive.html

16. FoxNews.com article: http://www.foxnews.com/us/2016/11/17/coddling-campus-crybabies-students-take-up-toddler-therapy-after-trump-win.html.

17. Twenge, *iGen*, 164.

18. Ibid.

19. *The Atlantic*, https://www.theatlantic.com/magazine/archive/2014/04/hey-parents-leave-those-kids-alone/358631/.

20. "Gen Z: The Culture, Beliefs and Motivations Shaping the Next Generation," Barna Group, January 23, 2018, 35.

21. https://www.theatlantic.com/magazine/archive/2014/04/hey-parents-leave-those-kids-alone/358631/

22. "Gen Z: The Culture, Beliefs and Motivations Shaping the Next Generation," Barna Group, January 23, 2018, 52.

23. Ibid.

Chapter 11: Ready, Set, Launch

1. Meg Meeker, M.D., *Boys Should Be Boys—7 Secrets to Raising Healthy Sons* (New York: Ballantine Books, 2008), 81.
2. Nicole Beland, "Babes in Boyland," *Men's Health* (October 2004).
3. Ibid.
4. Leonard Sax, M.D., PhD; *Boys Adrift* (New York: Basic Books, 2009), 142–43.
5. Ibid.
6. Albert Mohler, "What If There Are No Adults?" https://www.christianheadlines.com/columnists/al-mohler/what-if-there-are-no-adults-1413385.html, posted on August 19, 2005.
7. Sax, *Boys Adrift*, 136.
8. Ibid., 155.
9. Ibid., 123.
10. Lev Grossman, "Grow Up? Not So Fast," http://content.time.com/time/magazine/article/0,9171,1018089,00.html, posted on January 16, 2005.

Chapter 12: Family Man: An Endangered Species

1. http://www.chicagotribune.com/lifestyles/ct-marriage-in-decline-balancing-20150518-column.html
2. https://census.gov/data/tables/time-series/demo/families/marital.html
3. Jean M. Twenge, PhD, *iGen: Why Today's Super-Connected Kids Are Growing Up Less Rebellious, More Tolerant, Less Happy-and Completely Unprepared for Adulthood-and What That Means for the Rest of Us* (New York: Atria Books, 2017), 219.
4. Ibid., 220.
5. "Gen Z: The Culture, Beliefs and Motivations Shaping the Next Generation," Barna Group, January 23, 2018, 53.
6. Marcia Segelstein, "Late Dates: The Dangerous Art of Marital Procrastination," *Salvo*, Issue 8 (Spring 2009), www.salvomag.com.
7. Wendy Shalit, *Girls Gone Mild: Young Women Reclaim Self-Respect and Find It's Not Bad to Be Good* (New York: Random House, 2007), 4.
8. Ibid.
9. Segelstein, "Late Dates: The Dangerous Art of Martial Procrastination," 14.
10. Albert Mohler, "The Case Against Marriage," *Newsweek*, http://www.albertmohler.com/2010/06/25/the-case-against-marriage-courtesy-of-newsweek, posted on June 25, 2010.
11. http://www.foxnews.com/lifestyle/2017/09/02/cheap-sex-is-making-men-give-up-on-marriage-author-says.html
12. Ibid.
13. Ibid.
14. Joe S. McIlhaney, M.D., and Freda McKissic Bush, M.D., *Hooked* (Chicago, IL: Northfield Publishing, 2008), 101.

15. Ibid., 101–102.

16. Ibid.

17. Segelstein, "Late Dates: The Dangerous Art of Marital Procrastination."

18. Ibid.

19. Frederica Mathewes-Green, essay in "First Things," August/September 2005, http://www.firstthings.com, as cited in Albert Mohler, "What If There Are No Adults?" https://www.christianheadlines.com/columnists/al-mohler/what-if-there-are-no-adults-1413383.html, posted on August 19, 2005.

20. Ibid.

21. Jessica Bennett and Jesse Ellison, "The Case against Marriage," Newsweek, June 11, 2010, https://www.newsweek.com/case-against-marriage-73045.

22. Wendy Shalit, *Girls Gone Mild: Young Women Reclaim Self-Respect and Find It's Not Bad to Be Good* (New York: Random House, 2007), 19.

23. *Sex without Strings, Relationships without Rings: Today's Young Singles Talk about Mating and Dating*, A Publication of the National Marriage Project © 2000, www.marriage.rutgers.edu.

24. Pamela Smock, a family demographer at the University of Michigan, says about 70 percent of those who get married lived together first. "Cohabitation is continuing to grow, and it's become the model way of life."

25. *Sex without Strings, Relationships without Rings: Today's Young Singles Talk about Mating and Dating.*

26. The National Marriage Project's Ten Things to Know Series, "The Top Ten Myths of Marriage" (March 2002); Alfred DeMaris and K. Vaninadha Rao, "Premarital Cohabitation and Marital Instability in the United States: A Reassessment," *Journal of Marriage and the Family* 54 (1992): 178–90.

27. Naomi Schaefer Riley, "How Shacking Up Leads to Divorce," (February 9, 2015), https://nypost.com/2015/02/09/how-shacking-up-leads-to-divorce/.

28. "Sociological Reasons Not to Live Together from All about Cohabiting Before Marriage," http://www.leaderu.com/critical/cohabitation-socio.html.

29. Linda J. Waite and Kara Joyner, "Emotional and Physical Satisfaction with Sex in Married, Cohabitating, and Dating Sexual Unions: So Men and Women Differ?" 239–69 in E. O. Laumann and R. T. Michael, eds., *Sex, Love, and Health in America* (Chicago, IL: University of Chicago Press, 2001); Edward O. Laumann, J. H. Gagnon, R. T. Michael, and S. Michaels, *The Social Organization of Sexuality: Sexual Practices in the United States* (Chicago, IL: University of Chicago Press, 1994).

30. The National Marriage Project's Ten Things to Know Series, "The Top Ten Myths of Divorce" (April 2001). David Popenoe and Barbara Dafoe Whitehead, unpublished research by Linda J. Waite,

cited in Linda J. Waite and Maggie Gallagher, *The Case of Marriage* (New York: Doubleday, 2000), 148.

31. Twenge, *iGen*, 218.

32. Ibid., Shalit, *Girls Gone Mild*. "Marital Status and health: US 1999–2002," Report from Centers for Disease Control (2004). This study, based on interviews with 127,545 adults age eighteen plus, found that married adults were in better psychological and physical health than cohabiting, single, or divorced adults.

33. *Sex without Strings, Relationships without Rings.*

34. Ibid.

35. Ibid.

36. Meg Meeker, M.D., *Boys Should Be Boys—7 Secrets to Raising Healthy Sons* (New York: Ballantine Books, 2008), 173.

Chapter 13: Raising Up a Gentleman

1. "Reputation," Dictionary.com, http://dictionary.reference.com /browse/reputation (accessed July 22, 2010).

2. See http://www.quotationspage.com/quote/2871.html.

3. Rick Johnson, *That's My Son* (Grand Rapids, MI: Revell, 2005), 146.

4. Ibid.

5. https://www.russellmoore.com/2018/02/12/teach-boys-respect -women/

6. "Study: College Students More Narcissistic Than Ever," https:// www.foxnews.com/story/study-college-students-more-narcissistic-than -ever, posted on February 27, 2007.

7. Ibid.

8. Ibid.

9. Jocelyn Noveck and Trevor Noveck, "Poll: Family Ties Key to Youth Happiness," *The Associated Press* (August 20, 2007), http:// www.washingtonpost.com/wp-dyn/content/article/2007/08/20/AR 2007082000451.html.

10. Ibid.

11. Ibid.

12. Steve Gerali, *Teenage Guys* (Grand Rapids, MI: Zondervan, 2006), 208.

13. Stephen James and David Thomas, *Wild Things: The Art of Nurturing Boys* (Carol Stream, IL: Tyndale House Publishers, 2009.

14. Gerali, *Teenage Guys*, 244.

15. John Eldredge, *Wild at Heart* (Nashville, TN: Thomas Nelson Publishers, 2001), 62.

16. Gerali, *Teenage Guys*, 236–37.

17. Rick Johnson, *That's My Son* (Grand Rapids, MI: Revell, 2005),165.

18. Ibid., 162.

19. Leonard Sax, M.D., PhD; *Boys Adrift* (New York: Basic Books, 2009), 204–5.

Chapter 14: Grounded for Life

1. LifeWay Study about going to church after high school.
2. Jossey-Bass Study, San Francisco, 2009.
3. America's Changing Religious Landscape Study (Pew Research Center).
4. Christian Smith and Melinda Lundquist Denton, *Soul Searching: The Religious and Spiritual Lives of American Teenagers*, Oxford University Press, 2005.
5. "Gen Z: The Culture, Beliefs and Motivations Shaping the Next Generation," Barna Group (January 23, 2018), 97.
6. Ibid.
7. Ibid., 82.
8. Ibid., 88.
9. *Ladies' Home Journal*, December 1948, 185.
10. J. I. Packer, *Knowing God* (Downers Grove, IL: InterVarsity Press, 1973), 19.

Appendix: Talk Sheets

1. http://www.ns.umich.edu/new/releases/25302-kids-and-screen-time-signs-your-child-might-be-addicted Kids and screen time: Signs your child might be addicted, Dec 01, 2017
2. Ibid.
3. https://www.cdc.gov/std/life-stages-populations/YouthandSTDs-Dec-2017.pdf
4. *JAMA Pediatrics* (February 26, 2018), doi:10.1001/jamapediatrics.2017.5745
5. https://www.womenshealth.gov/relationships-and-safety/sexual-assault-and-rape/sexual-assault